T0113445

The Path to Genocide examines three aspects of the events leading up to the Final Solution in Nazi Germany. First, Professor Browning looks at how the Nazis tried to deal with the "Jewish problem" between the outbreak of war and the emergence of the Final Solution, a period that focused first on the possibility of expelling the Jews to Lublin or the island of Madagascar and later on ghettoization. Second, Browning discusses how other historians have attempted to explain the origins of the Final Solution. The last section of the book is organized around case studies of lower- and middle-echelon personnel, in an attempt to explain how such people conformed so quickly and easily to a campaign of mass murder.

THE PATH TO GENOCIDE

The Path to Genocide

Essays on Launching the Final Solution

CHRISTOPHER R. BROWNING
Professor of History, Pacific Lutheran University

CAMBRIDGE
UNIVERSITY PRESS

CAMBRIDGE UNIVERSITY PRESS
Cambridge, New York, Melbourne, Madrid, Cape Town, Singapore,
São Paulo, Delhi, Dubai, Tokyo, Mexico City

Cambridge University Press
32 Avenue of the Americas, New York, NY 10013-2473, USA

www.cambridge.org
Information on this title: www.cambridge.org/9780521558785

First published 1992
Reprinted 1993 (twice), 1994
Canto edition 1995
10th printing 2008

A catalog record for this publication is available from the British Library

ISBN 978-0-521-55878-5 Paperback

For My Mother
Eleanor Oechsli Browning

Contents

Preface

If the Nazi regime had suddenly ceased to exist in the first half of 1941, its most notorious achievements in human destruction would have been the so-called euthanasia killing of seventy to eighty thousand German mentally ill and the systematic murder of the Polish intelligentsia. If the regime had disappeared in the spring of 1942, its historical infamy would have rested on the "war of destruction" against the Soviet Union. The mass death of some two million prisoners of war in the first nine months of that conflict would have stood out even more prominently than the killing of approximately one-half million Jews in that same period. In the next eleven months, however, from mid-March 1942 to mid-February 1943, over one-half the victims of the Jewish Holocaust, or *Shoah*, lost their lives at the hands of Nazi killers. The Nazi regime called this attempt to murder every Jew in Europe the "Final Solution to the Jewish Question." It was a killing campaign that ever since has overshadowed National Socialism's other all-too-numerous atrocities.

Historians as well as others were puzzled and awed by murder on such an extraordinary scale carried out in such a systematic manner. Many could not reconcile the Final Solution with their positive notion of human nature and their belief in progress within the historical framework of Western civilization. Often their response was to treat the Holocaust as an aberration – a freakish and inexplicable event – not to be analyzed in the same way historians approach other occurrences and not to be assimilated into our self-understanding.

Gradually this situation has changed. In the past twenty years in particular, increasing numbers of historians have sought to study the Holocaust not as an inpenetrable mystery but rather as a man-made catastrophe, to be approached with the same tools of historical research and analysis that are applied to other events in our past.[1]

As the field of Holocaust studies has grown, it has developed three basic subdivisions or areas of specialization that focus respectively on the perpetrators, the victims, and the bystanders. Each area has had noted controversies, such as the role of the Jewish councils among the victims and the role of Pope Pius XII and Franklin Roosevelt among the bystanders. In the writing of perpetrator history, one of the longest ongoing controversies concerns the origins of the Final Solution. How was it humanly possible and how is it historically explainable that the government of a highly civilized European nation-state – one that in many respects represented the pinnacle of achievement in Western civilization – managed to launch a mass-murder campaign that aimed at killing all the Jews of Europe?

In *The Path to Genocide,* I have attempted to study Nazi Germany's systematic destruction of the Jews from three perspectives. The first is that of policy evolution. How did Nazi Germany try to solve its self-imposed "Jewish problem" between the outbreak of war in September 1939 and the emergence of a Final Solution based on mass murder? Here two kinds of policies were salient. The first was "resettlement" as Nazi leaders – especially Heinrich Himmler – sought to reorganize the populations of eastern Europe on the basis of Nazi racial principles. The "Jewish question" was to be solved within the framework of these resettlement plans through forced expulsion (first to the Lublin district in Poland and then to the island of Madagascar) and concomitant population decimation. The second was ghettoization, the concentration and isolation of the Jews until resettlement could take place. Resettlement was planned at the highest echelons of the Nazi government. Ghettoization, in contrast, emerged as an improvised response from local occupation authorities.

The second perspective is that of recent historiography. How have other historians in the past few years attempted to explain the origins of the Final Solution? In particular, how have they sought to explain the decision-making process that took Nazi Germany over the brink? Some

---

[1] For developments in the historiography of the Holocaust see Michael Marrus, *The Holocaust in History* (Hanover and London, 1987).

have found the driving force in one component of the Nazi coalition. Susanne Heim and Götz Aly have focused on the technocrats who saw the Jews as an obstacle to their plans for economic modernization. Arno Mayer has focused on the anti-Bolshevik paranoia of the conservative elites. The Nazi leadership has continued to attract attention as well. Philippe Burrin has focused on the ideology and personal role of Adolf Hitler; Richard Breitman on Heinrich Himmler and his working relationship with Hitler in shaping Nazi Jewish policy. Taking into account the new evidence and interpretations that have emerged in the past decade, I continue to argue that the Final Solution was not a premeditated plan of Adolf Hitler, but that he played the central role in the decision-making process.[2] The Final Solution emerged from a series of decisions between the spring and fall of 1941, usually taken when Hitler was elated and emboldened by the euphoria of seeming victory.

To some readers the attention historians have paid to the decision-making process and particularly its dating may seem inordinate and overblown. The argument can take on the quality of a scholastic splitting of hairs, as historians seem to quibble over a few months, weeks, or even days. However, I would argue, as does Richard Breitman, that the issue of dating is not a matter of arcane detail.[3] Unless the chronology is established accurately, the historical context for the fateful decisions remains illusive, as do purported explanations of motivation and causality.

Leaders, decisions, and policies are only part of the story. Hitler and a small clique of Nazi leaders did not act alone. Their decisions had to be embraced and their policies implemented by many others to realize a plan for mass murder on the scale of the Final Solution. The third perspective here, therefore, is the study of the lower- and middle-echelon personnel of what Raul Hilberg has called the "machinery of destruction" – a far-flung and multifaceted apparatus of power, "structurally no different from organized German society as a whole,"

---

[2] For my earlier historiographical survey of these issues and my own arguments concerning them see Christopher R. Browning, *Fateful Months: Essays on the Emergence of the Final Solution* (New York, 1985; revised ed., 1991), pp. 8–38.

[3] Richard Breitman, *The Architect of Genocide: Himmler and the Final Solution* (New York, 1991), p. 24.

that in one way or another contributed to carrying out the Final Solution.[4] By looking at a variety of such people – a ministerial bureaucrat in the Foreign Office in Berlin, the chief of the military administration in Serbia, the ghetto manager in Lodz, public health doctors in the General Government, and ordinary reserve policemen sent to do the killing – an attempt has been made to answer several questions. What role did such people play in the evolution of Nazi Jewish policy in this period? What did they think they were doing? How did these people react when Nazi Jewish policy turned to systematic and total murder? How could they be harnessed to a mass-murder campaign so quickly and easily?

Many were entangled in the web of Nazi Jewish policy before 1941 and, as enthusiastic and ambitious servants of the regime, had already committed themselves to finding a solution to the "Jewish problem." Frustrated by earlier failure, they were by 1941 receptive to a policy of mass murder. Some of them had even anticipated such a policy in advance of the regime's fateful decisions. The process of corruption was gradual but irreversible. For those abruptly thrust into the killing without warning or preparation, the stifling bonds of conformity within the group and the inability to assert moral autonomy against the majority of one's comrades and the authority of the regime were sufficient to turn most of them into killers.

The initial impetus for most of the essays in *The Path to Genocide* can be traced back to 1984 and 1985, when I took part in a year-long seminar sponsored by the Institute for Advanced Studies on the campus of the Hebrew University of Jerusalem. To my colleagues and friends who shared that extraordinary experience – Yehuda Bauer, Israel Gutman, Saul Friedlander, Otto Dov Kulka, Dinah Porat, Richard Cohen, Shmuel Almog, Michael Marrus, and Bernard Wasserstein – I am especially grateful. Subsequent research has been made possible by help from Alexander von Humboldt Foundation and Fulbright fellowships as well as a sabbatical leave and two Regency Advancement Awards from Pacific Lutheran University. The staffs at many archives were helpful in

---

[4] Raul Hilberg, *The Destruction of the European Jews* (New York, revised and expanded ed., 1985), p. 994.

providing access to the documentation – Shmuel Krakowski of the Yad Vashem Archives, Alfred Streim of the Zentrale Stelle der Landesjustizverwaltungen, and Helge Grabitz of the Staatsanwaltschaft in Hamburg deserve special mention here. The encouragement and helpful comments of many colleagues have been much appreciated, but I owe a very special debt to Peter Hayes, who not only conceived the idea for this collection of essays but also found its publisher.

My family has once again experienced the usual preoccupations and absences of the author that accompany the writing of any book. For their continued support I am very thankful.

PART I

The Prelude to Genocide

1

Nazi Resettlement Policy and the Search for a Solution to the Jewish Question, 1939–1941

In recent years the historiographical discussion of Nazi Jewish policy has reflected the wider debate on National Socialism between so-called "intentionalists" and "functionalists" and the even broader division within the historical profession between those who explain history through the ideas and decisions of individuals and those who explain history through the impersonal and underlying structures of society and institutions that limit and shape the actions of individuals.[1] The intentionalists concentrate for the most part on political and diplomatic history and have focused their interpretation of the Nazi period on the central role of Hitler and the continuity of his ideological goals from their crystallization in the 1920s through their realization in the early 1940s. The functionalists (also referred to as "structuralists") are generally social and institutional historians. They have emphasized the polycratic nature of the Nazi regime and have sought to explain the course of events during this period in terms of the improvisation and cumulative radicalization produced by the contradictory nature and chaotic decision-making process of this regime rather than by the dominant role of Hitler and the calculated pursuit of his ideological goals.[2]

Reprinted in slightly revised form with permission. From *German Studies Review*, 9/3 (1986), pp. 497–519.
[1] The research for this paper was undertaken while I had the privilege of being a Fellow of the Institute for Advanced Studies of the Hebrew University of Jerusalem.
[2] The terms "intentionalist" and "functionalist" were coined by Tim Mason, "Intention and Explanation: A Current Controversy about the Interpretation of National

Initially the debate on Nazi Jewish policy focused on the 1930s, with the intentionalists arguing that this policy was a conscious and calculated preparation for the realization of Hitler's "unalterable" program and the functionalists portraying it as a "planless" radicalization along the "twisted road" to Auschwitz.[3] More recently this controversy has centered on the events of 1941 and Hitler's particular role in the decisions and orders for the Final Solution in that year.[4] By the time these issues were debated at a conference in Stuttgart in May 1984, the lines of polarization, at least among German historians, had been clearly drawn.[5]

The functionalists who argued for an evolutionary view of Nazi Jewish policy in the 1930s claimed either that Hitler made no decision and issued no orders for the Final Solution in 1941 (Broszat and Mommsen) or did so only in the Fall of 1941 (Adam). In either case the Final Solution resulted primarily from the dashed expectations of the Russian

Socialism," Gerhard Hirschfeld and Lothar Kettenacker, eds., *Der Führerstaat: Mythos und Realität* (Stuttgart, 1981), pp. 21–40. The next two articles in this volume starkly contrast the two approaches: Hans Mommsen, "Hitlers Stellung im nationalsozialistischen Herrschaftssystem," pp. 43–72; and Klaus Hildebrand, "Monokratie oder Polykratie? Hitlers Herrschaft und das Dritte Reich," pp. 73–97.

[3] For contrasting views, see for instance: Lucy Dawidowicz, *The War Against the Jews* (New York, 1975), Karl Dietrich Bracher, *The German Dictatorship* (New York, 1968), and Helmut Krausnick, "The Persecution of the Jews," *Anatomy of the SS State* (New York, 1968) on the one hand, and Karl Schleunes, *The Twisted Road to Auschwitz* (Urbana, Illinois, 1970) and Uwe Dietrich Adam, *Judenpolitik im Dritten Reich* (Düsseldorf, 1972) on the other.

[4] Uwe Adam first articulated the functionalist side of this aspect of the debate in *Judenpolitick im Dritten Reich*, pp. 303–316. It was developed further by Martin Broszat, "Hitler und die Genesis der 'Endlösung.' Aus Anlaß der Thesen von David Irving," *Vierteljahrshefte für Zeitgeschichte* (hereafter cited as *VfZ*), 25/4 (1977), pp. 739–775. A "moderate functionalist" reply to Broszat can be found in Christopher R. Browning, "Zur Genesis der 'Endlösung.' Eine Antwort an Martin Broszat," *VfZ*, 29/1 (1981), pp. 97–109. A starkly intentionalist stand, which took aim at David Irving rather than Broszat, appeared with Gerald Fleming, *Hitler und die Endlösung. "Es war des Führers Wunsch. . . "* (Wiesbaden and Munich, 1982). A further articulation of the functionalist interpretation followed with Hans Mommsen, "Die Realisierung des Utopischen: Die 'Endlösung der Judenfrage' im 'Dritten Reich'," *Geschichte und Gesellschaft*, IX/3 (Autumn, 1983), pp. 381–420.

[5] The conference proceedings, both papers and debate, have now been published as Eberhard Jäckel and Jürgen Rohwer, eds., *Der Mord an den Juden im Zweiten Weltkrieg: Entschlußbildung und Verwirklichung* (Stuttgart, 1985).

campaign. Plans to solve the Jewish question by expulsion into the wastelands of conquered Russia had been thwarted. The eastward movement of Jews already underway was backing up, and whether by Hitler's decision or local initiative, mass murder emerged as the way out of the *cul-de-sac* into which the Nazis had maneuvered themselves.

For the intentionalists, in this case Eberhard Jäckel and Andreas Hillgruber, there was a fundamental connection in Hitler's mind between the acquistion of *Lebensraum* through the invasion of Russia and a solution to the Jewish question through systematic mass murder, which together constituted the nucleus or *Kernstück* of Hitler's racist ideology and were his conscious goals since the 1920s.[6] The Final Solution emerged in 1941 from a series of decisions taken by Hitler during the preparations for Barbarossa in the Spring of 1941 and the euphoria of victory in the following Summer that inaugurated policies to achieve these long-held and inextricably connected goals simultaneously.

In my opinion these contrasting positions are unduly polarized. A middle position that views the development of Nazi Jewish policy as evolutionary rather than programmatic but at the same time credits Hitler with making the key decisions in the Spring and Summer of 1941 in close connection with the preparations for and initial euphoria of the Russian campaign is not contradictory. What might seem a reckless jumping from the functionalist to the intentionalist horse in midstream turns out not to be a jump at all if one looks more closely at the relatively ignored interim years of 1939 and 1940 that lie between the two periods that have hitherto been the center of attention, that is the development of Nazi Jewish policy in the 1930s and the fateful events of 1941.[7]

---

[6] Andreas Hillgruber, "Die 'Endlösung' und das deutsche Ostimperium als Kernstück des rassenideologischen Programms des Nationalsozialismus," *VfZ*, 20 (1972), pp. 133–153, reprinted with updated footnotes in Manfred Funke, ed., *Hitler, Deutschland und die Mächte* (Düsseldorf, 1978), and "Die ideologisch-dogmatische Grundlagen der nationalsozialistischen Politik der Ausrottung der Juden in den besetzten Gebieten der Sowjetunion und ihre Durchführung 1941–1944," *German Studies Review*, II/2 (1979), pp. 263–296. Eberhard Jäckel, *Hitler's Weltanschauung: A Blueprint for Power* (Middletown, Connecticut, 1972).

[7] One important recent study that has in fact examined the relationship between the Nazi policies of expulsion and mass murder is that of the East German historian Kurt Pätzold, "Von der Vertreibung zum Genozid. Zu den Ursachen, Treibkräften und

Nazi Jewish policy in this interim period centered on the resettlement or expulsion schemes of the Lublin Reservation and the Madagascar Plan. For many historians these schemes have seemed too bizarre and feckless from the post-Auschwitz perspective to be taken seriously. For instance, the first historian to make a scholarly study of this subject, Philip Friedman, concluded in 1953 that "[a]midst all these projects for population transfers the deportation of the Jews could easily pass as a part of the general plan. There was therefore little suspicion, at first, that behind this innocent mask of 'resettlement' a scheme was in preparation of a quite different nature – nothing less than the total extermination of the Jews."[8] Another early historian of the Holocaust, Gerald Reitlinger, also treated these plans as a subterfuge, as did Lucy Dawidowicz some years later.[9] Hillgruber and Jäckel likewise were unable to fit these resettlement schemes into a programmatic view that emphasizes the continuity between Hitler's goals of the 1920s and policies of the 1940s. They therefore dismissed these resettlement schemes as "half-hearted" policies or "opportunistic detours" of a cynical and calculating Hitler who awaited the right moment for the realization of his long-held plans.[10] In his most recent book, *Hitler in History,* Jäckel stated emphatically of the Madagascar Plan in particular, "There is no indication that Hitler had ever intended it seriously."[11]

On the other hand, functionalists, who maintain that Hitler was envisaging an expulsion of Jews into Russia even as late as the Summer or Fall of 1941, have taken the seriousness of these resettlement schemes for granted. But they have not examined whether the frustra-

Bedingungen der antijüdischen Politik des faschistischen deutschen Imperialismus," *Faschismusforschung: Positionen, Probleme, Polemik* (Köln, 1980), pp. 181–208.

[8] Philip Friedman, "The Lublin Reservation and the Madagascar Plan: Two Aspects of Nazi Jewish Policy during the Second World War," *YIVO Annual of Jewish Social Studies,* VII (1953), pp. 151–177.

[9] Gerald Reitlinger, *The Final Solution: The Attempt to Exterminate the Jews of Europe, 1939–1945* (New York: Perpetua Edition, 1961), pp. 77–79; Lucy Dawidowicz, *The War Against the Jews* (New York, 1975), pp. 154–155.

[10] The term "half-hearted" is Hillgruber's. "Opportunistic detour" is a phrase used by Eberhard Jäckel in a paper "Hitler und der Mord an den europäischen Juden im Zweiten Weltkrieg" delivered in Warsaw in April 1983.

[11] Eberhard Jäckel, *Hitler in History* (Hanover, New Hampshire, 1984), p. 51.

tions and failures of these schemes might not have led the Nazis in general and Hitler in particular to take decisions for mass murder earlier than the military failure of late 1941. Nor have they sought to analyze what the shaping of Nazi Jewish policy in this interim period indicates about the key role of Hitler and the manner in which he made decisions setting the parameters within which the Jewish question was to be solved.

It is my argument that for any reassessment of the resettlement schemes of 1939 and 1940, the historian must avoid the distortion of hindsight and seek to understand Nazi Jewish policy in this period as the Nazi perpetrators themselves did. Seen in this perspective, Nazi Jewish policy was part of a wider demographic project that aimed at a racial restructuring of eastern Europe. But within this wider demographic project, Jewish policy did not *yet* have the priority or centrality in the Nazis' own sense of historical mission that has been argued for on the basis of what happened later. I do not dismiss the significance of Nazi ideology or Hillgruber's and Jäckel's characterization of it as racist and Social Darwinist in nature. But I do argue that such terms as *Lebensraum* and *Endlösung* were not rigidly programmatic, excluding all but one interpretation, and that Jewish policy was not always the undisputed priority or centerpiece of Nazi racial policy. Between 1939 and 1941 the Nazis understood *Lebensraum* and *Endlösung* differently than in the post-Barbarossa period, though not in a way inconsistent with Hitler's racist Social Darwinist outlook.[12] But the Nazis' self-understanding of their historical mission in this period was no less real for being superseded. This was not a "phony war against the Jews" awaiting the real offensive. Let us trace the outline of Nazi racial and

---

[12] In this regard I find myself closer to Martin Broszat, who sees Hitler's ideology not as narrowly programmatic, but rather as "goal-setting" or "direction-setting." However, I would give greater importance than does Broszat to Hitler's individual decisions, in response to changing circumstances, for determining how far in these directions Nazi policies would actually evolve. I would not go so far as Hans Mommsen who evaluates Hitler's statements on the Jews primarily from the "propagandistic aspect" as "threats" against the Allied governments presumed to be under Jewish influence. Martin Broszat, "Soziale Motivation und Führer-Bindung im Nationalsozialismus," *VfZ* 18/4 (1970), pp. 392–409. Hans Mommsen, "Die Realizierung des Utopischen," pp. 390–392.

demographic policy from September 1939 to March 1941, taking the Nazis' schemes for population resettlement as seriously as the Nazis did then.

Specific Nazi plans for racial policy and *Lebensraum* in Poland took shape only during September 1939, not before the invasion. Certainly there was a general consensus beforehand on a "fourth partition" of Poland and a "neutralization" of anti-German elements through mass arrests and shootings.[13] But it was only on September 14 that Heydrich reported to his division chiefs that "proposals are being submitted to the Führer by the Reichsführer [Himmler] that only the Führer can decide. . . . "[14] Thus it was in the euphoria of victory over Poland that Hitler approved a specific policy, with the results transmitted to the army commander-in-chief Brauchitsch on September 20 and to Heydrich's division heads and *Einsatzgruppen* commanders on September 21.[15] The border areas of West Prussia, the Warthegau, and East Upper Silesia were to become purely German through the expulsion of all Poles, Jews, and Gypsies, and the resettlement there of ethnic Germans or *Volksdeutsche* from eastern Europe. The Poles were to be deported eastward into what became the General Government, and deprived of

---

[13] National Archives Microfilm, T 175/239/2728499–502 (conference of Heydrich's division heads, September 7, 1939). Zentralstelle der Landesjustizverwaltungen in Ludwigsburg, "Einsatzgruppen in Polen: Einsatzgruppen der Sicherheitspolizei, Selbstschutz und andere Formationen in der Zeit vom 1. September 1939 bis Frühjahr 1940" (hereafter cited as "EG in Polen"), II, pp. 22–29. Helmut Krausnick and Harold Deutsch, eds., Helmuth Groscurth, *Tagebücher eines Abwehroffiziers 1938–40* (Stuttgart, 1970), p. 362 (Document Nr. 14, Groscurth memorandum over verbal orientation by Major Radke, September 22, 1939). *Nazi Conspiracy and Aggression* (hereafter cited as *NCA*), V, p. 769 (3047-PS: notes by Lahousen from diary of Canaris). For a general overview of the development of Nazi occupation policy in Poland: Martin Broszat, *Nationalsozialistische Polenpolitik* (Stuttgart, 1960); and Waclaw Dlugoborski, "Die deutsche Besatzungspolitik gegenüber Polen," in Karl Dietrich Bracher, Manfred Funke, and Hans-Adolf Jacobsen, eds., *Nationalsozialistische Diktatur 1933–1945* (Bonn, 1983), pp. 572–590.

[14] National Archives Microfilm, T 175/239/2728513–5 (conference of Heydrich's division heads, September 14, 1939).

[15] National Archives Microfilm T 175/239/2728524–8 (conference of Heydrich's division heads and Einsatzgruppen leaders, September 21, 1939); *NCA*, VI, pp. 97–101 (3363-PS: Heydrich *Schnellbrief* to Einsatzgruppen leaders, September 21, 1939); Helmuth Groscurth, *Tagebücher*, p. 362. Hans-Adolf Jacobsen, ed., Franz Halder, *Kriegstagebuch* (Stuttgart, 1962), I, pp. 79, 82.

potential leadership elites through systematic executions (and subsequently through the sifting out of those deemed racially suitable for "re-Germanization"). As for the Jews, they were to be deported to the furthest extremity of the German empire, the Lublin region between the Bug and Vistula rivers, with at least some of them being expelled over the demarcation line into the Soviet zone.[16] The Nazi plan thus envisaged three belts of population – German, Polish, and Jewish – from west to east. As Hitler told Rosenberg at the end of September, only time would tell whether – "after decades" – the German settlement belt would move yet further eastward.[17] The man appointed to be in charge of this vast movement of peoples, both coming and going, was Heinrich Himmler. Within the burgeoning SS, the Reich Commissariat for the Strengthening of Germandom (Reichskommissariat für die Festigung des Deutschen Volkstums – RKFDV) was created to coordinate ethnic German resettlement, while Heydrich's Reich Security Main Office (Reichssicherheitshauptamt – RSHA) handled expulsions eastward.[18] If the Nazis' self-imposed Jewish problem had mushroomed with the conquest of Poland, it is important to remember that in their own minds they now also had a Polish problem and a *volksdeutsch* problem of immense magnitude, and the attempt to solve all three of these simultaneously would often necessitate an ordering of priorities.

The first step in this grandiose program of population transfers was initiated by Gestapo chief Heinrich Müller on October 6, 1939, when he authorized Adolf Eichmann to contact the Gauleiter of East Upper Silesia concerning the deportation of Jews from that region. As Müller told Eichmann, "This activity shall serve first of all to collect experiences, in order . . . to be able to carry out evacuations of much greater numbers."[19] As the first step, Eichmann was to organize one train of

---

[16] The area east of Cracow and north of the Slovak border was initially earmarked as the *Judenreservat* until Germany unexpectedly found itself with the Lublin region instead of Lithuania by its treaty with the Soviet Union of September 28, 1939.

[17] Hans-Günther Seraphim, ed., *Das Politische Tagebuch Alfred Rosenbergs* (Göttingen, 1956), p. 81.

[18] Robert Koehl, *RKFDV: German Resettlement and Population Policy 1939–45* (Cambridge, Massachusetts, 1957). This important study deals primarily with the resettlement of the *Volksdeutsche* and only tangentially with the expulsion of Poles and Jews.

[19] Yad Vashem Archives (hereafter cited as YVA), 0-53/93/283 (Eichmann note, October 8, 1939).

deportees from Kattowitz and one from nearby Mährisch Ostrau in the Protectorate, where many Polish Jews had fled during the recent fighting. Eichmann immediately tried to shift the center of gravity of this deportation experiment from East Upper Silesia to his old stamping grounds, Austria and the Protectorate, with regular trains from there to a transit camp in Nisko in the Lublin region. From here the Jews were to be expelled eastward. Moreover, it was Eichmann's openly expressed expectation that within three to four weeks, his deportation program would encompass the Old Reich as well.[20] But no sooner had the first transport departed from Mährisch Ostrau than on October 19 Berlin ordered an end to Eichmann's increasingly ambitious program.[21] When the irate Gauleiter of Vienna vented his displeasure on Arthur Seyss-Inquart, Hans Frank's deputy, whom he blamed for preventing the deportation of the Viennese Jews, Himmler intervened and made clear in no uncertain terms that the decision to stop the Nisko transports had been his own – due, he said, to "technical difficulties."[22]

Why did the Nisko experiment come to such an abrupt halt? Many unconvincing reasons have been suggested. Protests from Hans Frank or local authorities in Poland against the unwanted influx could not have been decisive, for the Himmler decision was made even as the first of five transports was just arriving. Concern for Russian sensibil-

---

[20] Two recent studies of the Nisko plan are: Seev Goshen, "Eichmann und die Nisko-Aktion," *VfZ* 27/1 (January 1981), pp. 74–96; and Jonny Moser, "Nisko: The First Experiment in Deportation," *Simon Wiesenthal Center Annual*, II (1985), pp. 1–30. For the rapid expansion of Eichmann's plans from two experimental transports to a comprehensive deportation program, see: YVA, 0-53/93/258–9 and 284 (Günther notes on conferences of October 9 and 10, 1939), pp. 223–224 (memorandum of October 17, 1939 on Eichmann-Ebner-Becker meeting of October 16, 1939), p. 206 (note for Eichmann of October 18, 1939), p. 289 (Braune to Wagner, October 13, 1939), pp. 299–300 (Eichmann to Nebe, October 16, 1939), pp. 227–229 (Günther-Braune FS-Fernspräch, October 18, 1939); Eichmann Trial Document T-1135 (Löwenherz memorandum, October 10, 1939); Gerhard Botz, *Wohnungspolitik und Judendeportation in Wien 1938 bis 1945: Zur Funktion des Antisemitismus als Ersatz nationalsozialistischer Sozialpolitik* (Wien, 1975), pp. 164–186 (Document VII: Becker memorandum, October 11, 1939).

[21] YVA, 0-53/93/235–8 (Günther daily report, October 19, 1939), p. 220 (undated Günther telegram), and p. 244 (Günther note, October 24, 1939).

[22] NCA, VI, 116 (3398-PS: Seyss-Inquart to Himmler, November 4, 1939), and Botz, *Wohnungspolitik und Judendeportation in Wien*, p. 196 (Document X, Himmler to Bürckel, November 9, 1939).

ities was not crucial, for expulsions over the demarcation line continued into December. Demand for transport was indeed great, but Eichmann found upon inquiry that deportations were not totally excluded for this reason.[23] Nor was Eichmann being disciplined for improvising, given his subsequent appointment as Heydrich's specialist in charge of Jewish affairs and evacuations within the RSHA. In my opinion the decisive factor was the arrival of the first Baltic Germans in Danzig on October 15.[24] The problem of finding space in West Prussia and the Warthegau for the incoming *Volksdeutsche* now took priority over deporting Jews from East Upper Silesia and especially from Austria and the Protectorate. The deportation of Jews from those regions simply did not provide the lodging and livelihood for incoming *Volksdeutsche* where Himmler needed them. The consolidation of *Lebensraum* in the incorporated territories and solving the Jewish question were turning out to be competing rather than complementary goals, and as we shall see, the latter continually gave way to the former during the next year.

The next major impetus for setting in motion the Nazis' vast resettlement program was a Himmler order of October 30, 1939. By the end of February 1940, the Reichsführer wanted *all* Jews (estimated at 550,000) removed from the incorporated territories along with *all* so-called "Congress Poles" from West Prussia, and a sufficient number of anti-German Poles from the other incorporated territories to bring the total to one million.[25] Meanwhile the resettlement of Baltic Germans in West Prussia bogged down, as Gauleiter Albert Forster became increasingly uncooperative. His antipathy to Himmler was no secret; he had been overheard to say of the Reichsführer: "If I looked like him, I would not speak of race at all."[26] On November 28, Heydrich

[23] YVA, 0-53/93/256-7 (Brunner to Eichmann, October 28, 1939).

[24] Hans Umbreit, *Deutsche Militärverwaltungen 1938/39: Die militärische Besetzung der Tschechoslowakei und Polens* (Stuttgart, 1977), p. 218.

[25] *Faschismus, Getto, Massenmord* [Berlin (East) 1960], pp. 42–43 (NO-5586: Himmler Order of October 30, 1939). *Trials of the War Criminals before the Nürnberg Military Tribunal,* IV, p. 873 (NO-4095: General Orders and Directives of RKFDV, undated, signed by Creutz). YVA, JM 21/1, Frank Tagebuch: Streckenbach report of October 31, 1939.

[26] Fred Taylor, ed., *The Goebbels Diaries 1939–41* (London, 1982), p. 157 (entry of October 30, 1939); Koehl, *RKFDV,* p. 62; Herbert S. Levine, "Local Authority and the

intervened from Berlin, drastically scaling back the deportations ordered by Himmler one month earlier. As a short-range plan he ordered that 80,000 "Poles and Jews" were to be deported from the Warthegau by mid-December so that the incoming Baltic Germans could be lodged there instead of in West Prussia.[27] In a frightening display of brutality, the Warthegau Nazis exceeded this quota, deporting 87,833 people in 80 trainloads by December 17.[28] In some reports the unfortunate deportees were referred to collectively as "Poles and Jews," elsewhere only as Poles, and no German records ever distinguished the specific number of Jews involved. The primary thrust of what was to become known as the "first short-range plan" had not been to solve the Jewish question but rather to find space for the Baltic Germans. Many Jews were undoubtedly involved, but that was not what was on the Germans' minds at the moment.

Immediately following the conclusion of the Warthegau deportations of the "first short-range plan," Adolf Eichmann was appointed Heydrich's "special adviser" for evacuations and Jewish affairs.[29] Recalling Himmler's October 30th order, Eichmann lost no time in convening a Berlin conference on January 4, 1940, to announce once again the "urgent" deportation of *all* Jews from the incorporated territories in the coming months.[30]

This was Eichmann's second attempt to get massive Jewish deportations underway, but it fared no better than his Nisko venture. Sobered by the devastating and chaotic influx of Warthegau deportees in December, the Governor General Hans Frank balked at receiving more

SS State: The Conflict over Population Policy in Danzig-West Prussia," *Central European History*, II/4 (1969), pp. 331–355; "EG in Polen," II, p. 117.

[27] *Biuletyn Głównej Komisji Badania Zbrodni Hitlerowskich W Polsce* (hereafter cited as *Biuletyn*), XII (Warsaw, 1960), pp. 15F–18F (Heydrich to HSSPF Krakau, Breslau, Posen, and Danzig, November 28, 1939; and Heydrich to Krüger, Streckenbach, Koppe, and Damzog, November 28, 1939).

[28] Ibid., pp. 22F–31F (Rapp report of December 18, 1939); YVA, JM 3582 (Rapp report of January 26, 1940).

[29] YVA, JM 3581, Müller to all Staatspolizeileitstellen, December 21, 1939, and Heydrich to Sipo-SD in Krakau, Breslau, Posen, Danzig, and Königsberg, December 21, 1939.

[30] *Biuletyn*, XII, pp. 37F–39F (Abromeit note of January 8, 1940 on conference of January 4, 1940).

trainloads of starving, frozen, and penniless refugees. In this he was fully supported by the SS leadership of the General Government, a not very frequent concurrence of views. Heydrich thereupon counter-manded Eichmann's impending Jewish deportations in order to ensure at least the more urgent deportation of some 160,000 Poles to make space for the incoming Baltic and now Volhynian Germans. Only after the completion of deportations immediately connected with the *volks-deutsch* resettlement would the deportation of *all* Jews from the incor-porated territories, along with 30,000 Gypsies from the Old Reich, take place "as the last mass movement."[31]

A meeting of Himmler, Frank, the eastern Gauleiters, and Göring at the latter's Karinhall estate on February 12, 1940, did little to clarify the issue of deportation priorities. Göring opposed the deportation of any useful manpower, especially agricultural labor, from the incorpo-rated territories. The first priority, he stated unequivocally, was to strengthen the war potential of the Reich by making the new *Gaue* the granary of Germany. As for Jewish deportations, he was not opposed as long as the trains were sent in an orderly manner with prior notifi-cation. Frank openly allied himself with Göring's pragmatic stance. Himmler ignored Göring's offer to support Jewish deportations under orderly conditions but immediately emphasized the gravity of the *volksdeutsch* problem. He needed space for 70,000 Baltic Germans and 130,000 Volhynian Germans, and the latter had to be settled on Polish farms in a strip along the border with the General Government, i.e., precisely the disruption of agriculture that Göring opposed. Himmler volunteered to postpone the return of a further 220,000–270,000 Lithuanian, Bukovinian, and Bessarabian Germans, as well as the eth-nic Germans of the General Government. But the 30,000 *Volksdeutsche* east of the Vistula in the Lublin region had to be resettled too, because their present homeland was eventually destined to become the *Juden-reservat.* He did promise, however, that he and Frank "would agree upon the procedures of future evacuations."[32]

[31] *Biuletyn*, XII, pp. 44F–45F (NO-5322: conference of January 30, 1940).
[32] *Trials of the Major War Criminals before the International Military Tribunal* (here-after cited as *IMT*), vol. 36, pp. 300–306 (EC-305: Karinhall conference of February 12, 1940).

Himmler seemed to think that by scaling back the pace of ethnic German resettlement and indefinitely postponing Jewish deportations, he could sufficiently minimize disruption in both the incorporated territories and the General Government so as to continue with his cherished project for resettling *Volksdeutsche* and expelling Poles, despite the misgivings of Frank and Göring. For Himmler the rescue of the *Volksdeutsche* and the consolidation of *Lebensraum* in the incorporated territories clearly had priority over deporting Jews at this time. Frank's understanding of what had transpired at Karinhall was different. He assumed that Göring had given him the power to veto any undesired deportation. Moreover, he boasted,

> the great resettlement ideas have indeed been given up. The idea that one could gradually transport 7½ million Poles to the General Government has been *fully abandoned*. It is now only a question of the transfer of some 100,000–120,000 Poles, some 30,000 Gypsies, and a still to be determined number of Jews from the Reich, because the final goal shall be to make the German Reich free of Jews.

It was "indescribable" how Berlin still clung to the idea of a Jewish reservation east of the Vistula, Frank noted. However, "That that shall not occur in a year and especially not under the circumstances of war, Berlin also recognizes."[33]

In fact, even as Himmler was meeting with Frank and Göring at Karinhall, the SS was unilaterally launching new deportations – 1,000 German Jews from Stettin on February 12 (an exception to Heydrich's own rule against Jewish deportations from the Old Reich at this time) and 40,128 Poles from the Warthegau between February 10 and March 15, in what was known as the "intermediate plan."[34] Frank appealed to Göring, who specifically forbade further deportations of Jews without both his permission and proof of Frank's prior agreement.[35] Against the

---

[33] Italics mine. Hans Frank, *Diensttagebuch*, pp. 131 and 146–147 (Sitzung des Reichsverteidigungsauschuβ, Warsaw, March 2, 1940, and Dienstversammlung der Kreis- und Stadthauptmänner des Distrikts Lublin, March 4, 1940).

[34] YVA, 0-53/48/650-2 (Umwandererzentrale Abschluβbericht 1940).

[35] Politisches Archiv des Auswärtigen Amtes (hereafter cited as PA), Inland IIg 173, Göring telegram of March 23, 1940.

vociferous protest of Gauleiter Greiser, who was most anxious to expel the Jews of Lodz, Himmler agreed with Frank to postpone all Jewish deportations until August, when the Volhynian resettlement action –involving the expulsion of 120,000 Poles in the "second short-range plan" – was due to be concluded.[36]

Himmler's grandiose design for a sweeping racial reorganization of eastern Europe had been steadily whittled away. In the Fall of 1939, he had envisaged the deportation of about one million people (including all Jews) from the incorporated territories into the General Government by the end of February 1940, and eventually the removal of all so-called racially undesirable elements from these lands. By March 1940, however, Frank was boasting that the idea that one could gradually transport 7½ million Poles to the General Government had been "fully abandoned." Moreover, the Jewish deportations had been postponed repeatedly – most recently to August – and Göring had invested Frank with a virtual veto power over them. Even the resettlement of ethnic Germans had been scaled back. But if Frank could go over Himmler's head to Göring, Himmler now sought to re-legitimize his threatened dream by going over Göring's head to Hitler.

Since his pronouncements of the previous Fall, Hitler had played no visible role in shaping racial policy. In a typical example of the "institutional Darwinism" of the Third Reich, implementation had been left to a struggle between his subordinates, while the Führer himself turned his attention to loftier matters of grand strategy, in particular preparations for the offensives into Scandinavia, the Low Countries, and France. But by Spring Hitler seemed to have lost faith in his resettlement plan, at least insofar as it concerned the Jews in Lublin. According to Walther Hewel, Hitler told Colin Ross on March 12, 1940, that:

> the Jewish question really was a space question which was difficult to solve, particularly for him, since he had no space at his disposal. Neither would the establishment of a Jewish state

---

[36] Frank, *Diensttagebuch,* p. 158 (entry of April 5, 1940), and p. 204 (entry of May 19, 1940); *Dokumenty i Materialy Do Dziejow Okupacji Niemieckiej W Polsce,* vol. III, *Getto Lodzkie* (Warsaw, 1946), pp. 168–69 (Regierungspräsident to officials of Bezirk Lodz and Kalisch, May 8, 1940).

around Lublin ever constitute a solution as even there the Jews lived too close together to be able to attain a somewhat satisfactory standard of living. . . . He, too, would welcome a positive solution to the Jewish question; if only he could indicate a solution; this, however, was not possible under present conditions when he had not even sufficient space for his own people.[37]

The brilliant success of German arms in the first two weeks of the French campaign, however, gave Himmler the opportunity in late May to seek Hitler's approval for his racial design that stood in stark contrast to the pragmatic arguments of Göring and Frank and included an even more radical resettlement solution for the Jews than the now faltering Lublin Reservation.

Sometime in May 1940 Himmler drafted a memorandum, "Some Thoughts on the Treatment of Alien Populations in the East." The 15 million people of the General Government and the 8 million of the incorporated territories – "ethnic mush" in Himmler's view – were to be splintered into as many ethnic groups as possible for "screening and sifting." "The basis of our considerations must be to fish out of this mush the racially valuable, in order to bring them to Germany for assimilation." The ethnic identity of the leftovers, deprived of their racially valuable stock and dumped together in the General Government along with those from Germany "of the same racial and human type," would gradually disappear. This non-descript, denationalized population would then serve as a reservoir for migrant labor to Germany.[38]

The Jews were also to disappear but in a different way. "I hope completely to erase the concept of Jews through the possibility of a great emigration of all Jews to a colony in Africa or elsewhere." Concerning

---

[37] *Documents on German Foreign Policy*, D, VIII, pp. 912–913 (Hewel memorandum on conversation of Colin Ross and Hitler, March 12, 1940).

[38] Helmut Krausnick, ed., "Einige Gedanken über die Behandlung der fremdvölkischen im Osten," *VfZ* V/2 (1957), pp. 194–198 (NO-1880). Himmler did not start from scratch in writing this memorandum. A much longer study, "The Question of the Treatment of the Population of the Former Polish Territories according to a Racial-political Viewpoint," developing most of the ideas contained in the Himmler memorandum (with the notable exception of deporting the Jews to an African colony), had been submitted by Erhard Wetzel and Gerhard Hecht of the Racial Political Office on November 25, 1939. *Documenta Occupationis*, V (Poznan, 1949), pp. 2–28 (NO-3732).

this systematic eradication of the ethnic composition of eastern Europe, Himmler concluded: "However cruel and tragic each individual case may be, this method is still the mildest and best, if one rejects the Bolshevik method of physical extermination of a people out of inner conviction as un-German and impossible."

On May 25, a week after the German panzers reached the English Channel, Himmler submitted his memorandum to Hitler. Himmler's timing was impeccable, and he scored a great triumph. "The Führer read the six pages through and found them very good and correct," Himmler noted. Moreover, "The Führer desires that I invite Governor General Frank back to Berlin, in order to show him the memorandum and to say to him that the Führer considers it correct." Himmler then asked Hitler to authorize its distribution to the eastern Gauleiters and Göring, with the message that the Führer "had recognized and confirmed" the memorandum as containing authoritative guidelines. Hitler agreed once again.[39]

This episode is of singular importance, in that it is the only first-hand account by a high-ranking participant, i.e., Himmler, of just how a Hitler decision was reached and a *Führerbefehl* was given in the shaping of Nazi racial policy during this period. The initiative came from Himmler. However, he did not present Hitler with a precise plan. It was instead a statement of intent, a set of policy objectives. The details of implementation would be left to Himmler. Hitler indicated not only his enthusiastic agreement but also with whom this information could be shared. Hitler gave no specific orders to the likes of Göring, Frank, and the eastern Gauleiters. He simply allowed it to be known what he wanted or approved. Presumably business was often conducted in such a way in the Third Reich.

Himmler's enthusiastic memorandum-writing continued into June, when he encountered the argument that Polish labor would always be necessary in the incorporated territories for economic reasons. Himmler set out as his guiding principle: "One only possesses a land when even the last inhabitant of this territory belongs to his own people." Thus the alien population had to be forced off the land into construction work, with seven-eighths of them gradually deported to the east and

[39] Ibid., pp. 195–196 (Himmler memorandum, May 28, 1940).

one-eighth Germanized. "I am convinced that in the east we can get by without native Polish labor in the long run, and that we cannot and must not leave Poles in the eastern provinces even for economic reasons."[40]

The beleaguered Hans Frank thus not only faced the influx of Jews scheduled for August, but now also saw resurrected the very plan he thought "fully abandoned" in March, that is the deportation of more than seven million Poles from the incorporated territories into the General Government as well. Frank became increasingly desperate concerning the "catastrophic effects" of continued resettlement, when suddenly a surprising order from Himmler stopping the impending expulsion of the Jews into the General Government came to Frank as a veritable deliverance.[41] Himmler had found his colony in Africa for the Jews – the island of Madagascar!

Madagascar had long exercised a fascination among anti-Semites as the ideal dumping ground for the European Jews, but the idea did not take on real form as a concrete proposal among the Nazis until put forward by the Jewish expert of the German Foreign Office, Franz Rademacher, in early June 1940, when Germany's power to redistribute the French empire seemed at hand.[42] The alacrity with which the proposal was seized upon by the Nazi leadership is a measure of the frustration that had built up over the bottlenecks of demographic engineering in eastern Europe over the past nine months. By June 18 Hitler had informed Mussolini of his intention to use Madagascar as a Jewish reservation, and he broached the subject again with Admiral Raeder on June 20.[43] On June 24 the ever attentive Heydrich asserted

[40] National Archives Microfilm, T 175/122/2665958ff (Himmler memorandum, June 24, 1940).
[41] NG-1627 (Frank to Lammers, June 25, 1940). *Biuletyn* XII, 96F-97F (Note on Höppner-IV D 4 discussion, July 9, 1940).
[42] Leni Yahil, "Madagascar – Phantom of a Solution for the Jewish Question," in George Mosse and Bela Vago, eds., *Jews and Non-Jews in Eastern Europe* (Jerusalem, 1974), pp. 319–332. Christopher R. Browning, *The Final Solution and the German Foreign Office* (New York, 1978), pp. 35–43.
[43] Galeazzo Ciano, *The Ciano Diaries 1939–43* (Garden City, New York, 1947), pp. 265–266. Paul Schmidt, *Hitler's Interpreter* (New York, 1951), p. 178. Klaus Hildebrand, *Vom Reich zum Weltreich: Hitler, NSDAP, und koloniale Frage, 1919–1945* (Munich, 1969), pp. 651–652. In August Hitler told the German ambassador to France, Otto Abetz, that he intended to expel all the Jews from Europe at the end of the war. *Akten zur Deutschen Außenpolitik,* D, X, p. 389. Even American diplomats

his jurisdiction vis-à-vis the Foreign Office over Jewish resettlement there.[44] The news spread quickly eastward. On July 1, Adam Czerniakow, the head of the *Judenrat* in Warsaw, learned from an SD official, "that the war would be over in a month and that we would all leave for Madagascar."[45] Frank knew by July 10 that he was not only reprieved from the expected deluge of Jews from the Reich but would now be rid of his own Jews as well – a "colossal relief" he boisterously expounded upon to the *Heiterkeit* or "amusement" of his assembled court.[46] On Frank's orders ghetto building in the General Government came to an abrupt halt as pointless in view of the "plan of the Führer" to send the Jews to Madagascar.[47] If Frank was ecstatic, Greiser in the Warthegau was distraught. The Jewish deportations scheduled for August were cancelled, and he now faced the prospect of having to keep his own Jews for the duration of the war. His attempt in late July to get Frank to take the Warthegau Jews as an interim measure met with a flat refusal.[48]

Realization of the Madagascar Plan required the defeat of not only France but also Great Britain. By mid-September it was clear that this was not imminent, and the plan quickly faded. It was no less real for its brief existence, however. In cancelling the August deportations and halting ghetto construction in the General Government, Nazi leaders were not carrying out an elaborate sham to deceive future historians; they were making decisions based on the Madagascar Plan as the reality of Nazi Jewish policy in the Summer of 1940. Despite the constant postponements, the self-imposed "obligation" to solve the Jewish question still weighed heavily upon the Nazis. The greater the frustration, the lower the threshold to systematic mass murder. Thus

---

in Bucharest heard rumors of Hitler's mentioning the Madagascar Plan to Rumanian diplomats. *Foreign Relations of the United States*, II, p. 769. I am grateful to Itzhak Mais, director of the Yad Vashem museum, for this last reference.

[44] PA, Inland IIg 177, Heydrich to Ribbentrop, June 24, 1940.

[45] Raul Hilberg, Stanislaw Staron, and Josef Kermisz, eds., *The Warsaw Diary of Adam Czerniakow* (New York, 1979), 169 (entry of July 1, 1940).

[46] Frank, *Diensttagebuch*, p. 248 (entry of July 10, 1940), p. 252 (Abteilungsleitersitzung, July 12, 1940) and p. 258 (entry of July 25, 1940).

[47] *Faschismus-Getto-Massenmord*, p. 96 (report of Kreishauptmann of Minsk Mazowiecki, October 11, 1940) and p. 110 (Schön report of January 20, 1941).

[48] Frank, *Diensttagebuch*, pp. 261–263 (entry of July 31, 1940).

the Madagascar Plan was an important psychological step toward the Final Solution.

Even as Hitler in the last half of 1940 commenced planning for the invasion of Russia, which would fundamentally alter the Nazi perspective on eastern Europe, population transfer policies were not immediately affected. While neither the Lublin Reservation nor Madagascar Plan had been realized by the Fall of 1940, old habits, thought patterns, and temptations died hard. Through the Spring of 1941, the expulsion policy spasmodically revived as local Gauleiters along the borders of the Third Reich – both west and east – successfully prevailed upon Hitler to rid themselves of some of their undesired population through piecemeal deportations into Vichy France and the General Government. Hitler's open encouragement inspired the demographic engineers to produce yet another plan for massive population transfers of both Poles and Jews in early 1941, only once again to encounter insurmountable obstacles and cancellation.

With the defeat of France, Alsace and Lorraine had been reannexed to the Third Reich and joined to the Baden and Saarpfalz *Gaue*. Beginning in July the Germans began deporting Jews, Gypsies, asocials, criminals, mentally ill, and ardent French nationalists out of these newly annexed territories into France.[49] By mid-December the Germans had deported over 70,000 people, including 3,300 Jews, from Alsace-Lorraine, and barred the return of an even greater number who had fled.[50]

In this massive upheaval of humanity, it is not surprising that someone perceived the possibility of including the German Jews of Baden and Saarpfalz, thus making those *Gaue judenfrei*. According to Eich-

---

[49] That Himmler saw these population expulsions in the same light as the expulsions from the incorporated territories in the east can be seen in his speech to officers of the Waffen-SS in Metz: "Exactly the same thing took place in Poland at 40 degrees below zero, where we had to ship out thousands and tens of thousands and hundreds of thousands, where we had to have the toughness – this you should hear but then immediately forget – to shoot thousands of leading Poles." *IMT,* vol. 29, p. 104 (1918-PS: Himmler speech at Metz).

[50] For Lorraine: *IMT,* vol. 31 pp. 283–294 (2916-PS: overview of evacuations to November 15, 1940, compiled by the Chief of Sipo-SD). For Alsace: Akten der Partei-Kanzlei der NSDAP, 101 23821 (Chef der Zivilverwaltung im Elsass, April 22, 1941, to Bormann, on census of February 15, 1941).

mann, it was the Gauleiter of Baden, Robert Wagner, who made the proposal to Himmler, and the latter agreed "impulsively" without even considering the possible complications.[51] With Hitler's approval 6,504 Geman Jews were expelled into Vichy France on October 22–23 past the unsuspecting French border guards who assumed they were deportees from Alsace-Lorraine.[52] The ensuring diplomatic hassle at the armistice negotiations in Wiesbaden made further such deportations in the west impossible, however.

In the east the momentum behind expulsion policy was also decreasing, as Polish peasants stubbornly evaded roundups by spending their nights in the field or forest. Often only 40 percent of those earmarked for arrest could actually be seized.[53] No one was more pleased about this than Hans Frank. At a rare meeting of the eastern Gauleiters in Hitler's apartment on October 2, 1940, Frank could not resist boasting to Hitler about his success in the General Government, noting in particular the ghettoization of the Warsaw Jews then underway. Baldur von Schirach, the attentive Gauleiter of Vienna sitting on the other side of Hitler, immediately burst in that he had 50,000 Jews that Frank must take. Koch of East Prussia immediately proferred some Poles and Jews of his own. Hitler made no explicit decision and did not even mention the Jews specifically, but he did indicate his general line of thinking. The population density of the General Government was unimportant, he is alleged to have noted. It was only to be a "great Polish work camp."[54]

A month later Hitler, according to Frank, made clear to him his "urgent wish" that more Poles be taken into the General Government. In December Hitler was reported by Frank to have been even more insistent, declaring that "the Polish resettlement in the General Government was in line with his policy . . . . "[55] The renewed deportations were to

[51] Eichmann Interrogation, vol. I, pp. 141, 145.

[52] Bernhard Lösener, "Als Rassereferent im Reichsministerium des Innern," VfZ IX/3 (1961), p. 295.

[53] *Documenta Occupationis* (Poznan, 1959), VIII, p. 62 (Lodz Gestapo report, July 25, 1940).

[54] *IMT,* vol. 39, pp. 426–429 (Bormann note on Hitler discussion of October 2, 1940).

[55] Frank, *Diensttagebuch,* p. 302 (entry of November 6, 1940) and p. 327 (entry of January 15, 1941).

include not only Poles but also Jews, as Hitler intervened directly to authorize the expulsion of Viennese Jews to solve the housing shortage in that city.[56]

With Hitler's encouragement expulsion fever among the Germans was clearly on the rise. Eichmann's experts in the east were summoned to Berlin on December 17 for a meeting on the "third short-range plan" for the resettlement of ethnic Germans from Bessarabia, Bukovina, Dobrudja, and Lithuania.[57] To make room for the ethnic Germans, Heydrich intended to deport no less than 831,000 people in the coming year. In addition the army wanted 200,000 people relocated to the General Government to create vast training areas. Thus over one million people were to be moved to the General Government within the framework of the "third short-range plan." By its own statistics, that is not including the refugees who fled on their own and "wild" deportations, the SS had deported a total of 261,517 people to the General Government between December 1939 and January 1941.[58] Thus Heydrich was actually planning to deport four times as many people into the General Government in the coming year as had been deported in the last. In short, the Nazis hoped in 1941 to dwarf the demographic upheavals they had already engineered.

Once again, however, the grandiose schemes of the Nazis reflected their ambitions more than their capacities. The problem was no longer opposition from Frank, who now found Hitler's wishes in this matter all too clear.[59] Instead the transportation situation in the months before Barbarossa made realization of expulsions on the planned scale unattainable. The deportations, begun in late January, uprooted some 25,000 people – including 9,000 Jews – before they were abruptly stopped on March 15.[60]

---

[56] 1950-PS (Lammers to Schirach, December 3, 1940).

[57] YVA, 0-53/66/231 (Eichmann to Höppner, Krumey, Abromeit, Schlegel, and Riedel, December 12, 1940).

[58] YVA, JM 3582, Abschlussbericht 1941.

[59] Frank, *Diensttagebuch*, p. 309 (entry of December 2, 1940), and p. 326 (conference of January 15, 1941).

[60] YVA, 0-53/68/682–3 (report on Jewish evacuation in Danzig-West Prussia, February 19, 1941). YVA, JM 3582, Abschlussbericht 1941. Herbert Rosenkranz, *Verfolgung und Selbstbehauptung: Die Juden in Österreich 1938–1945* (Munich, 1978), pp. 261–

The repeated failure of German plans for massive population transfers, especially those for solving the Jewish question, frustrated not
only the demographic engineers of the SS but Hitler as well. According
to an account by Hitler's adjutant, Major Engel, the Führer ruminated
openly about the Jewish question before Bormann, Keitel, Speer and
Ley in February 1941. Hitler observed that while the war would speed
a solution, it also brought forth many more difficulties. Originally he
had thought only of breaking the power of the Jews in Germany, but
now his goal had to be the exclusion of Jewish influence in the entire
Axis sphere. "If [I] only knew where one could put several million
Jews, there were not so many after all," he lamented. When he remarked that he would make France provide Madagascar, Bormann
questioned how the Jews could be sent there during the war. Hitler replied that one would have to consider that problem. He would provide
the entire German navy for that purpose, except that he would not subject it to the risk of attack. According to Engel, Hitler then revealed
that he "was thinking of many things in a different way, that was not
exactly more friendly."[61]

Indeed, preparations for Barbarossa not only cut short the expulsions
of the "third short-range plan" but opened the way for Hitler and the
Nazis to think about many things in a "different way" by reorienting
and transforming the Nazi slogans of *Lebensraum* and *Endlösung*. As
articulated and practiced between 1939 and 1941, *Lebensraum* meant a
long-term process of racial consolidation in the incorporated territories. On several occasions Hitler remarked that his eastern Gauleiters
had ten years to tell him that Germanization of their provinces
was complete, and he would ask no questions about their methods.[62]

262. *Biuletyn*, XII, 138F–139F (Müller to Königsberg, Gotenhafen, Posen, Lodz,
Wien, March 15, 1941).
[61] Hildegard von Kotze, ed., *Heeresadjutant bei Hitler 1938–1943: Aufzeichnungen des
Majors Engel* (Stuttgart, 1974), pp. 94–95. Though cast in the form of diary notes
written at the time, this account was compiled by Engel later. The dating of events
has been shown to be unreliable in at least several instances (see the note of the editor
on p. 67).
[62] Groscurth, *Tagebücher*, p. 381 (Document Nr. 24, unsigned memorandum of October
18, 1939). *IMT*, vol. 39, pp. 426–429 (Bormann note of Hitler statement, October 2,
1940). *Hitler's Secret Conversations* (New American Library, 1961), p. 48 (entry of
August 1, 1941).

Likewise Hitler told Rosenberg in September 1939 that only time would tell if Germanization would – "after decades" – expand further east. Himmler's argument of June 1940 that a land belonged to the German people only when every last tiller of the soil was German also implied years, even generations, of consolidation. The *Endlösung* in this period meant the expulsion of the Jews to the furthest extremity of the German sphere of influence, first Lublin and then Madagascar. Little was done immediately to implement this version of the final solution, however. Of the nearly half-million Poles and Frenchmen expelled by the Nazi demographic engineers in this period, less than ten percent were Jews. Eichmann's frequent attempts to set full-scale Jewish deportations underway in October 1939, January 1940, and again in the Summer of 1940 all came to naught, for the Nazis temporarily conceded priority to the need to rescue and resettle endangered ethnic Germans. The Jewish question was just as important though not as urgent as *volksdeutsch* resettlement.

The decision to invade Russia brought about a reversal of these priorities. Driven on by his frustration with the military stalemate in the west, his own fervent anti-Bolshevism, his vision of Russia as a land destined for German expansion, his calculation that through the growth of the U.S. and USSR time worked against Germany, his increasing sense of himself as the man of destiny who must do all in his own lifetime, and the pervasive and ceaseless activism that possessed his own psyche as well as the Nazi movement, Hitler opted for Barbarossa.[63] The ideology of *Lebensraum* as practiced between 1939 and 1941 was radical in its methods but relatively conservative in its foreign policy implications. It did not compel an invasion of Russia; on the contrary,

---

[63] For the most recent discussion of Hitler's decision to invade Russia, see the contribution of Jürgen Förster in: *Das Deutsche Reich und der Zweite Weltkrieg*, vol. IV, *Der Angriff auf die Sowjetunion* (Stuttgart, 1983), pp. 3–37. Förster argues that Hitler's anti-Bolshevism and vision of *Lebensraum* in Russia dovetailed with the strategic impasse in which he found himself. "Das Ausgreifen nach Osten, *das* große außenpolitische Ziel seit den zwanziger Jahren, war für Hitler nun auch zum Mittel geworden, Deutschland aus der Zwangslage zu befreien, in die es durch seine axiomatische Grundvorstellungen, sein politisches Vabanquespiel, die nachgiebige Haltung der britischen Regierung sowie die konsequente globale Politik Roosevelts hineingeraten war." (p. 33)

it was transformed by that invasion from a doctrine of gradual racial consolidation into one of limitless expansion.

In the process the Nazi view of a final solution to the Jewish Question was radicalized as well. Limitless expansion into Russia meant ever more Jews. A problem that had already proved intractable threatened to reach immense proportions. The whole sequence of thwarted expulsion plans between 1939 and 1941 had both accustomed the Nazis to thinking in terms of an imminent final solution and frustrated them as, like a mirage, this vision of a *judenfrei* German empire continually receded before their advance. The time was ripe to break the vicious circle. Murder was in the air as the Germans prepared for a *Vernichtungskrieg* in Russia, and in these circumstances the Russian Jews could hardly be spared the fate awaiting so many others.

This whole tendency was intensified by the fundamental position of the Jewish-Bolshevik identity in Nazi ideology. When the Nazis invaded Poland in September 1939, the fate of the Polish Jews could wait but the fate of the Polish intelligentsia could not. The *Einsatzgruppen* were targeted to carry out the immediate genocidal elimination of all potential carriers of the Polish national identity. As the Nazis prepared to confront Bolshevism in 1941, neither the Russian commissars nor Russian Jews could wait; both would have to be eliminated by the onrushing *Einsatzgruppen,* for ultimately they were one – the political and biological manifestations of the same "Jewish-Bolshevik conspiracy."

Once underway the mass-murder of the Jews rapidly intensified. In the Summer of 1941, probably in July, Hitler indicated his approval for the preparation of a plan for the mass murder of all European Jews under Nazi control, though just how and when this was communicated to Himmler and Heydrich cannot be established. By October the plan for the Final Solution had emerged in the form of deportation to death camps equipped with poison gas facilities, and steps were being taken (the transfer of euthanasia personnel from Germany to Poland and the beginning of death camp construction at Chelmno and Belzec) that were inconceivable without Hitler's general approval.[64] The physical

[64] Christopher R. Browning, *Fateful Months: Essays on the Emergence of the Final Solution* (New York, 1985), pp. 8–38.

extermination of all European Jewry had become a top Nazi priority, while other visions of demographic engineering as outlined in the *Generalplan Ost* were for the most part postponed.[65]

Thus the achievement of *Lebensraum* through the invasion of Russia and the Final Solution to the Jewish Question through systematic mass murder were intimately connected and did indeed become the nucleus of Nazi policy, as Hillgruber and Jäckel have so cogently argued. But was this primarily the result of a clever and calculating Hitler awaiting the opportune moment to implement programmatic ideological goals that had crystallized in the 1920s? I would say no. The programmatic view is based primarily upon various statements made by Hitler, such as those in the late 1920s threatening a "bloody" solution "through the sword" or his famous January 1939 Reichstag prophecy that the outbreak of war would mean the destruction of the Jewish race in Europe.[66] My interpretation does not ignore such evidence or dismiss it as mere rhetoric. I am merely arguing that such statements should be seen in a pre-Auschwitz perspective, remembering that the reality of Auschwitz was literally inconceivable to its contemporaries.

If actually implemented, the Lublin Reservation or Madagascar Plan – with the inevitable decimation of the Jewish population that would have been involved – would not have been viewed as falling short of Hitler's pre-war threats of blood and destruction. In this light Hitler's remarks about "removal" or *Entfernung* of the Jews on the one hand and his threats of destruction on the other should not be seen as duplicity and camouflage juxtaposed with malevolent hints of the Final Solution to come. Rather they referred to one and the same general vision, the destructive expulsion of the Jews (first from Germany and then from a German-dominated Europe) as eventually embodied in the resettlement schemes of 1939–1941. Certainly, Hitler's explicit endorsement of and support for these expulsion schemes do little to sustain the idea that he did not take them seriously. Nor does the fact that Jewish emigration from Germany was permitted until October 1941 indicate that Hitler already had in mind the ultimate Final Solution, that

---

[65] Koehl. *RKFDV*, p. 146–162, 226–228. Helmut Heiber, ed., "Der Generalplan Ost," *VfZ*, VI (1958), pp. 281–325.

[66] Cited in Jäckel, *Hitler's Weltanschauung*, pp. 60–61.

is the compulsive attempt systematically to murder every last Jewish man, woman, and child within the German grasp. Thus the period of 1939–1941 was not a hiatus or detour from Nazi ideology but rather a real attempt to implement *Lebensraum* and the *Endlösung* as they were understood at the time. The transformation of these concepts was brought about in large part by the changing situation and cumulative frustration that the Nazis experienced.

A brief look at chronology would also suggest that the transformation may have been induced as much by Hitler's fluctuating moods as by a fanatically consistent adherence to a fixed program. In September 1939, in the flush of victory over Poland, Hitler approved the initial plan for a demographic reorganization of eastern Europe along racial lines. In May and June 1940, with the astonishing victory over France, he approved Himmler's memorandum on the treatment of the eastern populations and the Madagascar Plan. In July 1941, after Nazi armies had torn through Russian border defenses, encircled huge numbers of Russian troops, and raced two-thirds the distance to Moscow, he approved the drawing up of a plan for the mass murder of European Jewry. And in October 1941, with the great encirclement victory of Vyasma and Bryansk and a brief rekindled hope for final triumph before Winter, he approved the Final Solution.[67] Nazi racial policy was radicalized in quantum jumps that coincided with the peaks of German military success, as the euphoria of victory emboldened and tempted an elated Hitler to dare ever more drastic policies. It was with the end of military victories that Hitler clung stubbornly and fanatically to the precepts of 1941, investing them with a permanence and ultimacy they did not have until then.

[67] On Hitler's briefly renewed confidence in quick victory, recalling the atmosphere of July, see Andreas Hillgruber, *Staatsmänner bei Hitler* (Frankfurt, 1967), vol. I, pp. 626–627, 630.

2

Nazi Ghettoization Policy in Poland, 1939–1941

Nazi ghettoization policy in Poland from 1939 to 1941, like so many other aspects of Nazi Jewish policy, has been the subject of conflicting interpretations that can be characterized as "intentionalist" on the one hand and "functionalist" on the other.[1] The "intentionalist" approach views ghettoization as a conscious preparatory step for total annihilation. For instance, Andreas Hillgruber has described the ghettoization of the Polish Jews as a step parallel to Hitler's conquest of France; in both cases Hitler was securing himself for the simultaneous war for *Lebensraum* in the east and Final Solution to the Jewish question through mass murder. Together these steps constituted the nucleus of

Reprinted in slightly revised form with permission. From *Central European History*, 19/4 (1986), pp. 343–368. The research for this article was made possible by the generous support of the Institute for Advanced Studies of the Hebrew University of Jerusalem.

[1] The terms "intentionalist" and "functionalist" were coined by Tim Mason, "Intention and Explanation: A Current Controversy about the Interpretation of National Socialism," *Der Führerstaat: Mythos und Realität*, ed. Gerhard Hirschfeld and Lothar Kettenacker (Stuttgart, 1981), 21–40. Prime examples of the two interpretive approaches can be seen in the articles by Klaus Hildebrand and Hans Mommsen in the same volume. The intentionalists place primary emphasis on Hitler's ideology, leadership, and long-held "program" in explaining the course of the Third Reich. The functionalists emphasize institutional and social structures as more determinative than individuals and ideas. For a pro-intentionalist discussion of the historiography of the Nazi period, see: Klaus Hildebrand, *Das Dritte Reich* (Munich, 1979), now translated as *The Third Reich* (London, 1984). More sympathetic to the functionalists is Ian Kershaw, *The Nazi Dictatorship: Problems and Perspectives of Interpretation* (London, 1985).

his long-held "program."[2] Philip Friedman argued that Nazi Jewish policies in Poland from 1939 to 1941 "were not of a spontaneous or accidental nature, but were rather part and parcel of an unfolding plan, which began with the concentration and isolation of the Jews" and that the "ghettos were designed to serve the Nazis as laboratories for testing the methods of slow and 'peaceful' destruction of whole groups of human beings."[3] Less categorical but in the same vein, Isaiah Trunk, in his major work on the Jewish councils, concluded that Nazi ghettoization policy had the conscious goal or "set task" of decimating the Jewish population through pauperization, epidemic, and increased death rates – intentions that were partially frustrated by the last vestiges of humaneness among some German authorities and varying degrees of corruption among others.[4]

In contrast, the "functionalists" have argued that ghettoization played a vital role in the process of an unplanned "cumulative radicalization" that led to the Final Solution. Martin Broszat has suggested that because local authorities were appalled at the spectacle of the overcrowded ghettos that confirmed their image of the Jew as subhuman and were threatened by a further deluge of deportees from the Reich, they initiated local massacres that gradually took on the shape of a comprehensive program of mass murder.[5] And Hans Mommsen, generalizing from the notorious Höppner memorandum of July 1941,[6] has

---

[2] Andreas Hillgruber, "Die 'Endlösung' und das deutsche Ostimperium als Kernstück des rassenideologischen Programms des Nationalsozialismus," *Hitler, Deutschland, und die Mächte,* ed. Manfred Funke (Düsseldorf, 1978), 98–99.

[3] Philip Friedman, "The Jewish Ghettos of the Nazi Era," *Roads to Extinction: Essays on the Holocaust* (New York and Philadelphia, 1980), 61, 69.

[4] Isaiah Trunk, *Judenrat: The Jewish Councils in Eastern Europe under Nazi Occupation* (New York, 1972), 61.

[5] Martin Broszat, "Hitler und die Genesis der 'Endlösung': Aus Anlass der Thesen von David Irving," *Vierteljahrshefte für Zeitgeschichte* 25, no. 4 (1977): 753–55. This article is available in English translation as: "Hitler and the Genesis of the 'Final Solution': An Assessment of David Irving's Theses," *Yad Vashem Studies* 13 (1979): 61–98.

[6] *SS-Sturmbannführer* Rolf Heinz Höppner reported to Eichmann on a meeting of a group of SS men in Poznań, who had considered the possibility of killing the non-working Jews in the Warthegau with a "quick-acting agent" because this would be more "humane" than having them starve the following winter. Raul Hilberg, *Documents of Destruction* (Chicago, 1971), 87–88.

implied that local authorities could rationalize mass murder as a more "humane" alternative because they could not keep the ghettoized Jews from starving in any case.[7]

It is my contention that neither of these approaches adequately explains either ghettoization policy itself or its relationship to the subsequent program of systematic mass murder. Ghettoization was not a conscious preparatory step planned by the central authorities to facilitate the mass murder nor did it have the "set task" of decimating the Jewish population. Ghettoization was in fact carried out at different times in different ways for different reasons on the initiative of local authorities.

The pattern of local initiative in ghettoization, however, also provides no solace for the functionalist argument of automatic mechanisms of cumulative radicalization inherent in the structure of the Nazi political system. In the local policy disputes in Poland, moderates arguing for a rational exploitation of the Jews' productive potential as the way to keep the incarcerated Jews alive at least cost to the Reich prevailed over radicals arguing for deliberate attrition. Left to themselves, most local authorities followed a course of normalization, not radicalization. In the end only renewed intervention from Berlin induced an abrupt change of course from the policies of normalization to which they inclined.

To examine these arguments more closely, I would like to take as examples the two largest ghettos in Poland – Warsaw and Łódź – and examine three important aspects of Nazi ghettoization policy: first, the decision to create a sealed ghetto; second, the response to the crisis that sealing the ghetto inevitably produced, which took the form of a policy struggle or debate between two groups that I shall dub "productionists" and "attritionists"; and third, the problems that stood in the way of creating a viable and productive ghetto economy, above all the shortage of food.

[7] Hans Mommsen, "Die Realisierung des Utopischen: Die 'Endlösung der Judenfrage' im 'Dritten Reich'," *Geschichte und Gesellschaft* 9, no. 3 (Autumn 1983): 410–11, 414. This article is now available in English translation as: "The Realization of the Unthinkable: The 'Final Solution of the Jewish Question' in the Third Reich," *The Policies of Genocide: Jews and Soviet Prisoners of War in Nazi Germany,* ed. Gerhard Hirschfeld (London, 1986), 93–144.

I

In September 1939, Hitler, Himmler, and Heydrich envisioned a vast demographic reorganization of the newly-conquered territories. As part of this overall plan the Jews were to be concentrated in urban centers and then expelled to the furthest corner of the German empire – the Lublin district on the demarcation line with the Soviet zone. Initially, the deportation of Jews from the incorporated territories, to be completed by February 1940, was to have priority. As for the Jews who were temporarily concentrated "in ghettos" in the cities in order to facilitate "a better possibility of control and later deportation," Heydrich ordered no specific policies other than the appointment of Jewish councils. Though he noted that the concentration of Jews "for general reasons of security will probably bring about orders" restricting their movement, he also noted that "[o]bviously the tasks at hand cannot be laid down in detail from here. . . . " At the same time, Hitler met with Brauchitsch, the commander in chief of the German army, who reported that "the idea of ghettos exists in general" but the details had not yet been clarified. In short, *sealed* ghettos of *prolonged* duration were not part of any policy imposed by Berlin on local German authorities in Poland in September 1939.[8]

In the fall of 1939, therefore, the German authorities in the Warthegau (one of the four provinces composed of Polish territory annexed to the Third Reich) expected that their Jews would be deported eastward in short order. When the Łódź Jews were not included in the first wave of deportations,[9] Arthur Greiser, who as *Reichsstatthalter* and

---

[8] For the development of Nazi demographic plans, see: Christopher R. Browning, "Nazi Resettlement Policy and the Search for a Solution to the Jewish Question, 1939–41," *German Studies Review* 9, no. 3 (1986): 497–519. For Heydrich's instructions: National Archives Microfilm, T175/239/2726524–28 (protocol of conference of 21 Sept. 1939); and *Nazi Conspiracy and Aggression* (Washington, 1946), 6: 97–101 (PS-3363: Heydrich Schnellbrief of 21 Sept. 1939). For the Hitler-Brauchitsch meeting: Franz Halder, *Kriegstagebuch*, ed. Hans-Adolf Jacobsen (Stuttgart, 1962), 1: 82. For the expulsion of Jews from the incorporated territories: *Faschismus, Getto, Massenmord* (Berlin [East], 1960), 42–43 (NO-5586; Himmler order of 30 Oct. 1939); and *Trials of the War Criminals before the Nürnberg Military Tribunal* (Washington, 1949–53), 4: 873 (NO-4095: undated memorandum of Creutz).

[9] Deportation of the Łódź Jews was initially excluded by Higher SS and Police Leader Wilhelm Krüger at a conference of 8 Nov. 1939, because it was not yet clear whether

Gauleiter combined both state and party leadership in the Warthegau, decided in December to make a virtue out of necessity and exploit this delay. Arguing that the Jews had "hoarded colossally," Greiser ordered their ghettoization "until what they have amassed is given back in exchange for food and then they will be expelled over the border."[10] Thus the local Germans viewed the Łódź ghetto as a strictly temporary device for extracting Jewish wealth, a device which would end abruptly with the deportation of the impoverished victims. As the *Regierungspräsident* for the Łódź region, Friedrich Uebelhoer, put it, "The creation of the ghetto is of course only a transition measure. I shall determine at what time and with what means the ghetto and thereby also the city of Łódź will be cleansed of Jews."[11]

The ghetto was finally sealed at the end of April 1940, but much to the surprise of the Warthegau Nazis they could not deport the Jews as expected. In April 1940 Greiser's request for deportation was put off until August because the repatriation of ethnic Germans from the Soviet sphere was given priority.[12] As most Jews in the incorporated territories had already been stripped of their lodgings and livelihoods the previous fall, only the dispossession and deportation of Poles could provide the desired farms, businesses, and housing for the incoming *Volksdeutsche*. In the summer of 1940, the deportation of Jews to the General Government was cancelled entirely because the Madagascar Plan then in vogue called for the deportation of all European Jews in the other direction and out of Europe entirely. To no avail Greiser and

---

Łódź would be included in the "incorporated territories" annexed from Poland and allotted to the Warthegau or remain part of the General Government. *Biuletyn Głównej Komisji Badania Zbrodni Hitlerowskich W Polsce* (hereafter cited as *Biuletyn*) 12 (Warsaw, 1960): 11F–14F (conference of 8 Nov. 1939). Subsequently Łódź was included in the Warthegau.

[10] Berlin Document Center: Greiser Pers. Akten, Besuchs-Vermerk of the Staff of the Führer's Deputy, 11 Jan. 1940. I am grateful to Dr. Hans Umbreit for a copy of this document.

[11] *Faschismus, Getto, Massenmord*, 81 (Rundschreiben of Uebelhoer to party and police authorities, 10 Dec. 1939).

[12] *Dokumenty i Materiały Do Dziejów Okupacji Niemieckiej W Polsce, 3: Getto Łódzkie* (Warsaw, 1946; herafter cited as *DiM*), 168–69 (conference of 1 Apr. 1940, and Baur to Landräte, 8 May 1940).

his Higher SS and Police Leader Wilhelm Koppe frantically requested Frank to take the Łódź Jews as an interim measure because "the situation regarding the Jews in the Warthegau worsened day by day," and the ghetto there "had actually only been erected on the condition that the deportation of the Jews would begin by mid-year at the latest."[13]

In late summer of 1940, therefore, the Warthegau Nazis had to decide what to do with a ghetto that none of them had expected would still be in existence at that time. Since Berlin still expected the Jewish question to be solved through expulsion and refused officially to acknowledge that these plans had collapsed, local authorities were left to cope as best they could. The stage was set for the first debate over ghetto policy at the local level.

In contrast to Łódź, Warsaw experienced ghettoization in fits and starts. Ordered by local SS officials in the fall of 1939, ghettoization was put off by the military commander.[14] Instead the predominately Jewish section of the city was declared a quarantine area off-limits to Germans – the first of many occasions in which fear of the Jews as carriers of epidemic would play a role in policy decisions concerning the Warsaw Jews. A short-lived plan for a ghetto on the east side of the Vistula across the river from Warsaw was vetoed in the spring of 1940, as was the deportation of Warsaw Jews to the district of Lublin.[15] Again citing the danger of epidemic, however, public health officials of the General Government pressed successfully for the erection of walls around the quarantine area.[16] In the early summer of 1940, Warsaw officials pursued the idea of two suburban ghettos, until Frank ordered the cessation of all ghetto preparations as "for all practical purposes illusory" in view of the impending deportation of Europe's Jews to Madagascar.[17]

[13] Hans Frank, *Das Diensttagebuch des deutschen Generalgouverneurs in Polen 1939–1945*, ed. Werner Präg and Wolfgang Jacobmeyer (Stuttgart, 1975), 261–63 (entry of 31 July 1940).

[14] Yisrael Gutman, *The Jews of Warsaw 1939–1943: Ghetto, Underground, Revolt* (Bloomington, Indiana, 1982), 49.

[15] *Faschismus, Getto, Massenmord*, 108–9 (Schön report, 20 Jan. 1941).

[16] Yad Vashem Archives (hereafter cited as YVA), O-53/102/391–99 (Halbjahres Bericht von Dr. Kreppel, Abt. Innere Verwaltung, Warschau Distrikt, 14 May 1940).

[17] *Faschismus, Getto, Massenmord*, 109–10 (Schön report of 20 Jan. 1941).

In the end it was once again the persistent public health officials who prevailed, as they insisted in early September that ghettoization of the Warsaw Jews was an absolute necessity to ward off the threat of epidemic.[18] Frank agreed, and the Warsaw ghetto was sealed in mid-November.

II

If the Łódź and Warsaw ghettos were created at different times for different reasons, the existence of the ghettos themselves soon presented local German authorities with identical problems. Once the ghettos were sealed and all economic ties with the outside world had been broken, supplies within the ghetto were quickly exhausted and the incarcerated populations faced imminent starvation. Local German authorities had to decide whether to let the murderous attrition take its course or to take positive steps to mitigate the looming demographic disaster. While there were vigorous advocates of attrition and huge obstacles in the way of mitigation, nonetheless advocates of the latter prevailed in both cities.

When the Łódź ghetto had been sealed, German authorities had calculated that the Jewish wealth which they wished to extract would suffice to provision the ghetto until the end of July. After that the Jews would be gone. Jewish efforts to interest the Germans in the potential of Jewish labor were generally unsuccessful; the Germans felt that at most Jewish labor would contribute 15 percent of the food costs of the ghetto. Any greater effort to exploit Jewish labor would result in raw material shortages and distort the local economy, the Germans believed.[19]

---

[18] YVA, JM 814: Lambrecht report, 3 Sept. 1940, and report of Div. of Internal Affairs, 4 Sept. 1940. *Faschismus, Getto, Massenmord*, 110 (Schön report, 20 Jan. 1941). *Trials of the Major War Criminals before the International Military Tribunal* (Nuremberg, 1947–49), 29: 406(2233-PS: conference of 6 Sept. 1940). Frank, *Diensttagebuch*, 281 (Abteilungleiterssitzung, 12 Sept. 1940).

[19] YVA, JM 799/209 (Vermerk of conferences of 26 and 27 Apr. 1940); O-58/78/296–97 (Rumkowski to Marder, 6 Apr. 1940); JM 800/387–89 (Vermerk by Dr. Nebel of conference of 27 May 1940). *DiM*, 74–75 (Oberbürgermeister to Rumkowski, 30 Apr. 1940).

Contrary to the expectations of the Łódź officials, the ghetto was not dissolved in August. Instead the ghetto experienced skyrocketing death rates; one and one-half percent of the ghetto population perished in July and August alone.[20] The leader of the Łódź Judenrat, Chaim Rumkowski, told the Germans that money for purchasing food had been exhausted, and he urged that the Jews be given employment in order to finance provisions for the ghetto.[21] Alexander Palfinger, a German official of the ghetto administration lodged within the municipal government of the city of Łódź, dismissed this proposal contemptuously. He argued that the Jews were still hoarding their valuables. Thus gainful employment had to be prevented, for only the "most extreme exigency" would make the Jews surrender their last reserves.[22]

By the end of August, however, food supplies for the ghetto were piling up outside because the ghetto community had no more money with which to purchase them.[23] Even stopping food deliveries for several days in September produced no outpouring of hoarded valuables from the ghetto. The chief of the ghetto administration, Hans Biebow, a 37-year-old Bremen coffee importer who had joined the Nazi party in 1937 and taken up his position in Łódź in May 1940, then asked *Regierungspräsident* Uebelhoer to provide funds for further food deliveries.[24] This use of public money to buy food for the starving Jews of Łódź made a fundamental re-examination of German ghettoization policy inevitable.

Hans Biebow became the outspoken advocate for creating a viable ghetto economy, arguing that every effort had to be made "to facilitate the self-maintenance of the Jews through finding them work." This program would be impossible without "continuous and initially high subsidies" because the "large-scale employment of Jewish labor" required considerable lead time to procure contracts and erect factories. Moreover, stockpiling for the winter, for which the Jews had no funds either, could no longer be put off. Subsidies were therefore needed "as

---

[20] YVA, O-6/79, Report of the Statistical Office of Łódź on the Jewish population in 1940.
[21] YVA, JM 798, Activity report for July 1940.
[22] YVA, JM 799/139 (Palfinger Aktennotiz, 16 July 1940).
[23] YVA, JM 798, Activity report for Aug. 1940.
[24] YVA, JM 798, Auditor's report of Feb. 1941.

quickly as possible."[25] Biebow did not get all he wanted financially, but the Łódź Judenrat received a four and one-half percent six-month loan of three million Reichsmark – out of confiscated Jewish funds, naturally.[26] The loan represented a turning point in German policy. The ghetto was no longer a temporary device for extracting Jewish wealth prior to deportation, but would now become a long-term institution in whose economic productivity the Germans had a vested interest. This change of perspective was articulated at a meeting on 18 October 1940, where "it was established at the outset that the ghetto in Łódź must continue to exist and everything must be done to make the ghetto self-sustaining."[27]

Not everyone was reconciled to this basic change in German ghetto policy, however. Biebow's sullen deputy, Alexander Palfinger, argued that "especially in the Jewish question the National Socialist idea . . . permits no compromises." In a disparaging reference to Biebow's background, Palfinger argued that a solution to the Jewish question could not be attained purely through a "salesman-like negotiating ability." His idea of a solution ran along different lines: "A rapid dying out of the Jews is for us a matter of total indifference, if not to say desirable, as long as the concomitant effects leave the public interest of the German people untouched."[28]

The deputy mayor of Łódź and immediate superior to the ghetto administration, Dr. Karl Marder, sided with the "productionist" viewpoint of Biebow, not the "attritionist" policy advocated by Palfinger. As he explained later, as long as the ghetto was a "transition measure" not intended to last the year, the major task of the ghetto administration had been the "drawing off of the wealth of the ghetto in order to supply their necessities of life." Now the character of the ghetto had to be "fundamentally altered." It was no longer to be "nothing more than a kind of holding or concentration camp" but rather an "essential element of the total economy . . . a one-of-its-kind large scale enterprise."[29]

[25] YVA, JM 798, Activity report for Sept. 1940.
[26] YVA, JM 798, Auditor's report of Feb. 1941.
[27] *DiM*, 102–4 (conference of 18 Oct. 1940).
[28] YVA, O-53/78/76–82 (Palfinger's "critical report" of 7 Nov. 1940).
[29] *DiM*, 177–79 (Marder to Uebelhoer, 4 July 1941).

The disgruntled Palfinger left for Warsaw to see if he could get his way there. His parting gesture, an obvious ploy to attract attention to what he considered the intolerable coddling of the Łódź Jews, was to order from Berlin 144,000 eggs per week for the ghetto, leaving the embarrassed Biebow to explain that the request had been made without his knowledge.[30]

Palfinger arrived in Warsaw just as the ghetto was being sealed in mid-November 1940. Waldemar Schön, the head of the Resettlement Division that had jurisdiction over the Jews, immediately appointed him head of the so-called *Transferstelle*. This agency was to be the economic intermediary between the incarcerated Jews and the outside world. The job of the *Transferstelle* was to provide food and raw materials to the ghetto and to negotiate contracts with the outside on its behalf. The *Transferstelle* was the sole judge in assessing the value of Jewish goods to be used to pay for food. Palfinger was thus in a position to strangle the economic activity of the ghetto and starve its inhabitants, an "attritionist" policy he immediately set about implementing with the support of other like-minded local authorities.

At a meeting in early December 1940 the head of the Warsaw district's Division of Food and Agriculture, Karl Naumann, urged that the ghetto not be supplied with food that month in order to force the Jews to use up their smuggled food and hidden valuables. The district public health official, Dr. Arnold Lambrecht, who had earlier urged ghettoization as a measure to counter epidemic, protested against deliberately fostering the outbreak of just such epidemic through "artificial famine." Schön indicated his agreement with Lambrecht, but in fact two days later Naumann refused to import food into the ghetto anyhow.[31] This refusal apparently had Schön's tacit support, for neither the objections of public health officials nor the pleas of the Judenrat chairman, Adam Czerniakow, moved Schön, Palfinger, and Naumann to alter their starvation policy. As Schön cynically declared in February 1941, he had no interest in the complaints of the Jews with one

---

[30] YVA, JM 799/167–68 (Ribbe to Marder, 22 Nov. 1940).
[31] YVA, JM 1113, conference of 2 Dec. 1940; *The Warsaw Diary of Adam Czerniakow*, ed. Raul Hilberg, Stanislaw Staron, and Josef Kermisz (New York, 1979), 223 (entry of 4 Dec. 1940).

exception: "The delivery of soap . . . must be carried out, lest the Jewish council can rightfully maintain that German offices are increasing its difficulties in carrying out hygienic directions."[32]

By mid-January reports had reached Hans Frank's capital of the General Government, Kraków, that food supplies to the Warsaw ghetto had been stopped completely.[33] By March the indications of looming catastrophe in Warsaw prompted the head of the Economic Division of the General Government, Dr. Walter Emmerich, to present Frank with a 53-page report analyzing the economic viability of the ghetto.[34]

The crux of the problem for Emmerich was that once the ghetto had been sealed and its population cut off from its normal economic activity, it consumed more than it produced. This constituted a negative balance or deficit for the economy of the ghetto, whose duration he estimated at five years. Once the existing wealth of the ghettoized Jews had been liquidated, the Germans would have to face one of four choices: (1) subsidize the ghetto; (2) accept the consequences of inadequate provisioning; (3) harness the Jews to productive labor; or (4) loosen the seal around the ghetto to allow the resumption of direct economic ties with the surrounding population. The public health officials would oppose the last possibility, and the undesirability of the first required no comment. Thus one could either view the ghetto "as a means to liquidate the Jews" or as a source of labor that had to be sufficiently fed to be capable of productive work. The bulk of the report sought to analyze the conditions necessary to achieve the third option, a self-sufficient, working ghetto. It concluded that to provide minimal provisions for the ghetto inhabitants without a subsidy, 60,000 Jews would have to be employed producing "exports" for the outside world.

The existing policies of Schön and Palfinger were totally inadequate to this task. Schön claimed that the ghetto inhabitants possessed wealth worth six months' food supply and that "pressure" through a "ban on food deliveries" was necessary to extract this wealth before one could worry about organizing production. Emmerich's investigators insisted

---

[32] Ibid., 394 (appended document: conference of 3 Feb. 1941).
[33] Frank, *Diensttagebuch*, 328 (conference of 15 Jan. 1941).
[34] Ibid., 334 (entry of 22 Mar. 1941). YVA, JM 10016, "Die Wirtschaftsbilanz des jüdischen Wohnbezirks in Warschau," Mar. 1941. Trunk, *Judenrat*, 287.

that nothing approaching that kind of wealth existed in the ghetto and production had to be organized immediately. They also criticized the plan for the *Transferstelle*, working through the Judenrat, totally to control a highly centralized ghetto economy on the Łódź model. The Judenrat lacked sufficient authority and organization for such a task, and the *Transferstelle* could not possibly control every aspect of an economy of nearly 500,000 people.

Frank ordered Emmerich to obtain the views of the Warsaw district governor, Dr. Ludwig Fischer, and promised to schedule a meeting on the subject. What followed was a dramatic debate between the Kraków-centered "productionists" and the Warsaw "attritionists."

The confrontation began at an initial meeting on 3 April 1941, attended by leading officials from both Warsaw and Kraków. Governor Fischer of the Warsaw district presented a rosy picture: the ghettoized Jews had "considerable means" at their disposal so "in the next months there is no danger at all of famine"; the Jews were extensively employed and production was going forward.[35] Emmerich brushed this fantasy aside. "One must free himself from the notion that it is still going well in the ghetto and that supplies are still available there," he stated. As the ghetto had been created for the long haul, economic planning must be done accordingly. *"The starting point for all economic measures has to be the idea of maintaining the capacity of the Jews to live* [italics mine]. The question is whether one can succeed in solving this problem in a productive manner." Despite Schön's complaint that the ideas of the Kraków economists were "too theoretical," Frank left no doubt about his views. "The responsibility that the government took on with the creation of a Jewish district of 500,000 human beings [*Menschen!*] is very great, and a failure would always be blamed on the authorities of the General Government."[36]

Four days after this meeting, Palfinger composed a blistering "exposé" of the Emmerich report. It had been drawn up by "impractical

---

[35] That Fischer was simply trying to allay interference from Kraków and was a strong advocate of the attritionist policies of Schön and Palfinger can be seen from his statement quoted by Philip Friedman: "The Jews will disappear because of hunger and need, and nothing will remain of the Jewish question but a cemetery." Cited in: "The Jewish Ghettos of the Nazi Era," *Roads to Extinction,* 69.

[36] Frank, *Diensttagebuch,* 343–46 (conference of 3 Apr. 1941).

and unrealistic theoreticians" whose facts were wrong. Employment prospects in the ghetto were so good, Palfinger claimed, that soon the ghetto administration would be able "to stock a reserve fund." Moreover, these "theoreticians" failed to realize that economic considerations had to be subordinate to "purely political" ones. For example, they were so politically deficient that they calculated the needs of the ghettoized Jews as if they were Aryans. Palfinger provided a different measure.

> A work animal from whom a human being demands output was never the subject of profound contemplation concerning its needs. On the contrary . . . the one who maintains the animal regulates its food supply according to its productivity.

The authors of the report ignored the fact that for political reasons the highest authorities desired "a radical course" in the Jewish question and that the living standard of the ghetto inhabitants was to be depressed to the level of an "internment camp" (*Anhaltelager*) regardless of the total output of the Jewish masses.[37]

Palfinger's "exposé" was in vain. On 9 April 1941 Kraków officials submitted to Frank a draft decree for reorganizing the administration of the Warsaw ghetto. Responsibility for the ghetto would be taken from Schön's Resettlement Division and placed in the hands of a commissioner for the Jewish district who would supervise the *Transferstelle*. Policy was to be made "within the framework of guidelines provided by the central authorities" in Kraków. Such a stipulation was necessary, the drafters argued, "because the district chief of Warsaw wants to decide this question alone. . . . "[38] At a follow-up meeting of 19 April 1940, Frank imposed the new policy on reluctant Warsaw officials.[39]

The ensuing changes in Warsaw were astonishing. The Viennese banker, Max Bischof, hired to lead the *Transferstelle*, had the specific task of achieving economic self-sufficiency for the ghetto. He was

---

[37] Archiwum Państwowe m. st. Warszawy, Der Kommissar für den jüdischen Wohnbezirk in Warschau, Nr. 125, Palfinger Aktennotiz, 7 Apr. 1941.

[38] Ibid., 354–55 (conference of 9 Apr. 1941). *Documenta Occupationis* (Poznań, 1949), 6: 556 (Verordnung über den jüdischen Wohnbezirk in Warschau, 19 Apr. 1941).

[39] Frank, *Diensttagebuch*, 359–62 (conference of 19 Apr. 1941).

promised a government subsidy if it proved necessary. He also received the assurance that, once he had worked into the job, he could have Palfinger removed.[40] Schön was transferred to another position, and Heinz Auerswald, a lawyer who at least on one occasion could not even remember when he had joined the Nazi party, was appointed commissioner of the Jewish district.[41]

Upon taking up their positions, Auerswald and Bischof were unpleasantly surprised to learn that, despite past assurances of high employment in the ghetto, almost no one was working, and that the *Transferstelle* had in fact procured only 5–10 percent of the ghetto's needed food and supplies. Under the circumstances, gaps in the ghetto cordon would have to be tolerated, they concluded.[42]

Czerniakow's diary for the month of May records a truly astonishing turnabout in German behavior. The Warsaw diarist Emmanuel Ringelblum had previously noted of Palfinger, "The director of the Transfer Station makes it a practice not to talk to Jews. There are dignitaries like that, who won't see a Jew to talk with as a matter of principle. They order the windows of the Transfer Station kept open because of the stench the Jews make."[43] Now in early May the same Palfinger solicitously informed Czerniakow "that he will do everything to improve the food supply." A week later, on 12 May, Czerniakow had his first meeting with Auerswald who "announced that his attitude to the [Jewish] Council was objective and matter of fact, without animosity." On 21 May, Czerniakow was even received by the district governor, Dr. Fischer. "At the very beginning he contended that starving the Jews was not his objective. There is a possibility that the food rations would be increased and that there will be work or orders for the workers."[44] In May 1941, therefore, a fundamental change – parallel to that in Łódź the previous fall – occurred in German policy toward the Warsaw ghetto. The "attritionists" were out and the "productionists" had prevailed. The ghetto was not to be starved to death but made into a productive entity. And this took place, it should be noted, in the very

[40] YVA, JM 1112, Bischof Aktenvermerk on discussion with Fischer, 30 Apr. 1941.
[41] YVA, O-53/49/103–4 (personnel questionnaire of Auerswald).
[42] YVA, JM 1112, Bischof Aktenvermerk, 8 May 1941.
[43] *The Journal of Emmanuel Ringelblum*, ed. Jacob Sloan (New York, 1958), 158.
[44] *The Warsaw Diary of Adam Czerniakow*, 230–39 (entries of 6, 12, and 21 May 1941).

month in which the *Einsatzgruppen* were being assembled in their
training camps for the murderous assault upon Russian Jewry.

III

Even after the "productionists" had prevailed over the "attritionists"
in both Łódź and Warsaw, immense problems still stood in the way of
self-sustaining ghettos. In both cities the ghetto managers would succeed in creating novel economies, although along quite different lines.
But in neither ghetto could they cope adequately with the devastating
hunger and epidemic, for they encountered constraints more intractable
than the opposition of the "attritionists."

In terms of expectations, the ghetto was a temporary phenomenon –
existing longer than expected but nonetheless destined for liquidation at
some point in the future – and thus had a low ranking in any claim on
priorities. Ideologically, and perhaps most importantly, the inhabitants
of the ghettos were at the bottom of a racial hierarchy, in which even the
surrounding Polish population was being held, by Hitler's explicit order, to a bare subsistence standard of living and yet axiomatically had
a greater right to scarce wartime resources than the Jews. Against such
factors the ghetto managers could not fully prevail, and the decimation
of the Jewish population through hunger and disease was only partially
stemmed. Prior to the Final Solution, however, this on-going horror
and attrition in the ghettos was not the result of a "set task" of cynical
ghetto managers but of problems they could not overcome.

At the decisive meeting of 18 October 1940 in Łódź the German authorities had conceded that the ghetto would continue to exist and had
to be made self-sufficient. Just how this was to be done was the subject
of several subsequent meetings. The ghetto was still considered a "necessary evil." If it had to be fed, it was to be supplied with goods of the
lowest quality. The priorities were clear-cut; provisioning the civil population could not be "impaired or disadvantaged even in the slightest
for the benefit of the Jews."[45] It was finally agreed that the food supply
should be based upon the "nutritional minimum" of "prison fare."
Scarce food and energy would be stretched through the introduction of

[45] *DiM*, 241–42 (conference of 24 Oct. 1940).

large common kitchens and a ban upon the use of electricity and heating in the ghetto after eight o'clock in the evening.[46]

As for the construction of a ghetto economy, Biebow in Łódź was determined from the beginning to keep all the strings in his own hands. All requests for Jewish labor were to be directed solely to the ghetto administration. To enhance the ghetto's productive capacity, he first sought to procure all unused or non-functioning machinery that had been confiscated by the Germans in the Warthegau.[47] He then cast his sights further and arranged through the Finance Ministry in Berlin for the delivery of machinery confiscated from German Jews. By March 1943 Biebow boasted of a machine inventory of 18,000 (which included everything from sewing machines and work benches to more sophisticated equipment).[48] He also toured Germany looking for contracts and was constantly adding new workshops and factories. Though the initial emphasis was on textiles, by the spring of 1941, the ghetto was producing cabinets, furniture, shoes, and gloves, and performing tannery, furrier, upholstery, and locksmith work.[49]

Employment statistics reflected the economic transformation of Łódź into what Isaiah Trunk termed "the most industrialized ghetto in all of Eastern Europe."[50] In October 1940, 5,000 textile workers were employed in the ghetto. By December this figure had risen to 15,000. By the summer of 1941, 40,000 Jews were at work in the ghetto. In the spring of 1943, it was 80,000 (which is to say almost the entire ghetto population at that time).[51]

Biebow encountered numerous problems in his attempt to establish a viable ghetto economy. Two problems were particularly salient, however. The first was the constant attempt of various German authorities in the Warthegau to lay their hands on the wealth being produced by

[46] YVA, O-53/78/70–74 (conference of 9 Nov. 1940).
[47] Ibid.
[48] YVA, O-53/78/137-39 (Gettoverwaltung memorandum of 24 Mar. 1943); *DiM*, 114–16 (Biebow to Treuhandstelle Posen, 26 Mar. 1942).
[49] YVA, JM 798, Activity reports for Feb., Mar., Apr., and May 1941; JM 800/148 (Aktennotiz of 10 Mar. 1941).
[50] Trunk, *Judenrat*, 84.
[51] YVA, JM 798, Activity reports for Oct. and Dec. 1940; O-53/78/137–39 (Gettoverwaltung memorandum of 24 Mar. 1943). *DiM*, 177–79 (Marder to Uebelhoer, 4 July 1941) and 243–45 (Biebow to Fuchs, 4 Mar. 1942).

Jewish labor. Of all the aspiring predators, the most significant was *Gauleiter* and *Reichsstatthalter* Greiser, who initially wanted all proceeds above 10 pfennigs per hour paid by private firms for Jewish labor to be deposited into the *Gauleiter*'s own NSDAP account in the Warthegau. After prolonged negotiations, he finally settled for 65 percent with Jewish workers permitted to retain 35 percent as wages.[52] Greiser's outrageous share may have rendered more difficult Biebow's attempts to achieve a ghetto "balance of payments," but in the long run it did give the *Gauleiter* a huge vested interest in preserving the ghetto from total liquidation.

A second, even more intractable, problem was the ghetto food supply. In the fall of 1940 it had been agreed that the Jews would receive "prison fare," with the limiting proviso "that the Jews receive this food only to the extent that in no case will the provisioning situation in Litzmannstadt [Łódź] be negatively affected."[53] As the winter deepened and the food situation became increasingly desperate, Biebow saw his whole enterprise endangered and complained bitterly.

> The plight in the ghetto is so great that the Eldest of the Jews felt compelled to hand over to his communal kitchens the potato scraps that had been delivered for horse fodder, in order at least to be able to prepare lunch for the productively active workers in the workshops. . . . In practice the ghetto lives from hand to mouth, and each further shortfall in food delivery earmarked for the Jews results in inescapable famine. . . . In calculating the needs of the population in Litzmannstadt and in the resulting allotment and delivery for the German and Polish population, apparently the ghetto is never included. It would be advisable that the attitude of the market control authorities fundamentally changes, for the fact remains that the head as well as the other competent authorities of the ghetto administration must occupy themselves day after day with the question of feeding the ghetto, because either the

---

[52] YVA, JM 800/217–20 (Marder to Reich Trustee for Labor, Poznań, 21 Aug. 1940), 227–28 (Marder to Regierungspräsident, 10 Sept. 1940), and 239 (Aktennotiz, 17 Sept. 1940); JM 798, undated memo "Beschäftigung von Juden durch Privatunternehmungen".

[53] YVA, JM 798, Activity report for Nov. 1940.

deliveries are not as large as promised or released provisions are suddenly withdrawn for allegedly more urgent needs. Inevitably the necessity arises to drop other equally important tasks of the ghetto administration, which is especially disadvantageous to the mobilization of Jewish labor.[54]

In addition to the desperate food supply, Biebow noted that the shortage of coal was so great that meals could not be cooked even if potatoes were available, and workers were not coming to the unheated factories because they simply could not withstand the cold there, the intensity of which Biebow had convinced himself through personal inspection.[55]

In mid-January 1941 Biebow finally extracted the assurance that henceforth 10 percent of the Łódź coal allotment would be delivered to the ghetto, for otherwise the factories could not operate. No similar commitment was made concerning food supplies, though they fell well below "prison fare."[56] In February 1941, in fact, potato deliveries remained at a mere one-quarter of that level. Even the horses, so essential for transporting goods, were starving. "Catastrophe" and "famine" threatened, Biebow noted.[57] The auditor examining the books of the ghetto administration that month calculated that the Jews were being fed on 23 pfennigs per day, less than one-half "prison fare."[58]

Those trying to provision the ghetto did not mince words about the corruption and obstruction that they encountered. Biebow openly charged that the Łódź bakers were trying to enrich themselves by delivering underweight products to the ghetto.[59] And the auditor who drew up a 28-page report in February 1941 on the economic status of the ghetto administration noted the hostile and uncooperative atmosphere in which Biebow worked. There was a widespread lack of "proper understanding" concerning the ghetto, he observed. Not only requests for food but also for raw materials were met with the standard reply that nothing was available for the Jews. "It is thereby completely

---

[54] YVA, JM 798, Activity report for Dec. 1940.
[55] YVA, JM 798, Activity report for Nov. 1940.
[56] YVA, JM 800/160–61 (Aktenvermerk of conference of 14 Jan. 1941).
[57] YVA, JM 798, Activity report for Feb. 1941.
[58] YVA, JM 798, Auditor's report of Feb. 1941.
[59] YVA, JM 798, Activity report for Nov. 1940.

overlooked," he concluded, "that the requests serve much less the interest of the Jews than the appropriate exploitation of Jewish manpower for the good of the Reich."[60]

Only in March did Biebow note that food deliveries in some areas were reaching the level of prison fare. In April the food supply, with some exceptions, was even characterized as "satisfactory" for the Jews, though not yet for the horses.[61] The high point of optimism was reached just days before the invasion of Russia, when Biebow met with the *Gau* food authorities in Poznań on 7 June 1941.

> All participants recognized that the present provisioning of the Jews was irresponsible and without a quick improvement would result in famine, which 1) was incompatible with the enormous tasks that the Jews had been given in the skilled-labor area, and 2) ignored the great danger of epidemic outbreak in the ghetto. . . .

The Poznań authorities promised not just to obtain the approved ghetto rations but to increase them. For working Jews "Polish rations" were to be a minimum, while non-working Jews were to receive the long-promised "prison-fare."[62]

With the invasion of Russia and the fatal transformation of Nazi Jewish policy in the last half of 1941, the promised improvements did not in fact materialize. In vain Biebow continued to press for better provisioning of the ghetto even during the subsequent period of the deportations and mass murder in the nearby Chełmno death camp.[63]

Long before this, however, the terms of Biebow's argument had changed. Initially he had argued that the Jews must be put to work so that they could be fed. As the ghetto economy's contribution to the war effort increased while food supplies did not, he began to argue the other way around; the Jews had to be fed so that they could continue to per-

---

[60] YVA, JM 798, Auditor's report of Feb. 1941.

[61] YVA, JM 798, Activity reports for Mar. and Apr. 1941.

[62] YVA, JM 800/82–83 (Poznań conference of 7 June 1941) and 94 (Aktennotiz, 11 June 1941).

[63] *DiM*, 243–45 (Biebow to Fuchs, 4 Mar. 1942) and 245–47 (Biebow to Ventzki, 19 Apr. 1943).

form work vital to the war effort. But even the most cogent utilitarian arguments were to no avail as long as an improvement in the food supply to the Łódź ghetto meant diverting food supplies from someone else. As the mayor of Łódź, Werner Ventzki, informed Biebow, "The *Gauleiter* [Greiser] has repeatedly refused to improve the provisioning of the Jews *on principle* [italics mine], in view of the fact that supplying the German population involved not inconsiderable difficulties."[64] In Łódź, therefore, the triumph of the productionists over the attritionists was very incomplete at best. The ghettoized Jews continued to starve, albeit more slowly than the attritionists had wished.

In Warsaw the departure of the notorious attritionists Schön and Palfinger came too late to stem a skyrocketing death rate produced by a half-year's deliberate starvation. This death rate had risen above 1,000 in the month of February, above 2,000 in April, and then nearly doubled to 3,800 in May 1941. "A quantum leap in deaths for May of this year showed that the food shortage had already grown into a famine." Auerswald concluded. "The provisioning of food thus constituted our most urgent task." Auerswald did provide some extra supplies to the Jewish Self-Aid (JSS) to increase the daily meals it provided from 30,000 in May to 120,000 in August. "Due to the general impoverishment of the Jews prevailing since the outbreak of the war," however, these supplementary rations did not staunch the rising death rates until they peaked at 5,550 in July and 5,560 in August. Thereafter a modest decline and stabilization set in.[65]

As in Łódź in the early summer of 1941, the Germans briefly held out the prospect of "Polish rations" to the Warsaw Jews. These hopes were dashed in late August, as Czerniakow noted in his diary. "Auerswald declares that Kraków is also inclined not to starve out the Jews. However, the rations cannot be increased at this point because the newly captured territories absorb a lot of food."[66] In October 1941 Max Bischof complained that the "unconditionally necessary" provisions

[64] *DiM*, 248 (Ventzki Aktenvermerk, no date).
[65] YVA, JM 1112, Auerswald report of 26 Sept. 1941. *The Journal of Emmanuel Ringelblum*, 191–92. Gutman, *The Jews of Warsaw*, 63–65.
[66] *The Warsaw Diary of Adam Czerniakow*, 264 and 269 (entries of 7 July and 19 Aug. 1941).

for workers in the economy were lacking. He was supported vehemently by Auerswald. All aspects of his policy toward the Jews – tighter sealing of the ghetto, ending Jewish blackmarketeering and smuggling, preventing the spread of epidemics, as well as exploiting Jewish labor – depended on "securing a necessary nutritional minimum for the working Jewish population." The present rations, less than one-third the level provided in the Łódź ghetto, were "absolutely insufficient." Governor Fischer, the one-time "attritionist," continued to argue that the war was a conflict "with Jewry in its totality" and that the Germans would be justified in striking "annihilatingly" (*vernichtend*) against "these spawning grounds of Jewry, from which all world Jewry is constantly renewed." In the meantime, however, if the Jews were to work, they had to receive "sufficient rations."[67]

Frank, like Greiser in the Warthegau, refused any increase on principle, noting that "even for the Polish population hardly anything more can be provided." Bischof then attempted with some success to get private German employers with contracts for military production to provide supplementary rations to their workers, hoping that the increase in productivity that resulted would induce other employers to follow suit.[68]

Knowing that "the amount of legally delivered food is utterly insufficient effectively to counter the famine situation existing in the Jewish district," Auerswald initially took a relatively lenient view toward smuggling, provided that it could be accomplished without the spread of the ghetto epidemics that starvation had induced. Czerniakow noted, "He [Auerswald] indicated that so far as smuggling is concerned the authorities are looking the other way but that he will take the sternest measures against people leaving the ghetto. The reason – the epidemic."[69] As spotted fever spread beyond the ghetto and Auerswald blamed Jewish smugglers, his tone became harsher. "Only the most

---

[67] YVA, JM 1112, Transferstelle report of 8 Oct. 1941; Archiwum Państwowe m. st. Warszawy, Der Kommissar für den jüdischen Wohnbezirk in Warschau, Nr. 132, speeches by Ludwig Fischer, Max Bischof, and Heinz Auerswald, 15 Oct. 1941.

[68] YVA, JM 21/4 (Frank Tagebuch, 15 Oct. 1941); JM 1112, Transferstelle report of 7 Jan. 1942.

[69] YVA, JM 1112, Auerswald report, 26 Sept. 1941. *The Warsaw Diary of Adam Czerniakow*, 248 (entry of 13 June 1941).

drastic steps against vagabonding Jews (death penalty!) and above all the creation of borders that assure an actual demarcation and control can help here.''[70] In fact, both of Auerswald's remedies – a drastic shortening of the ghetto walls intensifying the overcrowding and the death penalty for leaving the ghetto – were instituted in the fall of 1941.

Four days after the first executions of Jews caught outside the ghetto had taken place in mid-November 1941, an extraordinary conversation occurred, in which Czerniakow talked with Auerswald for two and one-half hours about the latter's ''historical role and responsibility'' and the ''rationality of official measures.''[71] Perhaps because there was a significant decline in the incidence of epidemic,[72] perhaps because of Czerniakow's effort, Auerswald's attitude on the smuggling question softened. Instead of shooting all those caught leaving the ghetto, he acceded to Czerniakow's request to work for the release of many of them. When finally successful, he told Czerniakow that ''had he known how complicated the whole business was, he would not have undertaken it.'' Czerniakow replied that he should ''listen to the voice of his conscience above all.''[73]

If Auerswald did not solve the food problem and struggled ambivalently with the problem of smuggling, he and Bischof were more successful – though only gradually – in creating the basis for a ghetto

[70] YVA, JM 1112, Auerswald report, 26 Sept. 1941.

[71] *The Warsaw Diary of Adam Czerniakow*, 301 (entry of 21 Nov. 1941).

[72] YVA, O-53/101, Hummel's monthly reports to Bühler in Kraków from Dec. 1941 to July 1942. In Dec. 1941 1,971 new cases of spotted fever were reported. This dropped to 784 in Feb. 1942 and to a mere 67 in July 1942.

[73] *The Warsaw Diary of Adam Czerniakow*, 301, 330 (entries of 21 Nov. 1941 and 26 Feb. 1942). *The Journal of Emmanuel Ringelblum*, 234. I am more comfortable with the evaluation of Auerswald in Gutman, *The Jews of Warsaw*, 97–99, than the more negative one in Trunk, *Judenrat*, 294–98. Trunk bases his characterization of Auerswald as ''a successfully indoctrinated Nazi functionary who strictly abided by popular National Socialist slogans about the Jews'' in large part on the unsavory rhetoric of his report ''Zwei Jahre Aufbauarbeit im Distrikt Warschau: Die Juden im Distrikt Warschau.'' He does not note, however, that Auerswald's initial report of 26 Sept. 1941, both sober and critical, was rejected by the Kraków authorities as ''unsuitable'' for inclusion in a series of essays celebrating two years of Frank's rule in Poland. Auerswald was told to produce something more fitting for the occasion. See the correspondence concerning these two reports in YVA, JM 1112.

economy in Warsaw. When Auerswald and Bischof took up their positions, massive unemployment afflicted the ghetto. In June 1941 German statistics recorded 36,198 registered employed and 76,102
unemployed.[74] This stood in dismal contrast to Łódź, where at this
time 53,000 Jews were employed in a ghetto with only one-third the
population.

In Łódź Biebow presided over a totally controlled ghetto economy.
In Warsaw the German authorities instead attempted to foster a kind of
free-enterprise economy. To encourage economic activity confiscations
and other counter-productive interventions were halted. Various con-
trols on possession of currency were lifted, and an amnesty was decreed
for hidden wealth in order to encourage its use in the economy. The
Judenrat was allowed various banking and credit privileges previously
denied, and fees for economic transfers were sharply reduced. The various departments of the Judenrat that had hitherto handled economic
functions were dissolved and replaced by "corporations" that would
henceforth operate on a business rather than a bureaucratic basis. A
concerted attempt was made to attract German employers to the ghetto.
Articles about Jewish skilled workers were placed in various German
newspapers; newsletters were sent to various economic organizations in
Germany; the dispensers of public contracts were approached.[75]

The involvement of private capital, both German and Jewish, was
preferred to direct management of production by the ghetto administration. Thus the ghetto administration got out of the business of trying to
run workshops. "Since in the long run the *Transferstelle* could not assume the economic risk for these shops, German firms have been in-
troduced to direct the shops and obtain orders for them. . . . "[76]
Bischof also denounced Czerniakow's imposition of forced welfare
contributions on wealthier Jews on the grounds that "it is ruining the
capital market."[77] In this free-enterprise economy Bischof openly admitted that the *Transferstelle* was powerless even to enforce simple approval procedures for contracts and exchange of goods. Thus much of

---

[74] YVA, JM 1112, Auerswald report, 26 Sept. 1941.

[75] Ibid.

[76] *The Warsaw Diary of Adam Czerniakow,* 401 (appended document: Auerswald to
Medeazza, 24 Nov. 1941).

[77] YVA, JM 1112, Auerswald Vermerk, 4 Mar. 1942.

the ghetto's economic activity took place outside the knowledge and supervision of the *Transferstelle*.[78]

In the spring of 1942 the changing military situation greatly facilitated the efforts of Auerswald and Bischof to increase employment. With early victory no longer taken for granted, demands for Polish labor in the Reich increased, and even Russian prisoners of war, hitherto totally expendable, became a scarce commodity. Under the circumstances, local employers now turned to the ghetto as a reservoir of labor to fill the void.[79]

In the months of April and May demand for Jewish labor rose dramatically, and in May the monthly death-rate dropped below 4,000 for the first time in a year.[80] Production figures rose sharply. That portion of the economy registered in *Transferstelle* statistics had produced exports worth 3,736,000 złoty in January 1942. This increased regularly each month, so that in June this figure reached 14,458,200 złoty and in the first three weeks of July 15,058,558.[81] Thus despite all the disadvantages – starvation of the workers, round-the-clock power failures and cut-offs, frequent shortages of raw materials, constant transportation stoppages[82] – the ghetto economy in Warsaw had turned the corner. The liquidation of the ghetto which began in July 1942 was not the product of local initiative with frustrated ghetto authorities turning to outright murder either because the ghetto had stubbornly survived their attempts to starve it or because there was no other way out of an economic impasse in which the ghetto population could not be viably supported. In Warsaw the turn to mass murder would destroy an economic experiment of the ghetto managers that was in fact just beginning to bear fruit.[83]

---

[78] YVA, JM 1112, Transferstelle report, 7 Jan. 1942. Gutman, *The Jews of Warsaw*, 75; Trunk, *Judenrat*, 78–81.

[79] YVA, JM 3462, conference on Jewish labor of 20 Mar. 1942.

[80] YVA, JM 3462, Hoffmann reports of Apr. and May 1942, and Czerniakow report (no. 65) of May 1942.

[81] YVA, O-53/101, Hummel's monthly reports to Bühler for Jan. through May and the bimonthly report of June/July 1942.

[82] YVA, JM 1112, Transferstelle report of 7 Jan. 1942.

[83] Concerning the German data on economic activity in the Warsaw ghetto, Raul Hilberg has cautioned the historian that, "Standing alone, such data had a seductive effect; they implied productivity and viability. Economic enterprise could not, however,

IV

Raul Hilberg has estimated that over 500,000 Polish Jews died in the ghettos due to the terrible conditions under which they lived. They constituted nearly 10 percent of all victims of the Holocaust.[84] Even if the Final Solution through firing squad and death camp had not been subsequently implemented, the suffering and mass death of Polish Jewry in the ghettos in themselves would have been a tragedy of immense proportions. Nothing that has been said in this paper is meant to trivialize or minimize the magnitude of that tragedy.

It is my contention, however, that a better understanding of German ghettoization policy in Łódź and Warsaw is vital to the historian's wider understanding of the dynamics of Nazi Jewish policy in the 1939–41 period and the relationship of this policy to the Final Solution that followed. What light, then, does ghettoization policy in these two crucial examples shed on the wider question of Nazi Germany's path to the Final Solution? First, the concentration of Jews in Polish cities as a preliminary to their expulsion was part of a policy ordered by the central authorities in September 1939, but the subsequent creation of sealed ghettos was not. On the contrary, the sealed ghetto resulted from the failure of Berlin's expulsion policy. Local authorities were left to improvise and found their way to the sealed ghetto. They did so at different times and for different immediate reasons but always within the common ideological parameters set by the failed expulsion policy – namely that ultimately Jews and "Aryans" did not live together.

Secondly, the sealing of the ghettos produced within six months an identical crisis; once cut off from all economic ties with the outside world, the incarcerated inhabitants faced imminent starvation. This prospect of murderous attrition was welcomed by some local authorities, but they proved to be a minority. The prevailing view was that the

---

ensure survival." *The Warsaw Diary of Adam Czerniakow*, 53. If he means that the economic productivity of the ghetto could not alter the German decision for liquidation of the ghetto, he is most certainly correct. If he means that the bulk of the ghetto population would not have survived even if the ghetto population had not been deported to Treblinka, I disagree.

[84] Raul Hilberg, *The Destruction of the European Jews*, rev. ed. (New York, 1985), 1: 269 and 3: 1212.

Jews should be put to work to feed themselves. Production through Jewish labor was to be organized in the ghetto so as to make it "self-sufficient."

Thirdly, even as a productive entity the ghetto was viewed as a temporary phenomenon – a transition measure. It was a giant warehouse to store Jews at no expense to the Reich until Berlin decided what to do with them. As Dr. Moser, Uebelhoer's deputy in the Warthegau, remarked, the ghetto was a "necessary evil."[85] For Auerswald, "the best solution would apparently still be the removal of the Jews to some other place."[86] The ghetto managers always knew that one day the ghettos would disappear.

Fourthly, as a temporary measure and "necessary evil" inhabited by those deemed to be at the bottom of the Nazis' racial hierarchy, the ghetto had little priority. Here again ideology set crucial parameters within which the ghetto managers operated, even if it did not spell out clear programmatic goals. Thus the ghetto managers were free to improvise a ghetto economy only as long as they worked with marginal resources not hitherto claimed by someone else. What they could not do was to achieve a reallocation of resources, especially food, to benefit Jews at the expense of someone else. The continuing ravages of hunger and epidemic that afflicted the ghettos were not part of a covert scheme or "set task" on the part of local authorities to decimate the Jewish population. Men who conceive of themselves as part of such a scheme do not openly appeal for improved rations, or boast to their superiors of their success in combatting epidemic, lowering death rates, or harnessing the ghetto population to self-sustaining labor. While eventually the ghetto managers sought to overcome the constraints within which they operated by arguing that the Jews had to be fed if they were to continue performing vital work for the war effort, this must not obscure the fact that initially the argument had been the opposite: work had to be found for the ghettoized Jews so that they might be fed.

Finally, there is the question of the change in policy in 1941–42 from ghetto maintenance to liquidation of the ghettos and systematic mass

---

[85] *DiM*, 241–42 (conference of 24 Oct. 1940).
[86] *The Warsaw Diary of Adam Czerniakow*, 402 (appended document: Auerswald to Medeazza, 24 Nov. 1941).

murder of the Jews. I have argued that the behavior of the ghetto managers does not indicate the existence of a premeditated plan for such
mass murder, of which ghettoization was the initial or preliminary
stage. I have also argued that their behavior provides no evidence for
the existence of political mechanisms of automatic radicalization
through local initiative. How then does one account for the frictionless
transformation of ghetto managers into mass murderers?

Raul Hilberg has offered an interpretation of this transformation of
bureaucrats into murderers that implies the existence of a kind of "in-
visible hand" of bureaucratic structural determinism. German authorities were not operating according to any blueprint when they
ghettoized the Jews. Nonetheless, Hilberg argues, a "destruction process" has an inherent logic. "Concentration" of the victims was an
inevitable step in the sequence of policies carried out by a bureaucracy
that was seduced by a kind of Faustian temptation "to inflict maximum
damage" upon the Jews. Gradually a "shared comprehension" of their
destructive mission spread among the bureaucrats; they ultimately lost
patience and could not wait for attrition in the ghettos to annihilate the
Jews. "For the German decision makers, the pace was not fast enough.
They could not wait two or three decades. . . . They had to 'solve' this
problem, one way or another, right then and there."[87]

My own view is that this transformation was shaped less by an inherent logic in a seemingly autonomous and self-propelled destruction
process than by a combination of political decision-making at the center
and receptivity and accommodation at the periphery. I have argued
elsewhere that in the euphoria of victory of the summer of 1941, Hitler
solicited a plan for the systematic mass murder of the European Jews
and that the components of such a plan – deportation to camps
equipped with gassing facilities – were agreed upon by the end of October 1941, when construction of the first two death camps at Chełmno
and Belzec began.[88] News of these decisions was not disseminated systematically. Instead, by a haphazard and uneven process, signals ema-

---

[87] Raul Hilberg, *The Destruction of the European Jews*, 1: 54–55, 269, 3: 993–99.
[88] Ibid., 212–14. Christopher R. Browning, *Fateful Months: Essays on the Emergence of the Final Solution* (New York, 1985), 8–38.

nated from the center that increasingly indicated to local officials that a change of course had been made.

The invasion of Russia had already quickly brought an end to the promises of increased rations in Łódź and Warsaw that had been made in early June. No significant improvement in the food supply could henceforth be expected. In September 1941 officials in Łódź suddenly learned, much to their consternation, of Himmler's intention to deport additional German Jews and Gypsies to their ghetto, thus aggravating the tenuous situation even further. When local officials in Łódź complained vociferously, a *Sonderkommando* Lange (previously engaged in killing the mentally ill in East Prussia and the incorporated territories) was dispatched from Poznań to Chełmno near Łódź and equipped with two gas vans from the Security Police automotive department of the RSHA in Berlin.[89] Such intervention from the center could not have left the ghetto managers in Łódź any longer in doubt of the ultimate goal of Nazi Jewish policy.

As for the ghettos of the General Government, Frank in conversation with Rosenberg on 13 October 1941, was still trying to find a place to resettle his Jews in Russia.[90] In late November he received notice of a forthcoming conference on the Jewish question and sent his state secretary, Josef Bühler, to inquire about it.[91] On 16 December 1941, after Bühler's return from Berlin, Frank initiated his followers. Expulsion was impossible, for no one else wanted their Jews, he noted; thus they would have to liquidate the Jews themselves. How that was to be done, he did not yet know. But measures would be taken in conjunction with those being planned in the Reich.[92] As part of this coordination of Jewish policy with Berlin, Bühler attended the Wannsee Conference on 20 January 1942. Also travelling to Berlin at that time, presumably to be on hand for consultation if Bühler needed him, was none other than the commissar of the Warsaw ghetto, Heinz Auerswald.[93] Like Biebow in Łódź, Auerswald could no longer have been oblivious to the fatal turn

[89] Christopher R. Browning, *Fateful Months*, 30–31, 59, 62–63.

[90] Frank, *Diensttagebuch*, 413 (Aktennotiz, 14 Oct. 1941).

[91] Raul Hilberg, *The Destruction of the European Jews*, 2: 403.

[92] Frank, *Diensttagebuch*, 457–58 (Regierungssitzung, 16 Dec. 1941).

[93] *The Warsaw Diary of Adam Czerniakow*, 317–18 (entries of 19 and 23 Jan. 1942).

that had been taken, though he continued to operate on a business-as-usual basis until the ghetto-clearing units arrived in Warsaw six months later.[94]

Men like Biebow and Auerswald were neither hard-core party activists nor fanatic anti-Semites. But they had joined the party, and they had taken positions and made careers dealing with the ghettoized Jews. They never questioned that there was a Jewish question that had to be solved, and they never believed that the ghetto was the ultimate solution to that problem. They had committed themselves to a political movement, a career, and a task. When they worked to set up self-sustaining ghettos, it was because that is how they conceived of their duty to the Third Reich.[95] But they had arrived at that conception on their own. When signals came from Berlin that a new policy was at hand, that their duty lay in a different direction, their acceptance of and accommodation to this new policy was a foregone conclusion.

When the mass murder began, the perpetrators of the Final Solution would carry out their task with the same ingenuity and inventiveness that the ghetto managers had previously employed to maintain ghetto life under great constraints. The ghetto managers had acted in this way because that is what they thought was expected of them; now they knew differently. The absence of clear signals from Berlin in the first instance and the all-too-clear signals emanating from Berlin in the second were in both cases vital.

---

[94] Not only the Germans but also the ghettoized Jews of Warsaw were increasingly aware of their impending fate in the spring of 1942. See: Christopher R. Browning and Israel Gutman, "The Reports of a Jewish 'Informer' in the Warsaw Ghetto: Selected Documents," *Yad Vashem Studies* 17 (1986): 247–93.

[95] Even after the liquidation of the Warsaw ghetto, Auerswald did not attempt to rewrite with hindsight what he considered to be the successes of his term as commissioner of the Jewish district in order to make it appear as if he had prepared for and contributed to the subsequent mass murder. "Achievements of the Agency: simplification of the boundaries, construction of the wall, maintenance of peace (in May 1941 the Higher SS and Police Leader feared the outbreak of hunger revolts!), construction of an essentially satisfactorily functioning Jewish communal administration, improvement of the hygienic situation in the interest of combatting epidemic (decline of spotted fever), and – together with the Transferstelle – prevention of an initially feared economic failure (employment of a large number of skilled workers in armaments industries)." YVA, O-53/49/132 (Auerswald report on his activities in Warsaw, undated but after Jan. 1943).

PART II

Conflicting Explanations

3

German Technocrats, Jewish
Labor, and the Final Solution:
A Reply to Götz Aly
and Susanne Heim

In a series of recent studies, Götz Aly and Susanne Heim have posed
the question, "Was there an economy of the Final Solution?"[1] They
present the stimulating thesis that the economic and social planners
of the German occupation in eastern Europe saw in the mass murder
of the east European Jews the means for solving a problem of overpopulation that blocked the path to economic modernization. Seizing

[1] This chapter is reprinted in revised form with permission. It is based on the following
publications and presentations of Götz Aly and Susanne Heim, "Die Ökonomie der
'Endlösung': Menschenvernichtung und wirtschaftliche Neuordnung," *Beiträge zur Nationalsozialistischen Gesundheits- und Sozialpolitik,* vol. V, *Sozialpolitik und Judenver-
nichtung: Gibt es eine Ökonomie der Endlösung?* (Berlin, 1987), pp. 7–90; *Ein Berater
der Macht: Helmut Meinhold oder der Zusammenhang zwischen Sozialpolitik und Juden-
vernichtung* (Selbstverlag: Hamburg and Berlin, 1986), and "Die Ökonomie der 'Endlösung' am Beispiel des Generalgouvernements," paper presented at the Germany
Studies Association conference, St. Louis, October 1987. Subsequently Heim and Aly
have also published: "The Economics of the Final Solution: A Case Study from the
General Government," *Simon Wiesenthal Center Annual* V (1988), pp. 3–48; "Sozial-
planung und Völkermord: Thesen zur Herrschaftsrationalität der nationalsozialistischen Vernichtungspolitik" and "Wider die Unterschätzung der nationalsozialistischen
Politik: Antwort an unsere Kritiker," *Vernichtungspolitik: Eine Debatte über den
Zusammenhang von Sozialpolitik und Genozid im nationalsozialistischen Deutschland,*
ed. by Wolfgang Schneider (Hamburg, 1991), pp. 11–24 and pp. 165–175; and *Vor-
denker der Vernichtung: Auschwitz und die deutsche Pläne für eine neue eropäische
Ordnung* (Hamburg, 1991). My reply was initially published in *Konkret* (December
1989): 64–69, and subsequently in *Vernichtungspolitik,* pp. 37–51, under the title
"Vernichtung und Arbeit."

the opportunity that National Socialist conquest of eastern Europe offered them to implement their utopian modernization theories, they delivered a scientific rationale for the mass murder as a legitimate and necessary "development policy" (*Entwicklungspolitik*). Thus the Holocaust was not a mystical event beyond human understanding, but one that resulted from the rational means employed by German technocrats to get rid of a superfluous population. The contribution of these technocrats was not a peripheral phenomenon, for Heim and Aly assert that their research involved "the reconstruction of the course of decision-making at the center of the Nazi state."[2] This thesis, both strikingly original and based on arduous research into little-known sources, deserves careful study and assessment. Let us first examine the argument on behalf of Heim's and Aly's thesis in more detail.

Heim and Aly focus their research on a group of young technocrats whom they call the "planning intelligentsia" (*planende Intelligenz*). These men worked in a variety of obscure agencies such as the *Reichskuratorium für Wirtschaftlichkeit, Institut für Deutsche Ostarbeit, Reichsstelle für Raumordnung, Reichskommissariat für die Festigung des deutschen Volkstums*, and *Abteilung Bevölkerungswesen und Fürsorge*. In contrast to the rivalries and jurisdictional battles that permeated the higher echelons of the Nazi system, the planners cooperated closely with one another in an "interdisciplinary" fashion. A common vision and way of thinking—sober, problem solving, and rational – rather than a narrow-minded defense of their respective jurisdictional turfs (*Ressortblindheit*) characterized their labors.[3]

The starting point of their cooperative endeavors was a commonly shared analysis of the economic and demographic dilemma that faced Germany in eastern Europe. There the planners found a vicious circle of poverty, low productivity, and overpopulation. The ever-growing population prevented the capital accumulation needed to break out of the primitive subsistence economy. The consensus emerged that the east European Jews were not just part of the superfluous population, but a particular obstacle to modernization. Desperately poor but monopolizing the preindustrial handicraft sector, they not only prevented a

---

[2] Aly and Heim, "Die Ökonomie der 'Endlösung,' " pp. 7–9.
[3] Ibid., pp. 11, 14–15.

rationalization of industrial production but blocked the movement of the non-Jewish population from the countryside into the cities that was the only possibility for modernizing the agricultural sector as well. A removal of the Jews and confiscation of their property thus could solve a number of problems simultaneously. Population could be decreased. Small-scale manufacturing could be consolidated into fewer, more efficient, large-scale units. Poles could leave the countryside to find jobs in the newly rationalized and modernized industrial sector, and the restructuring of manufacturing could also lead to a restructuring of society (*Umschichtung*) – in particular, the emergence of a prosperous Polish middle class with a stake in the German New Order.[4] It was this heady vision that captivated the planners, and made them the "theoreticians of genocide"[5] (*Theoretiker des Völkermords*).

Aly and Heim assert that these planners not only counted on the removal of the Jews as a solution to their own problems, and were thus receptive to the Final Solution, but that from early on they actively strove for the solution through mass murder:

> It appears that between September 1939 and the summer of 1941 different groups of the planning German intelligentsia longed for the Final Solution for reasons that appeared logical to them at the time and that in the course of the preparations for the war against the Soviet Union they prevailed. . . . The Final Solution was gradually developed from their papers and proposals from the lower planning levels on up. It should be noted that these planners – who were not always significant in the hierarchy – did not decide, but they prepared the decisions of their superiors. . . . They were not to present recommendations but alternatives for decision.[6]

Without the contribution of such planners, Heim and Aly maintain, the race hatred of the regime would have led to pogroms and massacres but not to systematic genocide.[7]

As the prime example of the actual impact of the "planning intelligentsia" upon the formulation of Nazi policies leading to the Final Solution, Heim and Aly point to Walter Emmerich, chief of the Economic

---

[4] Ibid., pp. 30–67.   [5] Ibid., p. 17.   [6] Ibid., p. 14.   [7] Ibid.

Division of Frank's General Government, and his adviser, Rudolf Gater, the head of an economic "think-tank" called the *Reichskuratorium der Wirtschaftlichkeit*. Their initial experience in economic modernization had been in Austria following the *Anschluss* (annexation by Germany). Charged with raising the economy to a level competitive with the Reich, Emmerich and Gater had both rationalized the economy and compensated the Austrian *Mittelstand*, or lower middle class, through the expropriation and consolidation of Jewish property.[8] In a report of December 1940, Gater emphasized the crippling effect in Poland of overpopulation, which could not be solved through voluntary emigration, and in fact was fated to be aggravated by the expulsion of millions of Poles from the incorporated territories. Gater already accepted as a given the eventual departure of the Jews. Meanwhile, the exclusion of the Jews from trade and craft work was to be undertaken "in stages" (*in Etappen*) so that they could be replaced by retrained Poles who would constitute a viable middle class in a harmonious class structure. As for the displaced Jews, they would be registered and put to physical labor.[9]

Three months later, Gater and his deputy Meder wrote a further report on the economic difficulties posed by the creation of the Warsaw ghetto. Ghettoization had had beneficial consequences for the non-Jewish population, in that new employment possibilities had been created. But the ghetto itself, which they assumed would be in existence for at least five years, posed a severe economic dilemma. Employment of Jews outside the ghetto was uneconomical because of the added costs of guards and camp construction. Employment within the ghetto was difficult because at the moment there was no shortage of unskilled labor in the General Government. Yet at least 60,000 Jews had to be employed to produce "exports" from the ghetto, if an economic balance were to be maintained and the ghetto's needs were to be met. Thus the Germans faced four stark choices: (1) subsidize the ghetto, which no one advocated; (2) loosen the seal around the ghetto, so normal economic ties to the outside world could be restored, which the doctors rejected for public health reasons; (3) allow an underprovisioning "without regard" (*ohne Rücksicht*) for the consequences – in short, to

[8] Ibid., pp. 19–30.   [9] Ibid., pp. 67–70.

view the ghetto "as a means to liquidate the Jews" (*als ein Mittel . . .
das jüdische Volkstum zu liquidieren*); or (4) organize the effective
utilization of Jewish labor as quickly as possible, which was to be
accomplished not through the state as in Lodz but through private
enterprise.[10]

Following meetings on April 3 and 19, 1941, the Vienna bank director, Max Bischof, was put in charge of the Warsaw ghetto economy, in
order to attempt an "experiment limited in time" (*befristetes Experiment*) in developing a self-sufficient, free-enterprise ghetto economy.
He replaced Alexander Palfinger, who had clung too stubbornly to the
Lodz model of a state-organized ghetto economy. Simultaneously, however, the other "Gater-inspired" (*von Gater inspirierten*) policy of underprovisioning without regard for the consequences was also realized,
as attested to by the sky-rocketing ghetto death rate in the summer of
1941.[11]

By October 1941, the planners were convinced that the Bischof experiment was doomed to failure. According to Gater and his deputy Meder,
the feeding of unskilled Jewish labor was a "waste of capital" (*Kapital-
verschliess*) because despite the "hunger wages," machines could produce the same products less expensively. Bischof himself confessed that
economically the ghetto was a "field of ruins" (*Ruinenfeld*) that in the
long run could not cover all its costs. Emmerich pronounced the final
judgment "that the ghetto could not pay its way, could not live without
subsidies, if one set as a goal maintaining the Jews' capacity to live."[12]

Heim and Aly assert that the maintenance of cheap labor in the
ghetto became increasingly undesirable not only because of the intensifying food shortage in 1942, but also because their products undersold
businesses in the "Aryan" sector through "dumping prices" that hin-
dered modernization. The final disappearance of the Jews allowed the
planners, on the basis of labor shortage, to complete the rationalization
of the Polish economy through consolidation into labor-efficient, large-
scale units.[13]

Heim and Aly have articulated a brilliant and provocative thesis,
which is a "breath of fresh air" to a field of research no longer

---

[10] Ibid., pp. 71–74. [11] Ibid., pp. 74–75. [12] Ibid., pp. 75–76.
[13] Ibid., pp. 78–79.

passionate about the functionalist-intentionalist controversy and distracted by the *Historikerstreit*. However welcome, their contribution must still face critical scrutiny. In my opinion, they have convincingly demonstrated that by late 1941 at least some of the "planning intelligentsia" in the General Government were receptive to the murderous elimination of the Jews as a solution to their own problems. In this regard, these planners were not different from many other influential groups in German society.[14] The "planning intelligentsia" are one more piece in the mosaic of widespread receptivity to mass murder.

However, Heim and Aly claim much more for their study, namely that the cooperation and consensus among the "planning intelligentsia" transcended the polycratic rivalries of the Nazi regime, that these planners strove for a Final Solution long before 1941, that working upward from below they had a major impact on the decision-making process, and that without their input the racial hatred of the regime would not have gone beyond pogroms and massacres. I do not believe the study of Heim and Aly can sustain these conclusions.

Aly and Heim have convincingly demonstrated that the "planning intelligentsia" shared a common analysis of the economic and demographic problems of eastern Europe. Because the mass murder of the Jews could be construed as helping to solving these problems, however, does not mean that the "planning intelligentsia" uniformly and consciously worked for such a solution. A careful analysis of the political context within which the "planning intelligentsia" compiled their studies and made their recommendations raises serious doubts both as to whether they were immune to the polycratic rivalries that pervaded the Nazi system and as to whether most of them sought a Final Solution through mass murder long before 1941. It is the absence of this wider political context, in my opinion, that distorts some of the conclusions of the Aly-Heim study.

I have argued elsewhere that ghettoization of the Jews in the occupied Polish territories was a local response to the failure of the Nazi

---

[14] For the public health officials in the General Government, see Chapter 7 in this book. For the military, see my "Wehrmacht Reprisal Policy and the Murder of the Male Jews in Serbia," *Fateful Months: Essays on the Emergence of the Final Solution* (New York, 1985), pp. 39–56.

plans for massive expulsion and "resettlement."[15] The Jews were to be stored in ghetto "warehouses" until authorities in Berlin could decide how to move them out. The creation of sealed ghettos, however, soon presented local occupation authorities with a new dilemma. Cut off from the outside economy and quickly exhausting their own resources, the Jews in the ghettos were threatened with mass starvation. Rather than crystallizing a consensus to solve the Jewish question quickly by doing nothing at all, in fact, the looming demographic disasters in both the Lodz and Warsaw ghettos gave rise to a policy debate between two factions of local German authorities that I would dub the "productionists" and the "attritionists."

The crisis first became acute in Lodz in the late summer of 1940, when it became clear that the ghetto inhabitants had no further means to purchase food supplies. The head of the Lodz Jewish council, Chaim Rumkowski, urged that the Jews be given employment so that they would be able to purchase food. Alexander Palfinger, an official in the ghetto administration, argued that gainful employment had to be prevented, for only the "most extreme exigency" would make the Jews surrender the last reserves that he claimed they were still hoarding. Hans Biebow, the head of the ghetto administration, argued in contrast that every effort had to be made "to facilitate the self-maintenance of the Jews through finding them work," even at the cost of initial subsidies. Biebow prevailed. At a crucial meeting on October 18, 1940, "it was established at the outset that the ghetto in Lodz must continue to exist and everything must be done to make the ghetto self-sustaining." Palfinger argued unabashedly for a different policy: "A rapid dying out of the Jews is for us a matter of total indifference, if not to say desirable, as long as the concomitant effects leave the public interest of the German people untouched." Unable to prevail, Palfinger left Lodz for Warsaw.[16]

In Warsaw Palfinger was named head of the *Transferstelle*, the agency that was to be the economic intermediary between the newly sealed ghetto and the outside world. Palfinger found kindred spirits in Waldemar Schön, the head of the Resettlement Division that had jurisdiction over the Jews, Karl Naumann, the head of the district's Division

[15] See Chapter 2 in this book.   [16] Ibid.

of Food and Agriculture, and the district governor, Ludwig Fischer. These men did not proclaim their goal of attrition so openly as Palfinger had in Lodz, but they nonetheless set the ghetto on a starvation course. By mid-January reports reached Hans Frank's capital of the General Government, Kraków, that food supplies to the Warsaw ghetto had been stopped completely.[17]

This is the point at which Walter Emmerich, head of Frank's Economic Division, commissioned Rudolf Gater to compose his report on "The Economic Balance of the Jewish District in Warsaw" that is so central to the Aly-Heim study.[18] In their view the report presented a number of "value-free" alternatives, out of which the higher authorities in late April 1941 chose to pursue two: a limited experiment in a free-enterprize ghetto economy and continued starvation – the latter evidenced by the fact that the death rate continued to climb sharply into the summer of 1941.[19] I would suggest a very different interpretation, namely that a sharp policy dispute among the "planning intelligentsia" rather than consensus ensued and that Emmerich and Gater pushed for a productionist solution to maintain the Warsaw Jews rather than for attrition.

According to Gater's report on the economic viability of the Warsaw ghetto, the Germans faced the four options that have already been noted, namely: (1) providing a subsidy, (2) restoring economic ties to the outside world, (3) leaving the ghetto underprovisioned without regard for the consequences, that is, deliberate starvation, and (4) organizing a productive, self-sufficient ghetto economy. Gater concluded that the fourth option would require the employment of 60,000 Jews producing "exports" from the ghetto.

But the Gater report also dealt with another matter: the current policies of Waldemar Schön and Alexander Palfinger. Schön maintained that the Jews in the ghetto disposed of considerable wealth that would take at least one-half year to extract. To force the Jews to hand over

---

[17] Ibid.
[18] Yad Vashem Archives (hereafter cited as YVA), JM 10016, "Die Wirtschaftsbilanz des jüdischen Wohnbezirks in Warschau: Bericht des Reichskuratorium für Wirtschaftlichkeit, Dienststelle Generalgouvernement, Krakau, März 1941." The original is in the Archivum Panstwowe m. st. Warszawy (hereafter APW), Der Kommissar für den jüdischen Wohnbezirk in Warschau, Nr. 125.
[19] Heim and Aly, "Die Ökonomie der 'Endlösung,' " p. 75.

their gold, money, jewelry, and other valuables, he intended to exert pressure "through barring the delivery of food" (*durch Sperrung der Nahrungsmittellieferungen*). Gater's other sources disagreed with Schön's allegation of plentiful resources within the ghetto. Gater shared their more pessimistic estimation, for he concluded that if economic reorganization was not complete within three months, one would have to reckon with "a grave stoppage in the life" (*einer erheblichen Stockung des Lebens*) of the ghetto.[20]

On March 22, 1941, when Emmerich presented the Gater report to Frank, he made an explicit, indeed urgent, recommendation. "In the memorandum one comes to the conclusion that organizational and general changes must take place in this ghetto as quickly as possible, because according to the *Kuratorium* engaged by *Ministerialdirigent* Dr. Emmerich it cannot be maintained with the present economic policy." Frank directed Emmerich to obtain the position of district governor Fischer in Warsaw before he would call a meeting on the issue.[21]

Two days later Frank received quite contrasting news from Fischer, according to whom the ghetto was working out very well. Allegedly, 40,000 Warsaw Jews were already employed (15,000 within the ghetto and 25,000 in camps), and the epidemic situation had improved by 50 percent. According to Fischer, "If developments continue in this way, one need not reckon with special difficulties in the ghetto, all the less because provisioning is also guaranteed."[22] Fischer was supported by Palfinger, whose self-styled "exposé" faulted the Gater report on both the facts (the economic prospects of the ghetto were good) and the approach (these "theoreticians" failed to realize that economic considerations had to be subordinate to "purely political" ones). Rather than clinging to the Lodz model too closely, as Heim and Aly maintain, Palfinger harshly criticized Biebow's ghetto administration as the prime example of heretically putting economic interests before political principle.[23]

---

[20] YVA, JM 10016, "Die Wirtschaftsbilanz," pp. 34–35.

[21] *Diensttagebuch des deutschen Generalgouverneurs in Polen 1939–1945* (hereafter cited as DTB), ed. by Werner Präg and Wolfgang Jacobmeyer (Stuttgart, 1975), p. 334.

[22] Ibid., p. 337 (entry of March 25, 1941).

[23] APW, Der Kommissar für den jüdischen Wohnbezirk, Nr. 125, Palfinger Aktennotiz, April 7, 1941.

On April 3, 1941, the antagonists met in Warsaw in the presence of Hans Frank.[24] Governor Fischer continued his campaign of disinformation: The ghettoized Jews had "considerable means" at their disposal, provisioning was guaranteed, and thus "in the coming months there was no danger at all of famine." Emmerich brushed this fantasy aside: "one must free himself from the notion that it is still going well in the ghetto and that supplies are still available there." As the ghetto had been created for the long haul, economic planning had to be done accordingly. "The starting point for all economic measures has to be the idea of maintaining the capacity of the Jews to live. The question is whether one can succeed in solving this problem in a productive manner." Concerning the *Transferstelle*, Emmerich noted that the "question of personality" (*Persönlichkeitsfrage*) played a great role, as well as the problem of its autonomy. The latter was so great that constant conflict arose between the *Transferstelle* and the central government in Kraków.

Gater once again reviewed his calculations about the need to employ 60,000 Jews to achieve ghetto self-sufficiency – a calculation that Schön described as "too theoretical." To achieve this level of employment, Emmerich proposed enticing large German firms to move into the ghetto by granting them concessions over their Jewish employees. Frank then proposed a future meeting to finalize the details of a ghetto economy, but his support for the "productionists" was clear. "The responsibility, which the government undertook with the creation of a Jewish district of 500,000 human beings was very great, and a failure would always be blamed" on his regime.

On April 9, 1941, Kraków officials submitted to Frank a draft decree for reorganizing the administration of the Warsaw ghetto, taking responsibility from Schön's Resettlement Division and placing it in the hands of a commissioner for the Jewish district who would supervise the *Transferstelle*. "Such a policy was necessary," they argued, "because the district chief of Warsaw wants to decide this question alone." Frank "sharply" opposed this latter notion, and ordered Fischer to be informed accordingly.[25] At a follow-up meeting Frank imposed the new

---

[24] DTB, pp. 343–346 (entry of April 3, 1941).
[25] Ibid., pp. 354–355 (entry of April 9, 1941).

policy. Emmerich triumphed, as Fischer conceded that precautions had now been taken to ensure "that the entire ghetto question would be handled absolutely in accord with the guidelines of the Economic Division."[26]

The ensuing changes in Warsaw were dramatic. The Viennese banker, Max Bischof, was hired to head the *Transferstelle* with the specific task of achieving economic self-sufficiency for the ghetto. He was promised a government subsidy if it proved necessary. He also received the assurance that he could have Palfinger removed.[27] Schön was transferred to another position and replaced by Heinz Auerswald. Upon taking their positions, Bischof and Auerswald were unpleasantly surprised to learn the full extent of Schön's and Palfinger's mendacity and the degree to which an "attritionist" policy had been carried out under the cover of their false figures. Contrary to past assurances of high employment in the ghetto, almost no one was working. Rather than 25,000 Warsaw Jews working productively in labor camps in the spring of 1941, for instance, the maximum had been 6,100. Moreover, the camps had been such a disaster that they were in the process of being dissolved. The figures on provisioning had been just as misleading, as the *Transferstelle* had in fact procured only 5 to 10 percent of the ghetto's needed food supplies.[28]

Neither the policy struggle between "productionists" and "attritionists" nor its outcome in favor of the former can be easily reconciled with the portrayal of Heim and Aly of a close-knit group of "planning intelligentsia" working cooperatively and successfully toward a common goal of eliminating the Jews.

As Heim and Aly note, starvation continued in the ghetto and the death rate rose sharply. But was this because the Germans were simultaneously pursuing what Heim and Aly describe as a "Gater-inspired" (*von Gater inspirierten*) policy of deliberate underprovisioning? Auerswald's subsequent reports certainly do not indicate that he saw continued starvation as one of his tasks. "A quantum leap in the deaths for

[26] Ibid., pp. 359–362 (entry of April 19, 1941).
[27] YVA, JM 1112, Bischof Aktenvermerk on discussion with Fischer, April 30, 1941.
[28] YVA, O-53/105/II/415–7 (Vermerk: Betr.: Arbeitslager, June 30, 1941); JM 1112, Bischof Aktenvermerk, May 8, 1941.

May of this year showed that the food shortage had already grown into famine," he reported. "The provisioning of food thus constituted our most urgent task." Auerswald provided some extra supplies to the Jewish Self-Aid (JSS) to increase the daily meals it provided from 30,000 in May to 120,000 in August. "Due to the general impoverishment of the Jews prevailing since the outbreak of the war," Auerswald noted, the death rates did not peak until July and August. Thereafter a modest decline and stabilization set in.[29] Starvation indeed continued, but it was not the policy of Auerswald and Bischof, who had taken up their positions to carry out the economic program of Emmerich and Gater.

Aside from asserting the existence of a "Gater-inspired" starvation policy, the closest Heim and Aly come to implying that the "planning intelligentsia" had a direct impact on the decision-making process leading to the Final Solution is their account of the Warsaw meeting of October 15, 1941, attended by Hans Frank. The consensus of the meeting, according to Heim and Aly, was that the experiment in a self-sufficient ghetto economy had failed. According to Bischof, economically the ghetto was a "field of ruins" (Ruinenfeld). Auerswald and Emmerich both made reference to the future deportation of the ghettoized Jews. They were prepared therefore to view the ghetto as a "temporary concentration camp" in which, "in order to spare unnecessary work and expense, it would be most expedient to leave it essentially in its present situation."[30]

Indeed the meeting was not a celebration of economic success in the ghetto, but once again Heim and Aly miss an important dimension – namely, what the participants were actually proposing. The meeting was quite revealing about the intentions, goals, and hopes of the administrative and economic technocrats in charge of the Warsaw ghetto, Auerswald and Bischof. Earlier that month Bischof had already urged that "unconditionally necessary" provisions were lacking even for the workers.[31] In his presentation to the conference, Bischof again noted that ultimately the economic activity of the ghetto depended on the

---

[29] YVA, JM 1112, Auerswald report, September 26, 1941. Israel Gutman, *The Jews of Warsaw: Ghetto, Underground, Revolt* (Bloomington, Indiana, 1982), pp. 63–65.

[30] Heim and Aly, "Die Ökonomie der 'Endlösung,' " pp. 75–76.

[31] YVA, JM 1112, Transferstelle report, October 8, 1941.

food supply, for the current rations did not maintain the workers' strength. He also recapitulated the measures he had taken to restore economic incentive and private initiative to the ghetto economy by reducing the inhibiting control of the *Judenrat* and *Transferstelle*. As a result, there were already many positive developments in terms of increased employment, though as yet these were insufficient to sustain 500,000 ghetto inhabitants. He had thus advertised the availability of Jewish labor among German firms. The response had demonstrated an "urgent interest" in using Jewish labor, especially in the regions of Germany with good transportation connections to Warsaw. Bischof concluded: "Perhaps in this way, if ever, Jewish labor in Warsaw can in sufficient numbers successfully serve the needs of the Reich in its final struggle for the future."[32]

Auerswald also discussed labor and food. Unlike the western Jews who were predominately intellectuals and merchants, he noted, many eastern Jews were laborers and skilled workers. With proper coordination and direction, the systematic harnessing of Jewish labor was possible. But a "necessary minimal food supply" had to be provided for working Jews. Present rations, fixed before ghettoization and based on the assumption that the Jews could fend for themselves, were less than one-third those of the Lodz ghetto and "absolutely insufficient."[33]

Even Governer Fischer, the former supporter of the attritionists, confirmed that food supplies to the ghetto were too small to sustain life. If Jewish labor was to be maintained, additional rations were necessary. In contrast to the technocrats, however, Fischer was quite explicit about his preferred long-term goal. "Ultimately, however, this war is a conflict with Jewry in its totality. The publication of the American Jew Kaufmann clearly shows what we can expect from the Jews if they are victorious. I believe it would be justified if we struck annihilatingly at the spawning grounds of Jewry from which all world Jewry constantly renews itself"[34] (*Ich glaube, es kann verantwortet werden, wenn diese*

[32] APW, Amt des Distrikts Warschau, Nr. 132, pp. 22–32 (Bischof presentation, October 15, 1941).

[33] APW, Amt des Distrikts Warschau, Nr. 132, pp. 33–37 (Auerswald presentation, October 15, 1941).

[34] APW, Amt des Distrikts Warschau, Nr. 132, pp. 4–18 (Fischer presentation, October 15, 1941).

Brutstätte des Judentums, aus der sich das gesamte Weltjudentum stets von neuem ergänzt, von uns vernichtend getroffen wird).

The meeting of October 15 did not lead to an immediate improvement for the Jews. Frank was less supportive than he had been the previous spring and in fact refused increased supplies for the ghetto, noting that "even for the Polish population hardly anything more can be provided."[35] But the meeting clearly cannot be seen as an attempt by the technocrats to dismiss the potential of Jewish labor and speed the destruction process. On the contrary, they recommended better feeding and utilization of Jewish labor. The only call for annihilation came from Fischer, whose sentiments lend little support for the conclusion of Aly and Heim that Nazi race hatred would not have led to systematic genocide without the contribution of the economic planners.

Moreover, any assessment of the "planning intelligentsia" at this time that the Warsaw ghetto economic experiment was not going well, could not have been decisive even unintentionally in persuading the higher echelons to adopt a policy of mass murder, for that decision had already been taken. By October preparations for the construction of the first death camps at Belzec and Chelmno were underway. In my opinion, these preparations had been initiated several months earlier from above; they were not the product of local initiative from below.[36] The economic problems of the ghetto may help to explain why many local German administrators were so receptive to the impulses for mass murder emanating from the center, but these economic problems did not produce decisive local initiatives in mid-October 1941, which set the mass-murder program in motion.

Ultimately, Heim and Aly assert that the ideology of the regime sufficed to cause pogroms and massacres, but the economic calculations of the "planning intelligentsia" were a necessary – indeed the essential – ingredient for the Final Solution. But in asserting the primacy of economic calculation over ideology, Heim and Aly totally ignore the watershed change in economic perceptions that took place among Germans between the fall of 1941 and the spring of 1942, and the changing

---

[35] YVA, JM 21/4 (Frank Tagebuch, October 15, 1941).
[36] Christopher Browning, *Fateful Months: Essays on the Emergence of the Final Solution* (New York, 1985), pp. 8–38; and Chapter 5 of this book.

interplay between ideological and economic factors that resulted. The recent work of Ulrich Herbert is of fundamental importance in assessing this point.[37]

Ulrich Herbert notes that from September 1939 to September 1941, there was no conflict between ideological and economic considerations concerning the labor exploitation of Jews, Poles, and Russians. Victory would solve all economic problems, and Jews and Slavs were viewed as a "burden," not a source of potential labor. It was in such an atmosphere that the *Einsatzgruppen* commenced the mass murder of Russian Jewry, the Russian prisoners of war were allowed to die in mass, and preparations for a "total solution" to the European Jewish question were initiated.[38] Heim and Aly are correct in emphasizing that during this period there was no shortage of unskilled labor and therefore it was indeed difficult to find ways to employ ghettoized Jews. (In my opinion, however, they fail to observe that the prevailing faction of local German authorities nonetheless sought ways to employ ghettoized Jews, not for the intrinsic value of what they would produce but in order to have them fed at no cost to the state.)

In the fall of 1941, Herbert notes, a fundamental change occurred, leading to a conflict between *Vernichtung* and *Arbeit*, between economic interest and ideological primacy. In September 1941 a grave shortage of labor was first registered, and by late October Hitler for the first time had approved the labor exploitation of Russian prisoners of war. The rush of German industry for this labor pool quickly revealed that all but a fraction of the Russian prisoners of war had already died or were too physically ruined to work. Russian civilians were thus substituted, and no fewer than 1.4 million were rounded up and brought to Germany for forced labor in 1942. In Herbert's opinion it was precisely the decision for large-scale exploitation of Russian labor that permitted the Nazis to push ahead with their ideologically driven mass murder of the Jews without regard for the labor potential being destroyed.[39] Despite a very partial accommodation to economic considerations (the

---

[37] Ulrich Herbert, "Arbeit und Vernichtung: Ökonomisches Interesse und Primat der 'Weltanschauung' im Nationalsozialismus," *Ist der Nationalsozialismus Geschichte?*, ed. by Dan Diner (Frankfurt, 1987), pp. 198–236.

[38] Ibid., pp. 202–203.   [39] Ibid., pp. 213–215.

beginning of selections at Auschwitz, the postponement of the deportation of German Jews in the armaments industry), in fact the vast majority of Russian and Polish Jews were murdered in 1942 without the
slightest concern for their economic potential. This "primacy of destruction" over economic considerations led to objections from the
army and the civil administration. Himmler's response was to permit
a remnant of Jewish labor to work in SS camps. "However, there too
the Jews should, in accordance with the Führer's wish, disappear
some day."[40]

Herbert's scenario of an ideologically driven mass murder program
riding rough-shod over pragmatic economic calculations is criticized
by Heim and Aly for confusing the issue of overpopulation with that of
labor shortage.[41] Nonetheless, it is precisely the connection of labor
shortage with the allegedly superfluous Jews in the General Government that is reflected in the documents of the very echelon of local
planners and technocrats upon whom Heim and Aly focus. On March
20, 1942, a meeting was held in Warsaw to discuss the question of Jewish labor. It was attended by Auerswald as well as representatives of the
Transferstelle and the district-level Divisions of Labor, Internal Administration, Health, Food, and Economy among others. Hoffmann, the director of the ghetto branch of the Warsaw labor office (*Arbeitsamt
Warschau: Nebenstelle für den jüdischen Wohnbezirk*), noted the catastrophic lack of manpower that had arisen. Thus former objections to
the use of Jewish labor (health, race) had to be overridden. Even then,
Russians were being used in the Reich despite the health danger, he
noted. In fact, all Russian workers had been taken from the civilian section and 50 percent from the military sector to be sent to the Reich, as
were hundreds of thousands of Poles. Substitutes had to be found,
which meant using the reservoir of labor in the Warsaw ghetto for tasks
vital to the war effort. The representative for water control projects said
he could get no Poles or Russians and also needed Jews. Hoffmann replied that on the basis of past experience he wanted no round-up actions, "no camps of emaciated men, no impossible work demands that

[40] Ibid., pp. 216–223.
[41] Heim and Aly, "Wider die Unterschätzung der nationalsozialistischen Politik: Antwort an unsere Kritker," p. 171.

even German workers could not surmount." Besides, water control projects were long term, and only war-related work was important enough now to use Jews.[42]

Hoffmann's reports for April and May emphasized the burgeoning demand for Jewish labor to replace workers who had been taken to Germany. New Aryan firms had been formed in the ghetto, and the Wehrmacht demand for Jewish labor was "especially strong" (*besonders stark*).[43] Production figures rose sharply in the ghetto. In January 1942 the *Transferstelle* reported 3,736,000 zloty of exports; by June this figure had jumped to 14,458,200 zloty, and in the first three weeks of July to 15,058,558.[44]

In short, the economic situation of the Warsaw ghetto had been totally transformed between October 1941 and the summer of 1942. The very economic turnaround that Bischof had hoped for was underway. The pessimistic judgment of October 1941 – that in the long run the ghetto was economically unviable – was no longer valid. The ghetto was not liquidated because no employment could be found for its incarcerated inhabitants to cover the cost of its existence or because productivity was so low that machines were cheaper than paying starvation wages; rather it was liquidated in spite of the growing demand for Jewish labor and the ghetto's rapidly increasing production.

In summarizing his study of the impact of Nazi ideology on the use of forced labor, Herbert reaches the following conclusion: Economic considerations often led German employers to accept the massive loss of life among their laborers as a means to a particular production goal; but it was Nazi ideology that decreed the destruction of racial enemies as a goal, for which labor was on occasion allowed as a means. Thus, Herbert argues, any attempt to explain the mass-murder policies of the Nazi regime primarily from rational economic calcuation ignores the fact that for the Nazis the mass murder of ideological enemies was in

---

[42] YVA, JM 3462, meeting of March 20, 1942.

[43] YVA, JM 3462, Hoffmann reports of April and May 1942.

[44] YVA, O-53/101, Hummel's monthly reports to Bühler for January through May and the bimonthly report for June/July 1942. Heim and Aly, misleadingly in my opinion, suggest that the burst in productivity came only after July 1942 as Jews desperately sought work under the threat of deportation. "The Economics of the Final Solution," p. 33.

their minds already rationally justified, though they might support their murderous policies with economic, geopolitical, medical, and security rationalizations as well. Racism was not a delusion or myth hiding real economic interests but rather the "fixed point" of the system.[45] Such a viewpoint, which I find persuasive, is in stark contrast to the conclusion of Heim and Aly that only economic calculation moved the persecution of the Jews beyond pogrom and massacre to the Final Solution.

What can one say in conclusion? Heim and Aly have made a major contribution, both through their painstaking research into the obscure and hitherto unstudied ranks of lower echelon social and economic planners of the German occupation in eastern Europe and through their provocative and challenging theses that provide the impetus for reexamining important issues. Such is, after all, the purpose of historical scholarship. With their conclusions, however, I do not agree. Where they see cooperation and consensus, I see factionalism and infighting between rival groups that I would term "productionists" and "attritionists." Where they see long-term continuity and consistency of goals, I see changing circumstances and phases. Where they see local initiative and planning from below ultimately shaping the fundamental decisions from above, I see signals and impulses emanating from the center that meet with receptivity and accommodation on the periphery. Where they see economic calculation as the prime mover of the Final Solution, I see the Final Solution as a policy carried out in spite of its economic irrationality.

[45] Herbert, "Arbeit und Vernichtung," pp. 236, 288–289.

4

The Holocaust as By-product?
A Critique of Arno Mayer

The subtitle of Professor Arno Mayer's *Why Did the Heavens Not Darken?* is *The "Final Solution" in History.* Therein lies the major source of confusion and controversy in the book. Mayer does indeed attempt to set the "Judeocide" (a term he prefers to Holocaust) within various comparative frameworks, as the subtitle promises. But as the book progresses, the real thrust of Mayer's argument becomes apparent. He is not so much placing the "Final Solution" in a wider historical context as he is redefining it. Ultimately, Mayer does not believe there was a Final Solution, if one understands that Nazi euphemism to mean a conscious Nazi policy aimed at the systematic extermination of every last Jew in Europe. Instead Mayer sees the mass murder of European Jewry as a byproduct of Nazi Germany's anticommunist crusade on the one hand and its hyperexploitation of impressed labor on the other. Moreover, Germany's generals and industrialists share equal standing with Hitler and the Nazis as the perpetrators of this mass murder. This depiction of Nazi Jewish policy is, in my opinion, quite mistaken.

Mayer rejects the notion that the "Judeocide" was a uniquely twentieth-century phenomenon, characterized by "modern technology" and a "bureaucracy of violence." These elements facilitated the "Judeocide" but they were not its "mainspring." Mayer seeks the "driving force" behind the "Judeocide" in two earlier historical

Originally published as a book review (Arno Mayer, *Why Did the Heavens Not Darken? The "Final Solution" in History* [New York: Pantheon Books, 1989]) in *Dissent* (summer 1989), pp. 397–400. Reprinted in slightly revised form with permission.

parallels. The first is the Crusades, in which an ideologically driven "holy war" resulted in the massacres of Jews and Moslems. The second is the Thirty Years War of 1618–1648, a "total war" and "general crisis" of European society that involved enormous civilian casualties. For Mayer the second thirty years war of 1914–45 was a fusion of these elements – "ideological crusade" and "total" war. This fusion created "an enormous historical convulsion in which the Jews were the foremost but by no means the only victims."

How and why did the Jews become the most prominent victims of this second thirty years war? In his previous books Mayer has portrayed modern European history as a struggle between revolution and counterrevolution, between the forces of movement and the forces of order. Mayer sees European Jewry as caught in the middle of this conflict. In Western Europe the French and Industrial Revolutions brought emancipation and prosperity to the Jews. In Russia the Bolshevik Revolution opened the way to their more nearly equal participation in society. Not surprisingly, therefore, the Jews embraced liberalism and capitalism in the West and supported the Bolshevik Revolution in Russia. In the East European "rimland," however, the old order persisted, and the demographic center of European Jewry lay in countries characterized by hypernationalism, virulent anti-Semitism, and active illiberalism. A mass of unassimilated *Ostjuden*, strangers in their own lands, thus lived within a hostile political environment in the most "imperiled geopolitical zone" in Europe.

If Eastern Europe was fated to become the killing fields of the "Judeocide" and its dense population of unassimilated Jews the most numerous victims, the "epicenter" of the European "disequilibrium" was Germany. In what Mayer calls the "classic country of unsimultaneity," modern and traditional elements combined in an unreconciled and explosive mixture. Despite Germany's economic modernization, the old elites strove to maintain their domination. In desperation they turned to Hitler and his lower-middle-class supporters "to restabilize their endangered positions." One leitmotif of Mayer's book is the responsibility he heaps upon the old elites for the Nazi dictatorship, the war, and the "Judeocide." These sweeping condemnations, at least partially justified but usually devoid of the nuance and qualification that would shed more light than heat, reach their untenable extreme when Mayer writes, "In 1932–33 a self-appointed oligarchy of traditional conservatives and reactionaries had prevailed on Hitler to assume power."

Hitler's ability to forge an alliance between the antimodernist fears of the lower middle class and old elites derived from a "syncretic ideology" composed of anti-Semitism, social Darwinism, the geopolitics of eastern expansionism (*Lebensraum*), and anti-Marxism, all appropriated from the ideological arsenal of conservatism. Quite rightly Mayer emphasizes that for Hitler the Jew appeared in many different guises – "the antithesis of the German Aryan, the purveyor of modernity, the prime mover of parasitic capitalism, the agent of Marxist subversion, and the master of Bolshevik Russia" – and was thus the ideal "single enemy" to symbolize all the demons of his "syncretic ideology." But according to Mayer antimodernism was the key motive not only for the old elites and the lower middle class but for Hitler himself. "If Hitler's worldview had an epicenter, it was his deep-seated animosity toward contemporary civilization, and not his hatred for Jews, which was grafted onto it."

If Mayer captures the functional utility of Hitler's ideology, above all its capacity to offer something to almost everyone, in my opinion he misses its wellspring. Hitler's anticommunism and antimodernism were partial and qualified. He regarded Stalin as a great historical figure. He admired his ruthlessness and iron will, which were remaking Russia. He envied Stalin's ability, for instance, to murder the bulk of his officer corps. It was not the totalitarian terror of Stalinism but rather the emancipatory, egalitarian, and internationalist – that is the Jewish – aspects of Marxism that Hitler abhorred. Likewise, Hitler loved the gadgets of modern technology, from fast cars to V-2 rockets (might one add gas chambers?). It was the concomitant social change of the modernization process, again symbolized above all by Jewish emancipation, that he hated. In contrast, Hitler's racial anti-Semitism was total, implacable, and uncompromising.

Mayer's tendency to downplay the importance of Hitler and his anti-Semitism on the one hand and to emphasize antimodernism, anticommunism, and the role of the old elites on the other culminates in his interpretation of the relationship between the German attack on Soviet Russia – "Barbarossa" – and the Final Solution. Many historians have noted the close connection between Barbarossa and the Holocaust, but Mayer goes beyond this in arguing that the latter was "grafted" (this seems to be Mayer's favorite metaphor) onto the former. For Mayer "Nazi Germany's assault on Soviet Russia was *sui generis*" – an absolute or total war to conquer *Lebensraum* in the east but also a crusade to extirpate "Judeobolshevism."

Hitler, the SS, and the generals shared an "ideological-programmatic consensus" about this war of conquest and destruction, but it was not yet characterized by any fixed notion of killing all the Russian Jews. In the first four or five weeks of Barbarossa, Mayer argues, the Jews were subjected to "spontaneous" and "unpremeditated" pogroms by the vigilantes of the anti-Semitic and anticommunist "rimland" populations but not to systematic massacre. While the Germans eliminated Jewish communist functionaries like any other party cadres, they ghettoized the bulk of the surviving Jews, "apparently without any thought of exterminating them after victory. . . . " Instead, the Jews of Russia and the rest of Europe were to be resettled over the Volga or beyond the Urals. With the miscarriage of Barbarossa, particularly the delayed capture of Kiev in late September, the invading Germans – both army and SS – began "venting their rage" on the Jews out of fear of possible defeat. The starting point was the great massacre of nearly 34,000 Jews at Babi Yar outside Kiev on September 29–30. Thereafter, the more frustrated the Germans became, the more the "crusade within the war" intensified at the expense of the Jews.

As for the place of the Holocaust in history, therefore, it was not a decisive step in the creation of Hitler's New Order, but the most fatal convulsion of the Nazi Behemoth's death throes. With the courage of his convictions, Mayer does not shrink from the logical, albeit dubious, implications of his interpretation, namely that

> had the blitzkrieg succeeded in the east . . . Europe might iron-
> ically have been spared the worst horrors [and] the Jews, instead
> of being massacred, probably would have been deported. . . .
> Victory would have kept open the historical possibility of a sig-
> nificant remnant of Jews enduring. . . . In fact, the faster and

easier the victory, the larger this remnant and the better the chances for contingent survival would doubtless have been.

Mayer must ignore considerable evidence to sustain his view that the "derailment" of Barbarossa unleashed the "Judeocide" only in the fall of 1941. For instance, the advancing *Einsatzgruppen* almost immediately took control of the local anticommunist units, whose pogroms they had encouraged and incited. The initial pogroms – so emphasized by Mayer – constituted only a minute fraction of the killing subsequently carried out by these units under direct German supervision. The pace of systematic killing rapidly accelerated after mid-July 1941, when Himmler committed two SS brigades (over 11,000 men) to operate behind the fast-advancing and overburdened *Einsatzgruppen* force of three thousand men. In the month of August alone one of these brigades reported a body count of 44,000! In the first two weeks of August, Himmler toured the eastern front, encouraging his men in their onslaught against the Jews.

When confronted in mid-August with the complaints about the terrible psychological cost to his men of killing women and children, Himmler ordered his crime lab scientists to experiment with killing methods that would be "more humane" for his executioners. These experiments led directly to the gas vans, which went into use in the death camp at Chelmno in early December. Without waiting for such technological advances, *Einsatzgruppe A* reported a body count of 85,000 by September 19. Mass executions did not therefore begin only with Babi Yar. The evidence could be multiplied but the point is already clear: The notion of a systematic German assault on Russian Jewry dating only from the end of September and deriving from the frustration of defeat is simply fanciful. The vast intensification of the murder campaign against Russian Jewry dates from mid-July, at the height of victory euphoria.

If the mass murder of Russian Jewry is in Mayer's view "grafted" onto the spiraling brutality of the anti-Bolshevik crusade, the extension of the mass murder to the rest of European Jewry is seen within the context of the economic imperatives of total war, with the intensifying persecution of the Jews "calibrated in accordance with the productivity-utility precept." Following the "maddening winter of

1941–2," Mayer argues, the "deliberate mass murder of the Jews was set in motion" by a "program of extermination through forced labor." In Auschwitz and Majdanek, which contained both labor and death camps, there was a "conjuncture and inseparability between labor exploitation and extermination." Jews "were deported there as part of a vast impressment of all Europe for the benefit of Nazi Germany's overstrained war machine."

Because of his determination to emphasize the priority of labor over gassing, Mayer's logic and prose become increasingly tortured. He concedes the fact that – unlike non-Jews – Jewish women, children, and elderly were also sent to Auschwitz along with Jewish workers. This fact meant that the nonworkers were doomed to die in the terrible conditions there in any case. Thus "selection upon or after arrival was merely the logical consequence and implementation of this prior warrant for destruction. This is not the same as saying the 'preselected' Jews and Gypsies were sent to Auschwitz, especially Birkenau, to be gassed." Gassing developed only gradually and "may be said to have intensified the torment of the camp's Jews in degree, not in kind."

Mayer does not stop with this specious scholasticism but pushes his point even further. Certainly in Auschwitz and probably for all of Europe as well, he claims, more Jews died of "so-called 'natural' causes" (exhaustion, malnutrition, disease, exposure) than "unnatural" causes (gassing, shooting, injection). This extraordinary allegation, it must be said, finds no support whatsoever in any documents or historical studies that I have seen, and Mayer's book – without footnotes – provides no evidence for it.

Because the death camps of Chelmno, Belzec, Sobibor, and Treblinka had "none of the ambiguities" of Auschwitz and Majdanek and "had no function other than the mass murder of totally unarmed and helpless civilians," Mayer finds them "much more difficult to fit into historical focus." In fact for Mayer they admittedly "defy explanation." However, Mayer does not ask himself what the implications of this candid admission are for the adequacy of his interpretive framework.

Once again Mayer must ignore considerable evidence to sustain the notion that the gassing of Jews in the death camps emerged only after the winter of 1941–2 as a kind of afterthought to the "hyperexploitation'' of labor. Nowhere in Mayer's book do we learn that within two to three months of the invasion of Russia, Heydrich informed Eichmann of Hitler's decision for the physical extermination of all European Jewry. Nowhere in Mayer do we learn that Nazi ''Jewish experts'' traveling back from meetings in Berlin in October could casually inform their friends that ''in the near future many of the Jewish vermin will be exterminated through special measures.'' Nowhere in Mayer do we learn of the Berlin reply on December 18, 1941, to an inquiry about whether all Jews should be liquidated regardless of age, sex, and economic interest: ''In the meantime clarity on the Jewish question has been achieved through oral discussion: economic interests are to be disregarded in principle in the settlement of this problem.''

Not only did the middle-echelon officials know of the looming Final Solution in the fall of 1941, but concrete preparations were already underway. In October, during the great Nazi encirclement victory of Vyasma and Bryansk (and not during November as Mayer alleges), Herbert Lange toured the Warthegau looking for a proper site for the Chelmno death camp. In the same month SS officers arrived in Belzec, where camp construction began on November 1. The death camp was a totally unprecedented invention. If the death-camp solution had been approved and was being implemented in October, the problem must have been posed by Himmler and Heydrich to their SS planners much earlier. Himmler and Heydrich in turn must have been first incited to their task by Hitler earlier yet. We are once again led back to midsummer 1941 and the height of German victory for the genesis of the Final Solution. The mass murder of the European Jews was the first use to which German victory was going to be put; it was not the byproduct of desperate labor impressment to stave off defeat.

Mayer's attempt to correlate the Final Solution to Germany's sagging military fortunes works no better for the later years. Himmler's savage determination to kill all the Jews as fast as possible, and his impatience with a short stay of execution even for desperately scarce Jewish skilled workers, is well documented. Mayer sees such documents merely as evidence that Himmler was becoming ''more and more incoherent''! In fact Himmler was rapidly approaching his goal. By December 1942, one month before the debacle at Stalingrad and a full half-year before the Germans permanently lost the initiative at Kursk, perhaps 75 percent of all Holocaust victims were already dead. German defeat and Jewish death did not follow the same trajectory.

In the end one must return to Mayer's admission that the camps at Chelmno, Belzec, Sobibor, and Treblinka "defy explanation." One must be frank: They defy *his* explanation, and they do so because he refuses to understand the Final Solution for what it was – the Nazis' plan to kill every last Jew in Europe on whom they could lay their hands. For Mayer Jews were killed because they were identified with Bolshevism, because they were expendable labor, because they were easier prey than elusive partisan bands, because the camp and ghetto conditions were terrible, because the Germans were increasingly enraged over their impending defeat, and so on. They were killed, according to Mayer, for every conceivable reason but the most simple and obvious: They were killed because they were Jews.

Mayer's intention to set the Holocaust in a wider historical context and to explore its "linkages" to other Nazi concerns and obsessions is perfectly valid. Much of the best recent work in Holocaust studies, though not on the sweeping and ambitious scale attempted by Mayer, has been precisely along these lines. Mayer's desire to examine the correlation between Nazi Jewish policy and the course of the war is a promising approach if done accurately. His emphasis on anti-Bolshevism as the most crucial element for the old elites' participation in the genocide is sound. Mayer is also quite right to remind us that the anti-Semitism of Hitler and the leading Nazis was only part of the equation and that one must take into account the enabling and facilitating factors of the "Judeocide."

If Mayer's beginning conception and many of his insights are laudable, how did he go so wrong? I would suggest the following. In his discussion of Hitler's syncretic ideology, anti-Semitism is conceded and expansionism and anti-Marxism are explored, but the basic racist underpinnings of Hitler's *Weltanschauung* – his understanding of history as a struggle of races in which the Jews played the most nefarious role – is given short shrift. Although Mayer subsequently explores the "linkages" between Nazi Jewish policy, anti-Bolshevism, and total war, he ignores another key linkage – that between Nazi Jewish policy and Hitler's war aims, namely his schemes for a total reordering of Europe along racial lines.

Between 1939 and 1941, when Hitler was allied with Stalin and every war was a success, Hitler's demographic engineers were already preparing for a massive population shuffle in which the expulsion of the Jews was but one aspect. For the period after the defeat of the "Judeobolshevik" regime in Russia and the extermination of European Jewry, the even more grandiose schemes of *Generalplan Ost* were on the drawing boards, entailing the uprooting and removal of over thirty million people, solely on racial grounds. These plans had nothing to do either with an anti-Bolshevik crusade or the frustrations and exigencies of defeat in total war; they were racism gone berserk, and Mayer misses this point because he does not take Hitler's racism seriously. For the same reason, he cannot conceive of a Nazi program to kill Jews solely because they were Jews. "Biological politics" was fundamental to Nazism. As Mayer's book demonstrates, an attempt to situate the Nazis' Final Solution in history without taking this into account is bound to go astray.

5

Beyond "Intentionalism" and "Functionalism": The Decision for the Final Solution Reconsidered

From the mid-1960s to the mid-1980s interpretations of National Socialism for the most part have been divided between two schools characterized by Tim Mason as the "intentionalists" and the "functionalists."[1] The former focused on Hitler and his ideology. The course of the Third Reich, in their view, was primarily determined by the decisions of Adolf Hitler, which in turn were calculated or "intended" to realize the goals of an ideologically derived "program" to which he had clung with fanatical consistency since the 1920s. The latter focused on the structure and institutions of the Third Reich. They explained what happened in Nazi Germany as an unplanned "cumulative radicalization" produced by the chaotic decision-making process of a polycratic regime and the "negative selection" of destructive elements from the Nazis' ideological arsenal as the only ones that could perpetually mobilize the disparate and otherwise incompatible elements of the Nazi coalition.[2]

When these two approaches were applied to Nazi Jewish policy and the origins of the Final Solution, drastically different interpretations re-

[1] Tim Mason, "Intention and Explanation: A Current Controversy about the Interpretation of National Socialism," *Der Führerstaat: Mythos und Realität*, ed. by Gerhard Hirschfeld and Lothar Kettenacker (Stuttgart, 1981), pp. 21–40.
[2] See the starkly contrasting articles of Hans Mommsen, "Hitlers Stellung im nationalsozialistischen Herrschaftssystem," and Klaus Hildebrand, "Monokratie oder Polykratie? Hitlers Herrschaft und das Dritte Reich," ibid., pp. 43–97.

sulted. According to the intentionalists, Hitler decided on the mass murder of the Jews in the 1920s and thereafter worked with consciousness and calculation toward that goal. Insofar as Nazi Jewish policy in the 1930s could be seen as conscious preparation for mass murder, it was embraced as evidence of continuity; when it did not, it was dismissed as either temporary expediency or the irrelevant and unguided experiments of Hitler's subordinates. The ultimate decision to implement the Final Solution was tied to the invasion of Russia, for the conquest of *Lebensraum* and the total destruction of European Jewry were seen as so inextricably connected in Hitler's ideology that he inevitably sought to realize the two simultaneously.[3]

The functionalists eschewed this Hitlerocentric, ideology-focused interpretation. For them, the diversity and contradictions of Nazi Jewish policy in the 1930s – Karl Schleunes's "twisted road to Auschwitz" – were proof that Hitler and the Nazis were not operating programmatically toward a premeditated goal. Insofar as consensus was eventually reached in Nazi Jewish policy, it was for the expulsion of the Jews – a goal Hitler and the Nazis pursued well into the fall of 1941. Only when the failure of the *Blitzkrieg* in Russia blocked expulsion did mass murder emerge as a solution. According to Uwe Adam, the breakthrough to mass murder resulted from a belated Hitler decision. Martin Broszat and Hans Mommsen, however, argued that it occurred without any specific and comprehensive Hitler decision or order. The system's automatic mechanisms for "cumulative radicalization" more than Hitler's ideology and leadership explained the origins of the Final Solution.[4]

---

[3] Andreas Hillgruber, "Die 'Endlösung' und das deutsche Ostimperium als Kernstück des rassenideologischen Programms des Nationalsozialismus," *Hitler, Deutschland und die Mächte*, ed. by Manfred Funke (Düsseldorf, 1978), pp. 94–114; Andreas Hillgruber, "Die ideologisch-dogmatische Grundlagen der nationalsozialistischen Politik der Ausrottung der Juden in den besetzten Gebieten der Sowjetunion und ihre Durchführung 1941–1944," *German Studies Review*, II/2 (1979), pp. 263–296. Eberhard Jäckel, *Hitler's Weltanschauung: A Blueprint for Power* (Middletown, Connecticut, 1975). Lucy Dawidowicz, *The War Against the Jews* (New York, 1975). Helmut Krausnick, "The Persecution of the Jews," *Anatomy of the SS State* (New York, 1968). Gerald Fleming, *Hitler and the Final Solution* (Berkeley and Los Angeles, 1984).

[4] Karl Schleunes, *The Twisted Road to Auschwitz* (Urbana, Illinois, 1970). Uwe Adam, *Judenpolitik im Dritten Reich* (Düsseldorf, 1972). Martin Broszat, "Hitler und die 'Endlösung.' Aus Anlass der Thesen von David Irving," *Vierteljahrshefte für Zeitgeschichte* (hereafter cited as VfZ), 25/4 (1977), pp. 739–775. Christopher R. Browning, "Zur

88   *Conflicting Explanations*

This historiographical controversy climaxed in a series of international conferences held in Paris (1982), Jerusalem (1983), and Stuttgart (1984).[5] Neither of the interpretations in the paradigmatic and polarized form that I have sketched was able to bear the weight of the subsequent research it had helped to stimulate. On the one hand, the "ultra-functionalist" position of Broszat and Mommsen gained few additional adherents.[6] On the other hand, self-proclaimed "intentionalists" also began to modify their views in significant ways. I myself attempted to articulate a middle position, which I called "moderate functionalism," arguing that Hitler had not decided on the Final Solution as the culmination of any long-held or premeditated plan, but that he had indeed made a series of key decisions in 1941 that ordained the mass murder of European Jews. The key turning point, I argued, was July 1941, when in the euphoria of seeming victory Hitler solicited a plan to extend the killing process already underway in Russia to the rest of Europe's Jews.[7]

By the late 1980s, much of the drama had gone out of the historiographical controversy for two reasons. First, the rigidly drawn lines of battle began to waver as scholars searched for some form of synthesis incorporating elements of both the intentionalist and functionalist positions. Second, the whole controversy was overshadowed by the far more politically charged and emotionally laden but historically barren

Genesis der 'Endlösung.' Eine Antwort an Martin Broszat," VfZ, 29/1 (1981), pp. 97–109. Hans Mommsen, "Die Realisierung des Utopischen: Die 'Endlösung der Judenfrage' im 'Dritten Reich'," *Geschichte und Gesellschaft*, IX/3 (Autumn 1983), pp. 381–420.

[5] For the respective proceedings, see *Unanswered Questions: Nazi Germany and the Genocide of the Jews*, ed. by François Furet (New York, 1989); *The Historiography of the Holocaust Period: Proceedings of the Fifth Yad Vashem International Conference*, ed. by Israel Gutman and Gideon Greif (Jerusalem, 1988); and *Der Mord an den Juden im Zweiten Weltkrieg: Entschlussbildung und Verwirklichung*, ed. by Eberhard Jäckel and Jürgen Rohwer (Stuttgart, 1985).

[6] The most recent defense of the Broszat-Mommsen position can be found in Christian Streit, "Ostkrieg, Antibolschewismus und 'Endlösung'," *Geschichte und Gesellschaft* 17/2 (1991), pp. 242–255.

[7] Christopher R. Browning, "The Decision Concerning the Final Solution," *Fateful Months: Essays on the Emergence of the Final Solution* (New York, 1985), pp. 8–38.

Historikerstreit.[8] This latter controversy produced mountains of polemic and some recycling of what had long been known, but no new questions or promising lines of research about Nazi Germany and the Holocaust were raised. In short, it shed much heat but virtually no light on the genesis of the Final Solution, however revealing it may have been about the current state of academic politics in the Federal Republic. As the *Historikerstreit* has run its course, the time has come to reassess historiographical developments concerning the origins of the Final Solution that have taken place in recent years.

One common denominator of most recent scholarship on the subject has been the broadening of perspective beyond the narrow focus on the year 1941. In my own work on the 1939–1941 period (see Chapters 1 and 2), I have argued that neither the intentionalist nor functionalist approach adequately explains the Nazi policies of resettlement and ghettoization. Contrary to the intentionalist view, Hitler and the leading Nazis were initially quite serious about solving the Jewish question through resettlement, though this term must be understood as an euphemism for brutal expulsion and population decimation. Contrary to the functionalist view, Hitler was the key decision maker in authorizing the Lublin and Madagascar resettlement schemes, and these options were exhausted by the autumn of 1940. Resettlement was no longer a serious option in 1941.

Contrary to the intentionalist view, ghettoization was not a conscious preparatory step for the systematic mass murder that followed but rather an improvised response by local authorities to the failure of the expulsion plans. There was no need to wait until 1942 for the "opportune" moment to realize the long-held goal of killing Polish Jews. As early as 1940 some local authorities advocated the mass starvation of the ghettoized Jews, but they received no support from Berlin. If the

---

[8] Richard J. Evans, "The New Nationalism and the Old History: Perspectives on the West German *Historikerstreit*," *Journal of Modern History*, 59 (December, 1987), pp. 761–797, and *In Hitler's Shadow: West German Historians and the Attempt to Escape from the Nazi Past* (New York, 1989); Norbert Kampe, "Normalizing the Holocaust? The Recent Historians' Debate in the Federal Republic of Germany," *Holocaust and Genocide Studies*, II/1 (1987), pp. 61–80; Charles Maier, *The Unmasterable Past: History, Holocaust, and German National Identity* (Cambridge, Massachusetts, 1988).

polycratic model of the functionalists was confirmed in this regard, the predicted outcome was not. When local authorities were left to themselves, the "productionists" prevailed over the "attritionists." Relative moderation, not cumulative radicalization, was the result. Only intervention from above would reverse this trend.

Other historians linking the events of 1941 to a broader background also abandoned any strict adherence to a starkly intentionalist or functionalist position. One of the most noted intentionalists, Eberhard Jäckel, admitted the diversity and "planlessness" of Nazi Jewish policy before 1941 and conceded that the top Nazi leaders around Hitler did not know from the beginning that they were going to murder the European Jews. Jäckel emphasized the incremental nature of Hitler's decision making in 1941; the Final Solution did not result from a single, comprehensive *Führerbefehl*. In short, Jäckel accepted many aspects of the "functionalist" image of Nazi Jewish policy but with one absolutely vital exception. He still insisted that Hitler himself knew that his ultimate goal was the systematic mass murder of European Jewry, an intention he vainly tried to signal to Heinrich Himmler and others ever since the autumn of 1938. With the possible exception of Reinhard Heydrich, they could not or would not take the hint. The detours, delays, confusion, and incremental progress toward Hitler's goal were, in Jäckel's mind, to be explained by the difficulty Hitler faced in bringing the other top Nazis, especially Himmler, around to his own unprecedented radicality.[9]

In addition to Jäckel, two other modified intentionalist views have recently appeared: Philippe Burrin's *Hitler et les Juifs: Genèse d'un génocide* and Richard Breitman's *The Architect of Genocide: Himmler and the Final Solution*.[10] Burrin dubs his approach "conditional intentionalism." Hitler in the 1920s saw the solution to the Jewish question

---

[9] See Jäckel's remarks at Stuttgart as well as his paper, "Hitler und den Mord an den europäischen Juden im Zweiten Weltkrieg," delivered in Warsaw in April 1983; *Hitler in History* (Hannover, New Hampshire, 1984); and *Hitlers Herrschaft* (Stuttgart, 1985).

[10] Philippe Burrin, *Hitler et les Juifs: Genèse d'un génocide* (Paris, 1989); Richard Breitman, *The Architect of Genocide: Himmler and the Final Solution* (New York, 1991). A recent reiteration of the more traditional, "unmodified" intentionalist view can be found in Hermann Graml, "The Genesis of the Final Solution," *November 1938: From 'Kristallnacht' to Genocide*, ed. by Walter H. Pehle (New York and Oxford, 1991), pp. 168–186.

in terms of expulsion, resettlement, and hostage-holding, but not extermination, according to Burrin. By the mid-1930s, however, Hitler envisaged a potential alternative. On September 25, 1935, he intimated to Walter Gross concerning the Jews, that in case of a war "on all fronts," he was ready for "all the consequences."[11] Thereafter, Hitler followed a consistent policy. As long as he was successful, the Jews faced expulsion; once his expansionary goals were checked, the Jews faced extermination. This was the meaning of his threat in the Reichstag in January 1939: If the Jews provoked another *world* war, it would result in the destruction of the Jews in Europe.

In contrast to other intentionalists, therefore, Burrin believes Hitler took the Lublin and Madagascar plans seriously. Like the functionalists, he even argues that expulsion was still envisioned well into the summer of 1941. The *Einsatzgruppen* had no order for systematic extermination prior to the invasion. Among other reasons he offers, Burrin claims that the military and other conservative elites would not yet have tolerated such a policy. Only when the campaign in Russia began to falter did the Germans turn to the murderous alternative. From late July to late August, a growing murderous rage led from the selective killing of the Jewish leadership to the systematic killing of Jewish women and children. Hitler's precise role in this August turning point is scarcely examined by Burrin, however.

Thereafter the focus returns to the Führer. By mid-September an increasingly pessimistic Hitler clearly realized that Russia would not be defeated by the end of the year and that U.S. entry into the war was a foregone conclusion. Facing a prolonged world war on all fronts, Hitler ordered the destruction of European Jewry, as he had intended under such conditions since the 1930s. Burrin's key documentary discovery for the mid-September date is a Heydrich letter explaining the decision to allow the bombing of Parisian synagogues on October 2, 1941. According to Heydrich, the decision was taken "only at the moment when from the highest authority the Jews were emphatically branded as the incendiaries of Europe who must ultimately disappear."[12] In a brief interval of four weeks, between September 18 when Himmler announced the deportation of German Jews eastward, to October 18 when

[11] Burrin, *Hitler et les Juifs*, p. 48.   [12] Ibid., p. 141.

Himmler forbad further Jewish emigration, everything fell into place.[13]
The Final Solution was irreversibly under way, launched out of frustration, rage, and a burning desire for revenge rather than euphoria.

Burrin advances an interpretation, therefore, that embraces the intentionalist view of the centrality of Hitler and a long-held plan for extermination, albeit a conditional one. He accepts my scenario of the 1939–1941 period concerning the policies of resettlement and ghettoization. In the end he joins with the functionalist view of no preinvasion extermination orders for the *Einsatzgruppen* and a belated fall decision for the Final Solution motivated by frustration.

In *The Architect of Genocide*, Breitman offers yet another modified intentionalist view. He notes the deficiency of previous intentionalists in not assembling evidence connecting Hitler's ideological views with the actual decisions and preparations for mass murder. This is a deficiency he aims to remedy by tracing the key role of Heinrich Himmler in the decision-making process. Unlike Jäckel who posited a gulf of misunderstanding between Hitler and Himmler that was only bridged in 1941, Breitman feels that the Hitler-Himmler symbiosis is key. Both were secretive masters of deceit, and for Breitman the task is to expose the hitherto successful "cover-up" of their conspiratorial planning. The truth, he feels, lies not in the "carefully marked trail of neatly filed documents" but behind them. It is only by understanding this Hitler-Himmler modus operandi that the historian can parry the "tactics of deception that have misled a prominent school of historians," pick up the real clues, and uncover their "secret" plans.[14]

In a major modification of the intentionalist position, Breitman concedes that there was no prewar plan to murder all German Jews, much less all European Jews.

> The shift to a comprehensive plan for all Europe came considerably later. A program for the complete destruction of the Jewish people depended upon so many unrealized preconditions . . . that it is hard to see how anyone, even Hitler, could have made any kind of commitment, privately to himself or confidentially to others. He would undoubtedly seek to unleash his rage at the

[13] Ibid., p. 146.   [14] Breitman, *Architect of Genocide*, pp. 27–32.

Jews; how and when he did so depended upon the circumstances, opportunities, and plans presented to him.[15]

Quite moderately, Breitman argues that there were "signs" of a "preliminary plan" for "getting rid of as many [German Jews] as possible by force," if emigration failed to solve the Jewish question before the outbreak of war.[16]

By virtue of his methodology, Breitman downplays Himmler's well-documented role in planning the resettlement policies of 1939–1940. The "neatly filed documents" do not tell the real story. Madagascar, he suggests, was an "imaginary goal . . . serving as a cover" while "Himmler and the SS leadership had to work out the actual plans for disposing of large numbers of Jews in the East."[17]

Breitman's major claim is that Hitler took "a fundamental decision to exterminate the Jews" in early 1941 – "months earlier than the juncture most specialists have selected" – and that "[b]y March the Final Solution was just a matter of time – and timing."[18] Subsequent planning in the summer of 1941 merely involved "operational decisions" to implement the fundamental decisions and secret plans of early 1941. Breitman speculates liberally about many pieces of evidence, but ultimately his case for a fundamental decision and secret plan in early 1941 depends on one key document – a Propaganda Ministry memorandum of March 21, 1941, reporting on a meeting attended by Adolf Eichmann the day before. According to Breitman's interpretation of this document, "Eichmann revealed that about two months earlier Heydrich had presented a plan for the 'final evacuation' of the (German) Jews to Poland, and that only the limited absorptive capacity of the Government General [*sic*] was temporarily holding up implementation. In other words, Hitler had already approved it." At the same time Hitler assured the head of the General Government, Hans Frank, that his bailiwick would become the first territory to be made free of Jews. "There was only one way to have a 'final evacuation' of the Jews to Poland and simultaneously to make Poland free of Jews. . . ." Hitler, Breitman concludes, had already approved the mass murder of the Jews in Poland.[19]

---

[15] Ibid., p. 65.   [16] Ibid., p. 64.   [17] Ibid., p. 139.
[18] Ibid., pp. 153, 247.   [19] Ibid., pp. 152, 156.

By virtue of these quite contrasting modifications, a common intentionalist position has all but disappeared. Jäckel and Breitman disagree on the nature of the Himmler-Hitler relationship. Breitman and Burrin disagree on the timing of the decision. What they have in common, basically, is a concentration on the role of Hitler and the top leadership in the decision-making process. Two other recent contributions focus instead on impersonal factors, circumstance, and the input from below of the bureaucratic apparatus. Arno Mayer's *Why Did the Heavens Not Darken? The "Final Solution" in History* emphasizes the anti-Bolshevik consensus in German society and the economic exigencies of total war as the key factors in explaining what he terms the "Judeocide." Susanne Heim and Götz Aly focus on the "economy of the Final Solution" and the contribution of lower-echelon economic planners. As I have already discussed these contributions in Chapters 3 and 4, I would like to concentrate on the recent arguments and evidence put forth by Burrin and Breitman concerning three key periods in 1941: the late March events surrounding Eichmann's visit to the Propaganda Ministry, invoked by Breitman; the massive escalation of the mass murder of Jews in the Soviet Union in late July and early August and the assessment of Hitler's role therein; and finally the events of late September/early October and the relationship of these events to perceptions of Germany's military fortunes at that time. Is our view of the course of events in 1941 significantly altered by the research, evidence, and interpretations that have appeared recently?

Let us look first at an interesting episode in the spring of 1941 seized upon by Breitman. On March 17, Hans Frank came to Berlin and discussed the future of the General Government with Hitler for one and a half hours.[20] The following day Joseph Goebbels and Frank lunched at Hitler's apartment. Goebbels recorded in his diary: "Vienna will soon be entirely Jew-free. And now it is to be Berlin's turn. I am already discussing the question with the Führer and Dr. Frank. He puts the Jews to work, and they are indeed obedient. Later they will have to get out

---

[20] *Das Diensttagebuch des deutschen Generalgouverneurs in Polen 1939–1945* (hereafter cited as DTB), ed. by Werner Präg and Wolfgang Jacobmeyer (Stuttgart, 1975), p. 332 (entry of March 17, 1941).

of Europe altogether."[21] Clearly the deportation of Jews from Vienna, which Hitler had approved the previous December, was a topic of conversation. Heydrich had incorporated these Jewish deportations from Vienna (and Danzig) into his "third short-range plan" of December 1940/January 1941, which called for the deportation of more than a million Poles from the incorporated territories in the coming year. What apparently was not discussed was that Heydrich's "third short-range plan," including the Jewish deportations, had been ordered to a total halt just two days earlier, on March 15, as military preparations for Barbarossa monopolized all available rail transportation.[22] Goebbels apparently had reason to believe the time was ripe to expand the Jewish deportations to include Berlin.

Goebbels flew to Posen the following day, March 19, but obviously left instructions with his subordinates to pursue the topic of Jewish deportations raised at the Hitler luncheon. On March 20, Eichmann and a representative of Albert Speer's office attended a meeting in the Propaganda Ministry hosted by Goebbels's state secretary, Leopold Gutterer.[23] Gutterer informed his guests that

> when Dr. Goebbels was lunching with the Führer the topic of the 60–70,000 Jews still living in Berlin came up. In the conversation it was established that it was no longer tolerable that the capital city of the National Socialist Reich was still the residence of such a large number of Jews. . . . At this conversation the Führer admittedly did not personally decide that Berlin had to be made free of Jews immediately, but Dr. Goebbels is convinced that an appropriate evacuation proposal would certainly gain the Führer's agreement.
>
> Party Comrade Eichmann of the Security Main Office said that Party Comrade Heydrich – *who is entrusted by the Führer with*

---

[21] *The Goebbels Diaries: 1939–1941*, ed. by Fred Taylor (London, 1982), p. 272 (entry of March 18, 1941).

[22] See Chapter 1 in this book.

[23] National Archives Microfilm, T-81/R676/5485604-5 (note concerning the evacuation of Jews from Berlin, March 21, 1941). This document was first published in H. G. Adler, *Der Verwaltete Mensch: Studien zur Deportation der Juden aus Deutschland* (Tübingen, 1974), 152–153.

the final evacuation of the Jews [italics mine] – had submitted a
proposal to the Führer eight to ten weeks ago that has not yet been
implemented only because the General Government at the moment is not in the position to receive *one Jew or one Pole from the
Old Reich* [italics mine]. In any case there is a written order of the
Führer for the evacuation of 60,000 Jews from Vienna, that must
therefore be taken into the General Government. In Vienna only
45,000 Jews are on hand at the moment, so possibly one could
remove the remaining 15,000 Jews from Berlin.

Eichmann went on to warn that the war economy presently needed every Jew capable of work, though given the elderly character of the bulk
of the Jewish population in Germany, that was not a great number. The
conference concluded with Eichmann's agreement to prepare for Goebbels a proposal for the evacuation of the Berlin Jews.

Frank returned to the General Government where he reported on the
very satisfactory results of his conversations with Hitler. First Frank
sketched the long-term goal. "The General Government . . . will
above all be de-Judaized (*entjudet*). . . . with the Jews the Poles will
also leave this territory. The Führer has decided to make a pure German
country out of this territory in the course of 15–20 years." Frank then
turned to the short term.

[F]rom the broad perspective it is not practical to engage in racial
experimentation at the moment. As Reich Marshal Göring recently said: "It is more important to win the war than to implement racial policy." At present we must be happy over every Pole
whom we have in the work place. Whether the Pole or the Jew
suits us or not plays no role now; what is important is only that he
is indirectly in the service of the German people.[24]

Later the same day the Higher SS and Police Leader in the General
Government, Wilhelm Krüger, revealed that the deportation of Jews
and Poles into the General Government had been stopped. Only then,
seemingly as an afterthought, did Frank add that the Führer had promised him at their last meal together that the General Government would

[24] DTB, pp. 335–336 (first entry of March 25, 1941).

be the first territory made *judenfrei*. This was clearly not what he deemed to be the most important information he brought back from his meetings with Hitler.[25]

The following day Frank once again returned to the racial future of the General Government. "Within several decades" (*in einigen Jahrzehnten*) the General Government must become as purely German as the Rhineland. The Führer had assured him of his intention to make out of the General Government "the most aryan Gau of the German Reich. . . . The Führer promised me that in the foreseeable future (*in absehbarer Zeit*) the General Government will be completely freed of Jews."[26]

Clearly Frank, who had talked with Hitler at much greater length, had a different impression of Hitler's "timetable" for dealing with the Jewish question than did Goebbels. In the following month, April 1941, despite Hitler's assurances that the General Government would be the first territory made *judenfrei,* Frank approved the proposal of his economic advisers for a total reorganization of the Warsaw ghetto economy to place it on a self-sufficient basis. His advisers were estimating the duration of the ghetto at five years![27] Goebbels, in the meantime, returned from Posen to discover that he had been mistaken in interpreting Hitler's luncheon talk as a signal that the time was ripe for a proposal to deport the Berlin Jews. As he wrote in his diary, "the Jews, it turns out, cannot be evacuated from Berlin, because 30,000 of them are working in armaments factories."[28]

I would agree with Breitman that this episode is very illuminating, but I do not share his conclusions. Let us return to his analysis of the March 21 memorandum of the Propaganda Ministry. Breitman seizes on the expression "from the Old Reich," that is, the pre-1938 boundaries that did not yet include Vienna and the incorporated territories, as evidence that Eichmann was not speaking of Heydrich's well-documented "third short-range plan" (deporting Jews from Vienna and Poles from the incorporated territories). Then Breitman takes Eichmann's assertion of Heydrich's authority – he had been "entrusted by

---

[25] DTB, p. 337 (second entry of March 25, 1941).

[26] DTB, pp. 338–339 (entry of March 26, 1941).

[27] See Chapter 2 in this book.   [28] Goebbels, p. 277 (entry of March 22, 1941).

the Führer with the final evacuation of the Jews" – as the content of a second proposal to Hitler. Thus he cites this document as proof that the alleged second proposal was a "secret plan for the deportation of what seems to have been most Jews from the Old Reich . . . to the General Government." It was, moreover, a plan "already approved" by Hitler.[29] "It is likely," Breitman speculates further, "that the actual conception was to clear Jews from much of the continent, a fact which Eichmann had no need to reveal at the meeting."[30] If Hitler had already approved a secret plan to deport the Jews of Germany and much of the continent to Poland, while he simultaneously assured Frank that his territory would be the first to be made *judenfrei*, the implications are clear to Breitman; both the Jews in Poland and those to be sent there were to be murdered in mass. The decision for the Final Solution had already been made.

How compelling are Breitman's deductions? The key memorandum of March 21, it must be kept in mind, is not an internal SS document making careful distinctions between plans with which the writer was familiar. Rather it was the product of a note-writer in the Propaganda Ministry, briefly summarizing a lengthy discussion one day later. In these circumstances, a cryptic reference to an Eichmann statement about a plan whose details would have been totally unfamiliar to the writer cannot possibly provide the kind of precision that Breitman's interpretation demands. The fact that the reference was to "one Jew or *one Pole* [italics mine] from the Old Reich" suggests even more strongly that Eichmann was referring to the "third short-range plan" and not some secret second plan for deporting German Jews.

Furthermore, I would argue, the whole incident reveals a very different modus operandi than Breitman's conspiracy scenario, in which Hitler, Himmler, and Eichmann had hatched secret plans, which the loose-lipped Eichmann almost let out of the bag. On the contrary, Hitler seems to have spoken very generally to Frank about the long-term future of the General Government, in time spans of "several decades" and "15–20 years." At the luncheon the more immediate topic of the Vienna and Berlin Jews came up as well. What Hitler said, we do not know, but Hitler "admittedly" decided nothing. The overly eager

---

[29] Breitman, *Architect of Genocide*, p. 152.   [30] Ibid., p. 285, n. 32.

Goebbels clearly read into his remarks an invitation for a proposal to evacuate the Berlin Jews. This haphazard method of policy-making by soliciting proposals through hints and signals was not unusual for Hitler. But in this case Goebbels misjudged Hitler's intent. For the short term, both in Berlin and in the General Government, pragmatic considerations about Jewish labor were given priority over "racial experimentation." Heydrich's massive resettlement scheme had been halted due to the military's demands on transportation, and realistically no one could be planning anything about the Jews in Germany and Poland until the impending war with the Soviet Union was won. The fate of European Jewry hung on Germany's military success.

Let us turn to the next issue – the fate of Soviet Jewry. Though much has been published in recent years about preparations for Germany's "war of destruction" in the Soviet Union, little new has emerged about specific preinvasion decisions and plans concerning the Jews beyond the ongoing Krausnick-Streim debate. For the most part, that debate remained focused on the credibility of postwar testimony (each protagonist, of course, had his favorite witnesses).[31] Others who joined in the debate, however, increasingly switched the focus from the morass of postwar testimony to the documentable actions of the killers in the summer of 1941. The question, in short, was altered. Instead of asking what the perpetrators had or had not been told before June 22 (and trying to answer that question on the basis of postwar testimony), historians have increasingly asked what did the perpetrators do after June 22, and what can the historian infer from their patterns of behavior.

In his case study of Einsatzgruppe C, Yaacov Lozowick found no evidence of preinvasion orders for the total murder of Soviet Jews or of any early awareness within the unit that their killing of Jews was part of a Final Solution.[32] Nor did the unit radicalize its killings on its own initiative. At some point after the invasion, a new impetus came from above. Roland Headland focused on the *Einsatzgruppen* reports of just

[31] Alfred Streim, "The Tasks of the Einsatzgruppen," *Simon Wiesenthal Center Annual* (hereafter SWCA), IV (1987), pp. 309–328; and the exchange between Krausnick and Streim in SWCA, VI (1989), pp. 311–347.

[32] Yaacov Lozowick, *"Rollbahn Mord:* The Early Activities of Einsatzgruppe C," *Holocaust and Genocide Studies* (hereafter cited as HGS), II/2 (1987), pp. 221–241.

the first five weeks. He concluded that by the end of July the *Einsatz-gruppen* had already killed at least 62,805 civilians, the vast majority of whom were Jews. Only in relation to the even more intensive killings can *Einsatzgruppen* behavior in this period be seen as hesitant or re-strained. However uneven and ambiguous the policies of the *Einsatz-gruppen* may have been, Headland concluded, the leaders of the *Einsatzgruppen* knew what task they faced before the invasion and their undertaking "had as its goal the destruction of the Soviet Jews."[33] In short, the documentation of the *Einsatzgruppen* reports is sufficiently ambiguous that two scholars taking the same methodological approach and agreeing on the same general pattern of escalation after July none-theless came to opposite conclusions.

Perhaps the most promising new approach to shed additional light on this controversy was that of Yehoshua Büchler on the units attached to Himmler's own *Kommandostab*.[34] By shifting the focus from the *Ein-satzgruppen* to other formations that became involved in the killing campaign, he widened the field of investigation (and hence of potential documentation). Moreover, he opened the new dimension of manpower. Büchler's work made it clear that the August escalation in killing fol-lowed Himmler's decision in late July to reinforce the *Einsatzgruppen* with two SS brigades. Furthermore, his research established a far greater personal involvement on Himmler's part in the operations of one of these brigades than can be documented for any of the *Einsatz-gruppen* operations.

Surveying this confused historiographical terrain, which he termed a "zone of shadows," Philippe Burrin argued against the notion of any explicit preinvasion extermination order to the *Einsatzgruppen*.[35] Moreover, he doubted the existence of even a vague or implicit order, for only quite specific orders made any sense in the context of an ex-pected quick victory. Finally, Burrin argued, it was inconceivable in view of the sensibilities of the army, civil administration, and conser-

---

[33] Roland Headland, "The Einsatzgruppen: The Question of Their Initial Operations," HGS, IV/4 (1989), pp. 401–412.

[34] Yohoshua Büchler, "Kommandostab Reichsführer-SS: Himmler's Personal Murder Brigades in 1941," HGS, I/1 (1986), pp. 11–26.

[35] Burrin, *Hitler et les Juifs*, pp. 103–125.

vative elites, that the Nazi leadership could have given a preinvasion order for mass killing to be continued after quick victory. In fact, the first victims were primarily Jewish male leaders. Only in August did the killing of women and children become common; only in August did the documents refer for the first time to total extermination. Himmler seemed unprepared for mass killing on this scale, and as late as August 1, 1941, he was still talking about driving the Jewish women into the swamps rather than ordering his men to shoot them. Some time in August, Burrin concluded, the decision to kill all Soviet Jews was taken – though he strangely omitted any discussion of Hitler's own role in such a decision. Instead he suggested that a growing rage among the Germans over the military frustrations they were experiencing continued to intensify the killing of Jews well into the fall.

Accepting Burrin's starting point that any assessment of Nazi Jewish policy in the summer of 1941 must be tied to their contemporary perception of the war, and building on Büchler's approach of including the manpower dimension and the experience of other than *Einsatzgruppen* units, I would suggest the following scenario as most compatible with the existing state of research.[36] Before the invasion the *Einsatzgruppen* were not given explicit orders for the total extermination of the Jews on Soviet territory. Along with the general incitement to an ideological and racial war, however, they were given the general task of liquidating "potential" enemies. Heydrich's much-debated directive of July 2, 1941, was a minimal list of all those who had to be liquidated *immediately*, including all Jews in state and party positions. It is very likely, moreover, that the *Einsatzgruppen* leaders were told of the *future* goal of a *judenfrei* Russia through systematic mass murder. Though the time frame for this was left open, it was not as long term as the "several decades" Frank reported from his March conversations with Hitler about eliminating all Jews and Poles in the General Government. A mere force of 3,000 men, assigned to move as quickly as possible into the vast Russian interior behind the advancing German army, was

---

[36] At this writing I have seen only a few of the documents from the increasingly accessible Soviet and Czech archives. A large increase in documentation may substantially alter the historian's understanding of the course of the Final Solution on Soviet territory.

clearly not expected to accomplish such a task initially. They were, however, to incite pogroms and eliminate select categories of Jews.

As the *Einsatzgruppen* penetrated into Soviet territory, the killing units carried out executions while on the move that could in no way constitute a program of total extermination. They found that the so-called commissars – Jewish and otherwise – had for the most part fled. The overwhelming majority of executions in the first five weeks, therefore, were aimed at the closest approximation – the Jewish male leadership and intelligentsia.[37] In short, in the initial stage of killing, the bulk of the victims were adult male Jews, particularly those in leadership positions, but nonetheless the vast majority of Jews remained alive.[38]

Several documents from a later period imply that the *Einsatzgruppen* leaders knew of the final goal of total destruction at the beginning, even

---

[37] Consider the following excerpts from *The Einsatzgruppen Reports*, ed. by Yitzhak Arad, Shmuel Krakowski, and Shmuel Spector (New York, 1989): p. 2, Report No. 10, July 2, 1941 (EG C): "It is obvious that the cleansing activities have to extend first of all to the Bolsheviks and the Jews"; p. 9, Report No. 13, July 5, 1941 (EG C): "Leaders of Jewish intelligentsia (in particular teachers, lawyers, Soviet officials) liquidated"; p. 10, Report No. 14, July 6, 1941 (EG A): ". . . mainly Jews were liquidated. However, there were also Bolshevik officials and snipers among them . . ."; pp. 14–15, Report No. 17, July 7, 1941 (EG B): "According to instructions by RSHA, liquidations of government and party officials, in all named cities of Byelorussia were carried out. Concerning the Jews, according to orders, the same policy was adopted"; p. 22, Report No. 21, July 13 (EG B): ". . . about 500 Jews, saboteurs amongst them, are liquidated daily"; p. 28, Report No. 24, July 16, 1941 (EG A): "Actions against the Jews are going on in an ever-increasing number. . . . The Jewish families are being driven out of town by the Latvians; most of the men have been arrested. . . . The arrested Jewish men are shot without ceremony and interred in previously prepared graves"; Report No. 32, July 24, 1941 (EG B): "Mainly Jews between 20 and 40 years of age are rounded up, artisans and specialists being set aside as far as possible"; p. 46, Report No. 32, July 24, 1941 (EG B): "In Minsk, the entire Jewish intelligentsia has been liquidated (teachers, professors, lawyers, etc., except medical personnel)"; pp. 69–70, Report No. 43, August 5, 1941 (EG A): "On the one hand the operational activity in the Byelorussian area is geared to the principle of hitting the Jewish-Bolshevik upper class as efficiently as possible. . . . As was to be expected, almost the entire Bolshevik leadership has escaped. . . . The emphasis of the operational activity was, therefore, directed, first of all, against the Jewish intelligentsia."

[38] The only report of this early period that provides a statistical breakdown between total executions and Jews, male and female, is that of EK 3 for late July and early August. According to Report No. 54 of August 16, 1941, between July 22 and August 3, EK 3 executed 1,592 people. This included 1,349 male Jews and 172 female Jews. *The Einsatzgruppen Reports*, pp. 90–91.

if that policy was not immediately implemented. For instance, in the following January 1942, Rudolf Lange wrote: "The goal that the Einsatzkommando 2 had in mind from the beginning was a radical solution to the Jewish problem through the execution of all Jews."[39] More frequently cited is, of course, the Franz Stahlecker report of October 15, 1941. He discussed the initial policy of covertly inciting local antisemitic forces to carry out pogroms. However, "it was expected from the start that the Jewish problem would not be solved solely through pogroms." Thus "the security police cleansing work had according to basic orders the goal of the most complete removal possible of the Jews. Extensive executions in the cities and flat lands were therefore carried out through special units."[40] I argued earlier that such documents as these, along with the total absence in other documents of any reference to any postinvasion change in policy or new basic orders, point to the conclusion that from the beginning the *Einsatzgruppen* leaders had a general understanding of what was ultimately expected of them.[41] Arno Mayer has suggested that the Stahlecker report should be dismissed as a self-promoting document written in hindsight.[42] Burrin, too, implies that the document is tainted by hindsight, though on the part of historians who interpret it, not by Stahlecker himself. He thinks that the phrase about removing as many Jews as possible should be seen in the perspective of a very short war, after which large-scale executions would no longer be possible. The "most complete removal possible of the Jews" does not, he argues, imply total extermination.[43]

Another document that cannot be considered as tainted with hindsight, however, is Report No. 31 of July 23, 1941, containing an interesting comment from Artur Nebe, commander of Einsatzgruppe B, that he must have written and sent to the Reich Security Main Office

---

[39] Cited in Helmut Krausnick and Hans-Heinrich Wilhelm, *Die Truppe des Weltanschauungskrieges: Die Einsatzgruppen der Sicherheitspolizei und des SD 1938–1942* (Stuttgart, 1981), p. 534.

[40] *Trials of the Major War Criminals before the International Military Tribunal* (hereafter cited as IMT) (Nürnberg, 1947–49), Vol. 27, 687 (180-L).

[41] Christopher R. Browning, *Fateful Months: Essays on the Emergence of the Final Solution* (New York, 1985), pp. 19–20.

[42] Arno Mayer, *Why Did the Heavens Not Darken? The "Final Solution" in History* (New York, 1989), p. 259.

[43] Burrin, *Hitler et les Juifs*, p. 123.

(Reichssicherheitshauptam – RSHA) in Berlin many days earlier. Nebe reported that one and a half million Jews resided in the Byelorussian area. "A solution of the Jewish question during the war seems impossible in this area because of the tremendous number of Jews. It could only be achieved through deportations."[44] To "work out a flexible basis for the immediate future," therefore, he was installing Jewish councils, marking and ghettoizing the Jews, and putting them to work.[45] If expulsion of the Jews to Siberia was still being considered as the long-term solution and the *Einsatzgruppen* leaders had not yet received any indication of the final goal of extermination, as suggested by Burrin, Nebe's comment is puzzling. What was the intended solution made impossible by the large numbers of Byelorussian Jews? Why and to what was deportation posed as an alternative? This comment makes perfect sense, however, if Nebe knew he was ultimately responsible for killing one and a half million Jews but despaired of achieving that goal with a meager force of 600 to 700 men scattered all over White Russia and including an "advanced commando" (*Vorkommando*) that was to go all the way to Moscow.

The issue of manpower, I would argue, is as salient for the historian as it was for Nebe. If the historian wants to know when the Nazi leadership decided that the mass murder of Russian Jewry was no longer a future task but rather a goal to be achieved immediately, he must ascertain when the decision was taken to commit the necessary manpower. Establishing when this decision was taken will in turn help to elucidate the circumstances and motives behind it.

On July 16, Hitler spoke with Göring, Lammers, Rosenberg, and Keitel in a way that showed his clear conviction that victory was at hand. Some "fundamental observations" had to be made about German goals in the east. Germany would never leave these territories. The Crimea, former-Austrian Galicia, the Baltic, the Volga German settlements, and Baku were destined to become part of the German Reich. Out of the newly won territories in the east, he intended to create "a Garden of Eden." "All necessary measures – shootings, resettlements,

---

[44] *The Einsatzgruppen Reports*, p. 43.
[45] See also his subsequent remarks in Report No. 33, July 27, 1941. *The Einsatzgruppen Reports*, pp. 47–50.

etc." – would be undertaken to accomplish this. It was thus fortunate that the Russians had given the order for partisan warfare, for "it gives us the opportunity to exterminate anyone who is hostile to us. . . . Naturally, the vast area must be pacified as quickly as possible; this will happen best through shooting anyone who even looks askance at us."[46] As usual, Hitler was not giving explicit orders, but the tenor of his speech was unmistakable. What role could Jews have in a German Garden of Eden? What could be expected of his subordinates when Hitler urged the extermination and shooting of all hostile elements?

Himmler did not attend this meeting, though he received a copy of the minutes and he was in East Prussia in close proximity to Hitler's headquarters from July 15 to July 20.[47] What Hitler may have confided to him personally, we do not know. What he did in the following weeks can be adequately documented. As Yehoshua Büchler has shown in his pioneering work, on July 19 Himmler assigned the SS Cavalry Brigade to the Higher SS and Police Leader (HSSPF) Center, Erich von dem Bach-Zelewski, for an impending sweep of the Pripet marshes. On July 22 he attached the 1st SS Brigade to the HSSPF South, Friedrich Jeckeln. The SS Cavalry Brigade contained nearly 4,000 men, and the 1st SS Brigade over 7,200.[48] Within a week of Hitler's "victory speech," Himmler had more than quadrupled the number of SS men operating behind the advancing German army.

But that was only the beginning of the build-up. At least eleven battalions of Order Police (each of approximately 500 men) were part of the invasion force. These police battalions had initially been assigned to various military commanders in the rear areas. On July 23 Himmler reassigned them to the three HSSPF in north, central, and south Russia. As the war diary of Police Battalion 322 stated: "For the impending tasks of the battalion, it is placed directly under the HSSPF Gruppenführer von dem Bach."[49] The minimum of eleven police battalions constituted a reinforcement of another 5,500 to 6,000 men. By the end of

---

[46] IMT, vol. 38, pp. 86–94 (221-L: conference of July 16, 1941).

[47] Breitman, *Architect of Genocide*, pp. 184, 295.

[48] Prague Military Archives, Kommandostab-RFSS, sig. Ia 12/1, Kr. 10 (manpower strength of units under the Kommandostab-RFSS, July 19, 1941).

[49] Yad Vashem Archives (hereafter cited as YVA), O-53/127/53 (war diary of Police Battalion 322, entry of July 23, 1941).

the year there were twenty-six police battalions on Soviet territory.[50] Himmler was still not finished, however. One week later he was in Riga, where he ''mentioned that he intends to set up police formations consisting of Lithuanians, Latvians, Estonians, Ukrainians, etc., employing them outside of their own home areas. This is possible right away. . . .''[51] Units of native collaborators had already played a significant role in the killing process. At the end of 1941, the strength of these units had reached 33,000. By June 1942, it was 165,000; by January 1943, 300,000.[52] As Nebe rightly indicated, the task of killing Russian Jewry with the 3,000 men of the *Einsatzgruppen* was ''impossible.'' By the end of July 1941, Himmler's massive build-up ensured that the manpower to begin killing on such a scale was available.

What instructions were these units given? Burrin suggests that Himmler's cryptic order of July 30 to the 2nd SS Cavalry Regiment in the Pripet marshes – ''All Jews must be shot. Drive the female Jews into the swamp''[53] – demonstrates that even at that date he had not yet ordered – indeed that he had not yet ''dared'' to order – the shooting of women and children.[54] Some confusion surrounds this particular incident, but considerable evidence suggests it ought not be generalized.

On the eve of the Pripet marsh sweep, referring to the general population and not just Jews, Himmler ordered all units ''to shoot everyone suspected of supporting the partisans.'' Women and children were to be evacuated and the villages were to be burned down.[55] Order Police units from Police Battalion 322 clearing the Bielowies forest reported quite explicitly that they proceeded to shoot adult male Jews but evacuated their families. They did not begin killing women and children

[50] Berlin Document Center, O 464, Osteinsatz Polizei, ''Die im Osten eingesetzten Stäbe.''

[51] *The Einsatzgruppen Reports*, p. 83 (Report No. 48, August 10, 1941).

[52] For the June 1942 figure, see H. J. Neufeld, J. Huck, G. Tessin, *Zur Geschichte der Ordnungspolizei 1936–1945* (Koblenz, 1957), p. 101. For the growth from the beginning to the end of 1942, see NO-286 (Daluege's report of January 1943).

[53] *Justiz und NS-Verbrechen: Sammlung Deuschen Strafurteile wegen Nationalsozialistischen Tötungsverbrechen 1945–1966* (hereafter cited as JNSV) (Amsterdam), XX, No. 570 (LG Braunschweig 2 Ks 1/63), p. 44.

[54] Burrin, *Hitler et les Juifs*, pp. 126–127.

[55] *Unsere Ehre Heisst Treue*, p. 222 (Himmler *Sonderbefehl*, July 28, 1941).

until the end of August.[56] At the trial of the 2nd SS Cavalry Regiment in Braunschweig, however, it became clear that this unit had received the additional order from Himmler about driving the Jewish women into the swamp. *Sturmbannführer* Franz Magill reported on August 12, 1941, that the men of his four cavalry squadrons of the 2nd SS Cavalry Regiment had shot 6,529 "plunderers." (The entire brigade reported a total of 13,788 for the same period.) Magill elaborated that while "Jewish plunderers" had been shot, skilled Jewish workers employed by the army had been spared. "Driving women and children into the swamp was not successful, because the swamp was not so deep that sinking under could occur. After a depth of one meter, for the most part one hit firm ground (probably sand), so that sinking under was not possible."[57] Pretrial testimony revealed that most of the Jews killed by Magill's unit had in fact been adult male Jews fetched from Pinsk under the guise of rounding up labor. The killing actions did not take place in the marsh, and the few children who came along with parents were shot. In marshland villages women and children were shot on at least some occasions.[58] Magill's lengthy explanation about the shallow swamp remains puzzling, though perhaps he was trying to explain why Himmler's order was not taken more literally. In any case, he does not seem to have misunderstood Himmler's intent.[59]

Further south, in the Ukraine, Himmler apparently did not express himself ambiguously. When Reserve Police Battalion 45 reached the town of Shepetovka, its commander, Major Franz, was summoned by

---

[56] YVA, O-53/127/63-72 (war diary of Police Battalion 322, entries of August 2, 5, 9, and 15, 1941). Konrad Kwiet, "From the Diary of a Killing Unit," *Why Germany?* ed. by John Milfull (Oxford: Berg, forthcoming).

[57] *Unsere Ehre Heisst Treue.* p. 224 (1st Cavalry Brigade to HSSPF Central, August 13, 1941) and pp. 229–230 (Magill report of August 12, 1941).

[58] Staatsanwaltschaft Braunschweig, 2 Ks 3/63, indictment of Magill and others, pp. 32 and 53.

[59] This was not the only time Himmler used this expression about chasing Jews into the swamp. On the other occasion his intentions were perfectly clear. In his postwar testimony Friedrich Jeckeln told of a conversation concerning the resumption of transports of German Jews to Riga (where Jeckeln had been reassigned as HSSPF). "Himmler said that he had not yet decided in what way to destroy them. . . to shoot them in Salispils, or to chase them into the swamp." YVA, O-53/144/395-402 (interrogation of Friedrich Jeckeln, December 14, 1945).

the commander of Police Regiment South, Colonel Besser. Franz remembered vividly the conversation. According to Besser, Himmler had ordered that the Jews in Russia were to be destroyed and that Reserve Police Battalion 45 was to participate in carrying out this order. Several days later Besser instructed Franz to shoot the Jews – women and children included – in Shepetovka with the help of the local Ukrainian militia. When did this occur? The diary of one policeman reliably placed the battalion in Shepetovka between July 24 and August 1, 1941.[60]

Further east the commander of EK 5, Erwin Schulz, was summoned to Zhitomir by his superior, Dr. Dr. Otto Rasch of Einsatzgruppe C. In his detailed testimony to German judicial investigators in Köln in 1953, Schulz dated this meeting rather precisely to either August 10 or 12. Rasch let his officers know that he had been reproached for not treating the Jews sharply enough. HSSPF Friedrich Jeckeln had now ordered that all nonworking Jews, women and children included, be shot. Some of the officers replied that it was *already known* that Jeckeln's units were doing this. They noted that this practice had severe psychological effects on the men and led to increased support for the partisans. Rasch then invoked a binding order of Himmler. Schulz claimed that his commando continued to drag its feet in implementing this order. When Schulz returned to Berlin on August 24, Streckenbach confirmed to him that the order to kill women and children came from the highest authorities. Already considered "too weak," Schulz was able to procure a transfer.[61]

In the south it would appear that the murder order came from Himmler via the HSSPF Jeckeln and worked its way forward. Einsatzgruppe C, rather than being the cutting edge of the murder campaign, was in fact the last initiated into the next phase of the killing process.

---

[60] Zentrale Stelle der Landesjustizverwaltungen, II 204 AR-Z 1251/65 (LG Regensburg Ks 6/70, judgment against Engelbert Kreuzer), pp. 11–15.

[61] Landgericht Köln, 24 Ks 1/52, vol. III, pp. 747–755 (testimony of Erwin Schulz, February 3, 1953). Schulz's testimony is of course self-serving. But in evaluating it, one should keep in mind that he had already been tried and sentenced by the American military tribunal in Nürnberg in 1948 and he was serving his twenty-year prison term. His testimony was not helpful to the defendant in the Köln trial, Emanuel Schäfer. Moreover, Schulz was not part of what Streim considers the Ohlendorf conspiracy to coordinate testimony among the *Einsatzgruppen* officers on trial in 1948. He had testified in this vein, though in less detail, from the beginning.

Indeed, the SS brigade and police battalions under Jeckeln's direct command reported a victim total ("mostly Jews") for the month of August of 44,125.[62] This killing rate exceeded what any *Einsatzgruppe* had yet achieved.[63] Thus, I would argue that the dominant focus on the *Einsatzgruppen*, characteristic of previous scholarship, has in fact confused the issue, because different units of the *Einsatzgruppen* learned of the new turn at different times and in some cases rather belatedly.

In the Baltic, Stahlecker, the leader of Einsatzgruppe A, seems to have been completely initiated no later than Himmler's end-of-July visit to Riga. On July 27, 1941, the Reichskommissar for the Ostland, Hinrich Lohse, issued "guidelines" for the treatment of Jews that dealt with issues of foreign Jews, *Mischlinge*, marking, ghettoization, property, and forced labor. He neither consulted Stahlecker first nor delineated any sphere of responsibility for the Jewish question to the Security Police. The HSSPF North, Hans Adolf Prützmann, provided Stahlecker with a copy of the offending guidelines and offered the *Einsatzgruppe* commander the use of a plane to fly to Kovno for a meeting with Lohse, which he considered imperative.[64] Stahlecker had already received a copy of the guidelines from EK 3 commander Karl Jäger in Kovno. Stahlecker sent Jäger a three-page position paper on the guidelines, which the latter was to transmit to Lohse orally.[65]

Stahlecker's position paper – a recent "find" in the Soviet archives[66] – indicated that much more than a mere jurisdictional issue was at stake. "The new possibilities provided in the east for a cleaning up of the Jewish question had not been taken into consideration," Stahlecker noted. Lohse wanted to create conditions similar to those in the General

---

[62] *The Einsatzgruppen Reports*, p. 158 (Report Nr. 94, September 25, 1941).

[63] Once again it was Büchler (p. 17) who first suggested that the units of Himmler's *Kommandostab* were involved in total killing before the *Einsatzgruppen*, which were less closely supervised and had greater leeway.

[64] YVA, O-53/144/409-10 (Riga to Stahlecker, August 5, 1941).

[65] YVA, O-53/144/412 (Stahlecker to Heydrich, August 10, 1941).

[66] Historical State Archives, Riga: "Betrifft: Entwurf über die Aufstellung vorläufiger Richtlinien für die Behandlung der Juden im Gebiet des Reichskommissariates Ostland, August 6, 1941, Nowosselje," signed by Stahlecker. I am grateful to Professor Gerald Fleming for providing me a copy of this document. It is now printed in *Herrschaftsalltag im Dritten Reich*, ed. by Hans Mommsen (Schwann, 1988), pp. 467–471.

Government. "He thereby did not consider on the one hand the altogether different situation created through the impact of the eastern campaign and refrained on the other hand from keeping in mind the radical treatment of the Jewish question now possible for the first time." Lohse's measures indicated long-term ghettoization rather than "immediate measures" for the "resettlement of the Jews." Because of their Bolshevik connections, these Jews were much more dangerous than those in the General Government. The situation required "an almost one hundred percent immediate cleansing of the entire Ostland of Jews."

Stahlecker then provided Jäger with alternative measures to Lohse's guidelines, which were in effect a cover story. Jewish reservations were to be created in the wide expanses of the Ostland, and Jewish reproduction was to be prevented by separating the sexes. The reason for the cover story was made clear. In a hand-written note at the end of his position paper, Stahlecker noted that the Lohse draft "to a great extent touches on general orders from higher authority to the Security Police that cannot be discussed in writing." An indication of Stahlecker's orders that could not be put in writing can be found subsequently in the carefully collected statistics of Jäger himself. Beginning on August 15, 1941, the number of victims daily claimed by EK 3 jumped sharply and henceforth regularly included large numbers of women and children.[67]

Also on August 15, Himmler was concluding yet another of his visits to the killing units in the east and witnessed an *Einsatzgruppen* execution in Minsk. Though shaken by what he had seen, Himmler assured the men that he and Hitler alone bore the responsibility for their difficult but necessary task. Following his visit, Jewish women and children in that region were regularly included in the executions.[68] Faced with the complaints of Nebe and von dem Bach-Zelewski about the psychological burden on the men of killing women and children, Himmler ordered the search for alternative killing methods that led to the development of the gas van.[69]

[67] YVA, O-53/141/30-38 (Jäger report, December 1, 1941).
[68] JNSV, XIX, No. 567 (LG Kiel 2 Ks 1/64, concerning Einsatzkommando 8), pp. 795–796.
[69] Browning, *Fateful Months*, p. 59.

While the increasingly accessible Soviet and Czech archives may provide much additional documentation, I would suggest that the following scenario is most probable at this present juncture in historical research. In mid-July, convinced that the military campaign was nearly over and victory was at hand, an elated Hitler gave the signal to carry out accelerated pacification and racial "cleansing" of Germany's new "Garden of Eden." What had hitherto been seen as a future task was now to be implemented immediately. Himmler responded with a massive build-up of killing forces behind the lines. Moreover, he traveled through much of the eastern territory, personally contacting such people as von dem Bach-Zelewski, Stahlecker, and Nebe, and exhorting many of his killing units to carry out their difficult but historic task. For other units and leaders not graced with a visit from the Reichsführer-SS, the orders filtered eastward more slowly and less systematically. Reserve Police Battalion 45, for instance, learned of the new policy before the end of the month, but the officers of Einsatzgruppe C were officially initiated only on August 10 or 12, though they had already heard of the new turn of events informally before that. The complete extermination of Russian Jewry that Hitler had at least roughly envisioned in the spring and had instigated in mid-July was in full swing by mid-August.

If the context for this turning point was the premature euphoria of victory, not growing frustration, and Hitler's mid-July instigation was decisive, then Burrin's thesis of "conditional intentionalism" is endangered. Burrin himself concedes that a thesis of a vague or imprecise order at the beginning and intensification by stages is "credible,"[70] but it cannot be easily reconciled with his notion that Hitler would not and could not have given the order for systematic killing until convinced that his military aspirations had been thwarted. In order to sustain his thesis, I would suggest, Burrin has drawn a less probable conclusion from the very evidence he himself has assembled.

Let us turn to the third issue at hand. What can be said about Hitler's role in extending the killing to the rest of European Jewry? What was the timing and military context for this decision? Breitman has Hitler making the basic decision for the extermination of all European Jews in

---

[70] Burrin, *Hitler et les Juifs,* pp. 118, 125.

early 1941, followed first by a pause and then by a series of "operational decisions" taken by Himmler in July and August. Breitman concludes, "[T]he Final Solution came about gradually. Himmler's approval of a specific continent-wide program drawn up by subordinates, however, occurred in late August 1941, after he had settled upon the idea of gas chambers in extermination camps." The military context for the operational decisions of this gradually developing Final Solution was confidence in victory.

Burrin postulates a very late Hitler decision in mid-September, marked by the point at which he approved the immediate deportation of German Jews. This decision was followed by a flurry of activity in which "everything fell into place in an interval of four weeks, between September 18 and October 18."[71] The military context was Hitler's recognition that the Russian gamble had failed and he faced a prolonged war on all fronts, which he intended to fight to the end. On this aspect of the decision-making process, opinion can be so varied precisely because the evidence is so ambiguous. The historian here must weigh probabilities. In doing so, his sense of how the Nazi system worked – how decisions were taken and implemented – will invariably tilt the scales.

My own view is that Breitman's approach – with Hitler, Himmler, and Eichmann making secret plans that they did not begin to implement through "operational decisions" until months later – is too conspiratorial. The gap between basic decisions and operational decisions is too long, and the distinction between the two somewhat artificial. I think Burrin's contrasting view that everything came together in a brief four weeks once the Führer had finally spoken is also unrealistic. It provides too short a time span, given the unprecedented nature of the task.

In assessing the realistic time span necessary to implement a large-scale killing program, it is instructive to review the stages of policy development for the destruction of Soviet Jewry. In late February and March 1941, Hitler made a number of statements in which he outlined his vision of a war of destruction – an ideological and racial war – in the Soviet Union. In April, May, and June various institutions of the Nazi regime attempted to cast Hitler's pronouncements into policy. Most prominent were the negotiations between the army and SS over the jurisdiction of the *Einsatzgruppen*, the assembly and training of the

---

[71] Ibid., p. 146.

Einsatzgruppen in Pretsch, and the drafting of the *Kommissarbefehl* and Barbarossa decree. Following the invasion initial aspects of the war of destruction commenced, especially the selective killing of the communist and Jewish leadership. Following Hitler's pronouncements of mid-July, Himmler threw more than 16,000 additional Germans as well as numerous auxiliaries into the campaign to murder the Jews and personally visited many of the units. Rather than being unprepared as Burrin suggests, Himmler seemed quite prepared to react immediately when Hitler gave the signal. By mid-August the mass murder of Soviet Jewry was in full swing. The entire process stretched over six months.

Is it reasonable to expect that launching the unprecedented and vastly more complex "Final Solution of the Jewish question in Europe" could have taken place more quickly? Hitler's mid-July instigation for the complete destruction of the Soviet Jews, in my opinion, was also the starting point of a second decision-making process for the destruction of the European Jews. Victory in Russia was assumed; the whole continent lay at Hitler's feet. Pragmatic considerations about Jewish labor no longer seemed relevant. The time for uninhibited "racial experimentation" on a continent-wide scale had come.

But how was the task to be accomplished? Here, perhaps more than ever, the historian must attempt to balance historical perspective informed by hindsight with an effort to recapture the sense of uncertainty with which the perpetrators must have faced the future in the summer of 1941. What they were being asked to accomplish was at the time totally unprecedented. At this stage every step was uncharted, every policy an experiment, every action a trial run. In this regard it is worth noting the jubilant Nazi reaction *eight months later* when *for the first time* an entire ghetto – the Jewish community of Lublin – was in the process of being deported and gassed at Belzec within a time span of a few weeks: "The Jewish resettlement has proven, therefore, that such an action even on a large scale can also be carried out for the entire General Government."[72] Until that time they did not know – indeed could not have known – if the plans they had been formulating would even work. In such a state of uncertainty, historians can in fact read documents *too closely*, gathering clues and making deductions on the

---

[72] YVA, O-53/134/1816 (weekly report of March 28, 1942, of the Hauptabteilung Propaganda in the General Government).

assumption that the document writers were precise and coherent, when they were actually tentative and groping. This uncertainty on the part of the perpetrators is one reason why the documentary trial between July and October 1941 can be read and interpreted in different ways. Murder was in the air, many avenues were being explored, but little was settled other than that at least Himmler and Heydrich now knew what they were looking for – a way to kill all the Jews of Europe.

Having received the "green light" from Hitler to prepare what was in effect a "feasibility study" for the Final Solution, Heydrich drafted his famous "authorization" to prepare and submit a plan for a "total solution" of the Jewish question in Europe. He then visited Göring on July 31 and obtained the latter's signature. This was only the first move in a process that would stretch out over months. A clear concept of how they would first attempt to implement the Final Solution – through massive deportation to factories of death equipped with facilities to kill on an assembly-line basis through poison gas – would emerge by October. The physical and political preparations to begin carrying out this policy would only be in place in the Warthegau in December 1941 and in the General Government in the spring of 1942. Only at the end of this journey of innovation did the Final Solution take on an air of obviousness and inevitability that could not have been apparent to the perpetrators at the time.

In August, first Heydrich and then Goebbels proposed commencing the deportation of Jews from the Third Reich. Hitler vetoed both proposals; deportations would not begin "during the war." Hitler did, however, allow Heydrich to work on a proposal for a "partial evacuation of the larger cities." If Goebbels did not get everything he wanted, he did come away from his August 19 meeting with Hitler confident that the Führer's Reichstag prophecy "is coming true in these weeks and months with a certainty that appears almost sinister. In the East the Jews are paying the price, in Germany they have already paid in part and they will have to pay more in the future."[73] What was not yet certain was exactly how and when his prophecy would be fulfilled.

---

[73] Bernhard Lösener, "Als Rassereferent im Reichsministerium des Innern," VfZ, IX/3 (1961), 303; Goebbels diary entries of August 19 and 20, 1941, cited in Martin Broszat, "Hitler und die Genesis der Endlösung," pp. 88–89.

Gradually others were brought into the planning process. Some time between late August and late September (two to three months after the invasion), Eichmann was initiated.[74] Sometime in the summer Rudolf Höss was also initiated, as was Odilo Globocnik. Breitman suggests that July 13 through July 15 was the most likely date for Höss,[75] and July 20 was the earliest possible for Globocnik. Both could have been in August. Some time after August 24, 1941, Philipp Bouhler, who ran the euthanasia program out of the Führer Chancellery, was approached about providing manpower. He then visited Lublin.[76] Unfortunately, none of these dates can be established with the precision the historian would desire.

Beginning in mid-September the dating becomes more certain. On September 18, Himmler informed the Gauleiter of the Warthegau, Arthur Greiser, "The Führer wishes that the Old Reich and Protectorate be emptied and freed of Jews from west to east as quickly as possible." Thus "as a first step" Jews were to be deported into the incorporated territories "in order to deport them yet further to the East next spring."[77] On September 23-24, Hitler met with Himmler, Heydrich, and Goebbels. The Propaganda Minister learned: "The Führer is of the opinion that the Jews are to be removed from Germany step by step. The first cities that have to be cleared of Jews are Berlin, Vienna, and Prague. . . . *This could occur as soon as we arrive at a clarification of the military situation in the East*" [italics mine]."[78] On October 6, Hitler again spoke of deportations. "All Jews have to be removed from the Protectorate, not only to the General Government but

---

[74] On the problems of placing dates on Eichmann's account, see Browning, *Fateful Months*, pp. 23–26.

[75] Breitman, *The Architect of Genocide*, p. 189.

[76] Burrin, *Hitler et les Juifs*, p. 144.

[77] National Archives Microfilm, T-175/54/256695 (Himmler to Greiser, September 18, 1941).

[78] Goebbels diary excerpts of September 23 and 24, cited in Broszat, "Genesis der 'Endlösung'," p. 91. Hitler's adjutant, Engel, wrote of an October 2 meeting with Hitler, Heydrich, Keitel, and Jodl, in which Himmler reported on the deportation of Jews. *Heeresadjutant bei Hitler 1938–1943: Aufzeichnungen des Majors Engel*, ed. by Hildegard von Kotze (Stuttgart, 1974), p. 111. Engel's dating is an unreliable postwar reconstruction, and both Burrin and Breitman note that Himmler was in Kiev on October 2. In contrast to the dating, the substance of Engel's account has in general held up well.

straight on to the East. *Only the great shortage of transport prevents this being done at once* [italics mine]. Together with the Jews of the Protectorate all the Jews of Vienna and Berlin must disappear."[79] If Hitler was still hesitating, Heydrich was already speaking in continental terms. As Burrin notes, on October 4, in a meeting with officials from the *Ostministerium*, Heydrich remarked on the danger that many in the economy would classify their Jewish laborers as indispensable and make no effort to replace them. "This would ruin the plan for a total resettlement of Jews out of the territories occupied by us."[80] Clearly Heydrich was contemplating a deportation program more comprehensive than the one for deporting large numbers of German Jews that autumn.

Apparently Hitler's remaining concerns about the military situation in the East and the related transportation situation were soon resolved. In Prague on October 10, Heydrich announced "the Führer wishes that by the end of the year as many Jews as possible are removed from the German sphere. . . . "[81] Between October 15 and November 11, twenty trains left the Third Reich, carrying Jews to Lodz. Five Gypsy transports were dispatched to Lodz as well. Other trains subsequently departed for Kovno, Minsk, and Riga. When the first wave of deportation came to an end in February 1942, the number of Jewish transports had reached a total of 46.[82] The deportees in all five transports to Kovno and the first to Riga were massacred immediately on arrival. The rest were granted a very temporary stay of execution, if they could survive the rigors of winter life in the ghettos of Lodz, Minsk, and Riga.

In fact, the deportation program – set in motion by Hitler in early October – had developed more quickly than the search for an alterna-

---

[79] Koeppens's note of October 7, 1941, cited in Broszat, "Genesis der 'Endlösung'," p. 90.

[80] Burrin, *Hitler et les Juifs*, p. 139. This is a Nürnberg document (NO-1020) which has been strangely overlooked.

[81] H. G. Adler, *Theresienstadt 1941–45* (Tübingen, 1960, 2nd ed.), pp. 720–722 (protocol of conference in Prague of October 10, 1941.)

[82] No comprehensive list of Jewish transports from the Third Reich has yet been compiled or published. These figures are based on my as yet incomplete research in that direction.

tive killing method to shooting. During his trips to Russia, Himmler had learned of the psychological impact on the killers posed by the shooting of women and children on such a huge scale. On August 15 he commissioned Nebe to explore psychologically less burdensome ways of killing. After tests with explosives had failed gruesomely, Nebe's crime lab scientists tried engine exhaust gas. This line of experiment eventually led to the production of the gas van.[83] Meanwhile, on September 3, 1941, the first test of Zyklon B was undertaken in Auschwitz. Sometime in September, Bouhler and a few of his experts in euthanasia gassing (using carbon monoxide) visited Globocnik in Lublin.[84]

Just when the Nazis settled on gassing as their preferred method of killing cannot be pinpointed. Breitman's guess of late August is at the early end of the range of possibilities. When Eichmann visited Belzec sometime in the first half of October, the question had already been settled, for there he learned for the first time of the plans to construct gas chambers.[85] Likewise in October, experimental gassing was carried out in the old crematory in Auschwitz, the sending of a scientist to Riga to supervise constructing gas vans was discussed, and the site for the future camp at Chelmno was selected.[86] Only on December 8, 1941, however, did systematic gassing begin for the first time at the Chelmno camp near Lodz, the destination of the first Jewish transports nearly two months earlier. Probably Himmler submitted for Hitler's approval the concept of the extermination camp at the same time as he presented his deportation plans in late September. He himself must have opted for such a solution even earlier.

I think, therefore, that Burrin is correct that the pieces fell into place between September 18 and October 18, 1941. However, this is only the concluding phase of a longer process that began in mid-July, and Burrin's scenario does not allow nearly sufficient "lead time" to explain plausibly how everything could have come together so quickly at the end. The extermination camp equipped with gassing facilities was not, after all, an obvious invention, immediately self-evident the moment Hitler decided to kill the Jews.

[83] Browning, *Fateful Months*, pp. 59–62.   [84] Burrin, *Hitler et les Juifs*, p. 144.
[85] Browning, *Fateful Months*, pp. 25–26.   [86] Ibid., pp. 29–31.

If the decisions of late September and early October were crucial, what was the military context within which they were taken? Burrin concedes that Hitler launched Barbarossa in great confidence. However, he argues, beginning in the second half of July, Hitler experienced a growing unease and foreboding. By the beginning of August he was contemplating the possibility of a long war.[87] By the end of August, Hitler knew the war would continue into the next year and that American entry into the war was very probable. His growing frustration and disappointment were accompanied by a growing rage against the Jews, culminating in his mid-September decision for the Final Solution. Statements by Hitler that indicated a contrary mood are dismissed by Burrin as putting on a good face.[88]

Hitler's mood was not one of steady degeneration from confidence to despair. Rather his mood fluctuated. Furthermore, one can chart a striking coincidence between the peaks of German military success and Hitler's key decisions. At the time of Hitler's July 16 "victory speech" calling for the intensified pacification of Germany's new "Garden of Eden," the pincers of Army Group Central had closed behind Smolensk a mere 150 miles from Moscow. Even in the south, where German success had developed less slowly, the Ukrainian front had just been severed.[89] As Burrin himself points out, on July 14 Hitler had just approved a major reorientation in German armaments for the postwar period.[90] This was precisely the period when Hitler conveyed to Himmler and Heydrich his desire for both the immediate destruction of the Soviet Jews and a "feasibility study" for the Final Solution.

Hitler then attempted to persuade his generals to consolidate the central front, while the bulk of the armored forces there were to be turned to the north and the south. Hitler made clear that he gave priority to the capture of economic targets over Moscow, which he dubbed a "mere geographical concept." The generals resisted stubbornly, dragging their feet until Hitler unequivocally imposed his will on August 18. In the end Hitler successfully insisted that there would

---

[87] Burrin, *Hitler et les Juifs*, p. 162.   [88] Ibid., p. 165.
[89] Alan Clark, *Barbarossa: The Russian-German Conflict 1941–45* (New York: Signet Edition, 1966), p. 155.
[90] Burrin, *Hitler et les Juifs*, p. 155.

be no resumption of an offensive against Moscow until all his goals in the south and north had been achieved.[91] It was during this period of strategic stalemate with his generals that Hitler also resisted the pressures of Goebbels and Heydrich to begin immediate deportations from the Third Reich.

The Ukrainian campaign that Hitler imposed on his reluctant generals was a tremendous success. On September 12 Ewald von Kleist's tanks broke through the Russian lines behind Kiev. On the same day German forces cracked the Russian perimeter around Leningrad. In the words of Alan Clark, this day could be "reckoned the low point in the fortunes of the Red Army for the whole war." By September 16 Kleist had joined up with Heinz Guderian at Lokhvitsa to complete the vast Kiev encirclement.[92] By September 26, Kiev had fallen and 665,000 Russian prisoners had been taken.[93]

As Hitler experienced triumph in the Ukraine, he became increasingly amenable to proposals for immediate deportation that he had vetoed a month earlier. On September 18, it may be recalled, Himmler informed Greiser of Hitler's decision to shift German Jews eastward into the incorporated territories. On September 24, Goebbels noted that deportations "could occur as soon as we arrive at a clarification of the military situation in the East."

That clarification was not long in coming. On September 6 Hitler had ordered Army Group Center to prepare for a decisive campaign to destroy the Russian forces facing it.[94] On September 30, just four days after the fall of Kiev, Guderian's army began the offensive, and on October 2 the rest of the forces of "Operation Typhoon" struck along the Russian front. By October 7 the Germans had completed the double encirclement of Vyazma and Bryansk that ultimately led to the capture of another 673,000 Russian troops. According to Ernst Klink, "Unanimity over the favorableness of the situation reigned everywhere."

---

[91] The struggle over strategy can be traced in the appendixes of *Kriegstagebuch des Oberkommandos der Wehrmacht 1940–1941*, ed. by Percy Schramm (Munich, 1982), pp. 1029–1068. See also Ernst Klink, "Die Krieg gegen die Sowjetunion bis zur Jahreswende 1941/42," *Das Deutsche Reich und der Zweite Weltkrieg*, IV, *Der Angriff auf die Sowjetunion* (Stuttgart, 1983), pp. 489–507.

[92] Clark, *Barbarossa*, p. 166.   [93] *Kriegstagebuch des OKW*, p. 661.

[94] Klink, "Die Krieg gegen die Sowjetunion," p. 569.

(*Überall herrschte Übereinstimmung über die Gunst der Lage.*)[95] According to Andreas Hillgruber, Hitler exuded a "spirit of total victory" (*voller Siegesstimmung*) reminiscent of mid-July.[96]

On October 6, one day before the double encirclement was complete, Hitler apparently still had reservations concerning the deportation of Jews, noting that "only the great shortage of transport" prevented them from commencing at once. This was the last hesitation, however. On October 15, resistance died in the Vyazma pocket, and panic spread through Moscow. On that same day the first deportation train left Vienna for Lodz. By the time the Bryansk pocket was liquidated on October 18, three more Jewish transports had departed from Prague, Luxembourg, and Berlin.[97] The deportation program was well underway.

German expectations of quick victory foundered by the end of the month. The bad weather, terrible roads, shortage of supplies, exhaustion of German troops, and stubborn retreat of the remnants of the Red army all combined to bring the Wehrmacht to a halt. There was no open road to Moscow. But just as Hitler later could not contemplate a strategic withdrawal from any of the territories his armies had conquered, so he could not now contemplate retreating from his latest decisions on Jewish policy. The trains continued to roll, the extermination camps continued to be built. The Soviet Union was saved, the Jews of Europe were not.

Over a period of twenty-five months – from September 1939 to October 1941 – Nazi Jewish policy had evolved into a program that aimed at the physical extermination of all European Jews within the German grasp. What can be said about Hitler's role in this fateful evolution? First, he was an active and continuing participant in the decision-making process. There is not the slightest evidence that any major change in Nazi Jewish policy took place without the knowledge and approval of Adolf Hitler. Second, while we do not know the details of the decision-making process in all cases, in those we do know about, Hitler's participation was usually indirect. Hitler would give signals in the

---

[95] Ibid., pp. 576–577.

[96] *Staatsmänner bei Hitler: Vertrauliche Aufzeichnungen über Unterredungen mit Vertretern des Auslandes 1939–41*, ed. by Andreas Hillgruber (Frankfurt/M., 1967), p. 626.

[97] *Kriegstagebuch des OKW*, pp. 702 and 708, for the end of resistance at Vyazma and Bryansk.

form of relatively vague statements that established the priorities, goals, prophecies, and even "wishes" of the Führer. Others, especially Heinrich Himmler, responded to these signals with extraordinary alacrity and sensitivity, bringing to Hitler more specific guidelines for his approval, the classic example being Himmler's memorandum on the treatment of alien populations in eastern Europe of May 1940. On occasion, not only guidelines but quite concrete proposals – such as those for marking the German Jews or commencing the deportations of Jews from particular cities in the Reich to the east – were submitted to Hitler as well.

Third, Nazi Jewish policy between September 1939 and March 1941 cannot easily be characterized as a detour or hiatus during which Hitler either marked time while waiting for the opportunity to carry out his premeditated plan for mass murder in conjunction with the invasion of Russia or struggled to bring around his recalcitrant followers. One continuity that emerges is the close and sympathetic relationship between Hitler and Himmler in the formulation and implementation of Nazi Jewish policy. If one wants to know what Hitler was thinking, one should look at what Himmler was doing. In 1939 and 1940, Himmler was deeply involved in resettlement. Only when that option was exhausted did Nazi Jewish policy radicalize further.

Fourth, the chronology suggests a rather consistent pattern between victory and radicalization, indicating that the emergence of the Final Solution may have been induced as much by Hitler's fluctuating moods as by a fanatically consistent adherence to a fixed program. In September 1939, in the flush of victory over Poland, Hitler approved the initial plan for the demographic reorganization of eastern Europe, including the Lublin Reservation. In May and June 1940, with the astonishing victory over France, he approved Himmler's memorandum on the treatment of the eastern populations and the Madagascar Plan. In July 1941, with the stupendous early victories of the Russian campaign, he accelerated the *Einsatzgruppen* campaign and solicited the Final Solution. In late September and early October 1941, with the capture of Kiev and the great encirclement victory of Vyazma and Bryansk, he approved deportations from the Third Reich. At the same time death camp construction commenced. It would appear that the euphoria of victory emboldened and tempted an elated Hitler to dare ever more drastic policies.

PART III

*The Perpetrators:
Accommodation, Anticipation,
and Conformity*

6

Bureaucracy and Mass Murder: The German Administrator's Comprehension of the Final Solution[1]

In his incomparable work, *The Destruction of the European Jews,* Raul Hilberg argues that the Final Solution was an administrative process involving the participation of bureaucrats from every sphere of organized life in Germany. In what will surely be one of the most quoted passages of the revised and expanded edition of this work, Hilberg writes that a consensus for mass murder emerged among these bureaucrats that "was not so much a product of laws and commands as it was a matter of spirit, of shared comprehension, of consonance and synchronization."[2] But how did this shared comprehension, this consonance and synchronization, come about? If the German bureaucrats' collective actions are relatively well-documented for the historian, the latter encounters much greater difficulty when he enters the realm of individual consciousness. Few bureaucratic documents reveal the intellectual and moral odyssey of their authors. If sweeping generalizations are presumptuous,

Reprinted in slightly revised form with permission. From *Comprehending the Holocaust: Historical and Literary Research,* Asher Cohen, Yoav Gelber, and Charlotte Wardi, eds. (Frankfurt am Main: Verlag Peter Lang, 1988), pp. 159–177.

[1] Research for this paper was made possible by support from the DAAD, the Alexander von Humboldt Foundation and the Institute for Advanced Studies of the Hebrew University of Jerusalem.

[2] Raul Hilberg, *The Destruction of the European Jews.* New York: Revised and expanded edition, 1985, p. 55.

nonetheless the path to and comprehension of mass murder for some individuals can be traced.

For this purpose I would like to take as case studies three German bureaucrats whose considerable involvement in handling so-called Jewish affairs within the German government preceded the Final Solution. Representing the Jewish experts of the Berlin ministries will be Franz Rademacher of the Foreign Office. For the military administration of the occupied territories, there is Harald Turner in Serbia. And managing the second largest ghetto of eastern Europe is Hans Biebow, of Lodz. In all of these cases, three questions will be posed: (1) How did these bureaucrats conceive of a solution to the Jewish question before the policy of mass murder was inaugurated? (2) How did they first perceive or learn that the policy of mass murder was going to be implemented? (3) How did they respond to this information?

Let us first examine the background of these three men and their respective conceptions of a solution to the Jewish question prior to the fall of 1941. Franz Rademacher was a self-made man whose father, a locomotive engineer, had insisted that young Franz pursue an education rather than a career in the navy. Often earning his own way, Rademacher completed his legal studies at the Universities of Munich and Rostock, passed the required exams for state service, and served his bureaucratic apprenticeship in the Mecklenburg judicial system. Along with thousands of other ambitious civil servants, Rademacher joined the Nazi party in March 1933. A judicious blend of political enthusiasm and career opportunism can be detected in Rademacher, evidenced first by his joining the SA in the summer of 1932, before Hitler's assumption of power, and then by his leaving that increasingly suspect organization in the spring of 1934 shortly before the Roehm purge. In 1937 Rademacher was called to the Foreign Office and posted to Montevideo. He returned to Germany in the spring of 1940 and was immediately assigned to head the Jewish desk of the newly formed *Abteilung Deutschland*. He quickly arranged, through the courtesy of Albert Speer's office, to have a Jewish apartment evacuated for himself. In the true spirit of the self-made man, he ordered numerous books on the Jewish question in order to attain the expertise expected of his new position, and he cultivated the acquaintance of noted anti-Semites such as the foreign editor of Streicher's *Der Stümer*, Paul Wurm.[3]

Among our case studies, Rademacher most fully recorded his vision of a solution to the Jewish question before the era of systematic mass murder, for he was the enthusiastic author and advocate of the Madagascar Plan. In early June 1940, Rademacher suggested to his superior, Undersecretary Martin Luther, that his desk, the *Judenreferat*, should no longer concentrate its work on the various mundane bureaucratic tasks of the past that involved above all foreign complications arising from anti-Jewish measures within Germany. As foreign repercussions no longer weighed so heavily, the Jewish desk should now concentrate its efforts on shaping Nazi Jewish policy in accordance with Germany's overall war aims. This was particularly urgent, he suggested, since the traditional, that is to say less Nazified, elements in the German Foreign Office would otherwise shape war aims securing the political, military, and economic conditions necessary for Germany as a world power, while ignoring those measures necessary for the "liberation of the world from the chains of Jewry and free masonry." One possible policy in this latter regard, he suggested, was the resettlement of European Jewry on the island of Madagascar.

Foreign Minister Ribbentrop agreed that Rademacher's desk should undertake preparatory work on the solution to the Jewish question within the framework of the seemingly imminent peace treaties with France and Great Britain. Ribbentrop also carried the Madagascar idea to Hitler. Bandied about among anti-Semites in the past, it was an idea whose time had come. On June 18, 1940, Hitler told Mussolini of his intention to use Madagascar as a Jewish reservation, and by June 23, the attentive Reinhard Heydrich was insisting on *SS* jurisdiction in any "territorial" solution to the Jewish question being planned in the Foreign Office. Rademacher spent the summer of 1940 in frenetic activity on his pet project. The goal was clear. "The imminent victory gives Germany the possibility and, in my opinion, also the obligation to solve the Jewish question in Europe," he wrote. "The desirable solution is: All Jews out of Europe." When Great Britain was not beaten,

---

[3] Christopher R. Browning, *The Final Solution and the German Foreign Office.* New York: 1978, pp. 29–30.

the Madagascar Plan collapsed. The "desirable solution" had proven unrealizable. But the "obligation to solve the Jewish question" remained, an obligation that Rademacher would not escape.[4]

Our second example, Harald Turner, was a man of unusual background. His great grandfather had been an English cavalryman in the Peninsula campaign and had fought at Waterloo. His English father married a German woman, settled in Germany and served in the Prussian army. Harald Turner likewise pursued a military career and was wounded on both the western and eastern fronts in the First World War. After the defeat he dabbled in *Freikorps* activities, held various government jobs, and completed legal studies at the University of Giessen. He joined the Nazi party in 1930 and the *SS* in 1932. As a civil servant with *alte Kämpfer* credentials, he rose quickly after the *Machtergreifung*. Göring became his patron, making him first *Regierungspräsident* of Koblenz and then bringing him to Berlin where by 1936 he rose to the position of *Ministerialdirigent* of the Prussian Finance Ministry. He received commensurate *SS* promotions during this rapid rise. After serving in the occupation regimes in both Poland and France, he was made chief of the military administration in Serbia in April 1941.[5]

In Serbia Turner conceived of his task as a dual policy of *Aufbau* and *Ausschaltung*. By the first, Turner meant the "construction" of a collaborating Serbian administration and police force, a policy which would find increasing disfavor among hardliners, including the officers of the *SS-Einsatzgruppe* under his command, who felt that no Serbs could become trusted tools of Nazi rule. *Ausschaltung* was less controversial, for by that Turner meant the "elimination" of all "unreliable elements" but "first of all Jews."[6] Initially *Ausschaltung* involved rapidly imposing registration, marking, exclusion from many occupations and social activities, expropriation of property, and forced labor. But such measures were not enough for Turner. He wanted to be rid of the Jewish population entirely, and thus in mid-August asked the Ger-

---

[4] Ibid., pp. 35–43.

[5] Berlin Document Center (hereafter cited as BDC): *SS* and *RuSHA* files.

[6] Bundesarchiv-Militärarchiv Freiburg (hereafter cited as BA-MA): RW 40/183, Turner report of May 26, 1941, and RW 41/115, Abschlussbericht der Militärverwaltung Serbien, May 10, 1945, p. 79.

man ambassador in Belgrade, Felix Benzler, to inquire whether the Jews could be deported down the Danube to Romania or to the General Government.[7] This request was repeated two more times in early September, with Russia added as a possible reception area for the Serbian Jews.[8] In instigating this request Turner was not of course envisaging the later deportation program of the Final Solution, for the death camps did not yet exist. Turner was only trying what the *Gauleiter* of Baden, Saarpfalz, the Warthegau and other regions had already tried with mixed success, that is, to dump their own Jews on someone else. To add weight to the request, Turner and Benzler emphasized a connection between the Jewish presence in Serbia and the intensifying partisan uprising, though by mid-August virtually all the male Jews were already interned and could not possibly have been involved in the partisan activity they allegedly inspired. This request for deportation, sent through Franz Rademacher at the Foreign Office Jewish desk, was rejected for reasons that we shall soon examine in closer detail. Turner, like Rademacher, was on record concerning the urgent need to solve the Jewish question but had found his desired solution of Jewish expulsion thwarted.

The third subject of our study, Hans Biebow, was the son of a Bremen insurance director. He had hoped to succeed his father but the business was ruined by the inflation. The younger Biebow then successfully founded his own coffee import company, which he built up by 1939 to a large firm employing 250 people.[9] He joined the Nazi party in 1937 and took up the position of head of the Office of Food Supply and Economics in Lodz in May 1940, at which point the ghetto of 160,000 Jews had just been sealed.[10] As part of his duties in the city administration, Biebow became "ghetto manager." Greiser, the Warthegau *Gauleiter,*

---

[7] Landgericht Nürnberg-Fürth 2 Ks 3/53 (Rademacher trial), Hauptakten II, 266 (Benzler affidavit, 1949), and XI, 1911 (Benzler testimony, 1968). Politisches Archiv des Auswärtigen Amtes (hereafter cited as PA), Inland II A/B 65/4, Benzler to Foreign Office, August 14, 1941.

[8] *Akten zur deutschen Aussenpolitik* (hereafter cited as ADAP), D, XIII, Part 1, 378; PA, Inland IIg 194, Benzler to Foreign Office, September 12, 1941.

[9] *Dokumenty i Materialy Do Dziejow Okupacji Niemieckiej W Polsce,* vol. III, *Ghetto Lodzkie.* Warsaw: 1946 (hereafter cited as DiM), 252 (Hans Biebow Lebenslauf).

[10] Lucjan Dobroszycki, "Introduction," *The Chronicle of the Lodz Ghetto.* New Haven: xliii; DiM, 256 (Vollmacht of 4.5.40).

had originally decided upon a ghetto in Lodz in December 1939, as a way of extracting from the incarcerated Jews their alleged hoards of wealth in exchange for food, before they were expelled into the General Government.[11] It was expected initially that the Jews would be deported in the spring of 1940; when this plan was not realized, deportations were rescheduled for August of that year.[12] Thus when Biebow arrived on the scene in Lodz, the Germans still viewed the ghetto as a short-term arrangement for extracting Jewish wealth, and no plans existed for either funding an on-going provisioning of the ghetto or exploiting it as a potential source of labor. Jewish resources, it was estimated, would last through July.[13] After that the Jews would be gone.

In July, however, news of Hitler's support for the Madagascar Plan reached the incorporated territories and the General Government. Since it was now intended to deport overseas all Jews from both these territories as soon as the war was over, the August deportations from Lodz to the General Government were cancelled. In late July *Gauleiter* Greiser and his Higher *SS* and Police Leader Wilhelm Koppe literally begged Hans Frank to take the Lodz Jews into the General Government as an "interim solution" because "the situation regarding the Jews in the Warthegau worsened day by day." The ghetto there "had actually only been erected on condition that the deportation of the Jews would begin by mid-year at the latest. . . ."[14] Frank was unmoved, and the Lodz Jews were thus "stuck" for an indefinite period. It was left to the local authorities, Biebow in particular, to cope with the unexpected situation.

Since the spring of 1940, the chairman of the Lodz Jewish council, Chaim Rumkowski, had been urging the German authorities to permit the employment of the ghettoized Jews in order to earn money for the

[11] BDC: Greiser Pers. Akten, Besuchs-Vermerk of the staff of the Führer's Deputy, January 11, 1940; *Faschismus – Ghetto – Massenmord.* Berlin: 1960, pp. 78–81 (Rundschreiben of Uebelhoer, December 10, 1939).

[12] Hans Frank, *Das Diensttagebuch des deutschen Generalgouverneurs in Polen 1939–1945.* Edited by Werner Präg and Wolfgang Jacobmeyer, Stuttgart: 1975, p. 158 (entry of April 5, 1940); DiM, 168-9 (Regierungspräsident to officials of Bezirk Kalisch and Lodz, May 8, 1940).

[13] *Yad Vashem Archives* (hereafter cited as YVA), JM 800/387–9, Vermerk by Dr. Nebel of conference of May 27, 1940.

[14] Frank, *Diensttagebuch.* pp. 261–2 (entry of July 31, 1940).

purchase of food supplies. By July Rumkowski argued that the ability of the Jews to purchase food out of their own resources had been exhausted. Biebow's deputy, Alexander Palfinger, refused to believe this assertion, arguing that the Jews were merely trying to find other ways to provision the ghetto rather than give up their dearest possessions. Only "the most extreme plight" would pry loose their last reserves, he argued. Biebow was more cautious, reserving judgment.[15] By September, however, Biebow was convinced Rumkowski had been right, as the death rate in the ghetto had soared in July and August and food supplies for the ghetto were simply piling up outside because virtually no one within had the means any longer to make purchases. After Biebow asked *Regierungspräsident* Uebelhoer for funds to resume food deliveries, the ghetto manager concluded that every effort had to be made "to facilitate the self-maintenance of the Jews through finding them work." This self-maintenance would require "initially high subsidies" both to stockpile provisions for winter and to procure contracts and erect factories in the ghetto.[16] A meeting of local German officials on October 18, 1940, confirmed Biebow's viewpoint: "It was established at the outset that the ghetto in Lodz must continue to exist and everything must be done to make the ghetto self-sustaining."[17] The Jewish council was granted a 4½ percent six month loan of 3 million Reichsmark, naturally out of confiscated Jewish funds, to finance this process.[18]

Not everyone agreed with this approach. Alexander Palfinger bitterly criticized a policy based on "salesman-like negotiating ability" instead of national socialist principles. What he meant by the latter was quite clear. "A rapid dying out of the Jews is for us a matter of total indifference, if not to say desirable, as long as the concomitant effects leave the public interests of the German people untouched."[19] But Palfinger did not prevail, and he departed for Warsaw to try his methods there.

[15] YVA, JM 798, Activity report of July 1940: JM 799, Palfinger Aktennotiz, July 16, 1940.
[16] YVA, JM 798, Activity report of September 1940.
[17] DiM, 102-4 (conference of October 18, 1940).
[18] YVA, JM 798, Activity report of October 1940 and Auditor's report of February 1941.
[19] YVA, O-53/78/76-82. Palfinger "critical report" of November 11, 1940.

Bürgermeister Dr. Karl Marder, Biebow's boss, subsequently summarized the change in perspective that had taken place. As long as the ghetto was a "transition measure," not intended to last the year, the major task of the ghetto administration had been the "drawing off of the wealth of the ghetto inhabitants in order to supply their necessities of life." Now the character of the ghetto had been "fundamentally altered." Instead of a "holding or concentration camp," it was to become an "essential element of the total economy . . . a one-of-its-kind large scale enterprise."[20]

It was within this framework that over the next year Biebow fought to overcome the many obstacles that stood in the way of procuring for the ghetto equipment and orders on the one hand, and an increased food supply on the other. He was more successful in the former than the latter, a matter over which he never ceased to complain. Some progress was made in the late spring of 1941, and in early June Greiser even held out the prospect of "Polish rations" for the ghettoized Jews, though this prospect evaporated with the invasion of Russia weeks later. As the economic importance of Lodz increased, slowly and perhaps even unconsciously the terms of Biebow's argument altered. If initially he had argued that without work the Jews could not be fed, by August 1941 he was arguing that without food the Jews could not continue to work, and vital economic activity would be endangered.[21] For Biebow the productivity of the ghetto had become an end in its own right, not the means to relieve the Reich of the cost of feeding Jews. The events of autumn 1941 would push this logic to a fatal turning point; those Jews who could not work ought not to be fed.

What conclusions can be drawn from the pre-Final Solution careers of these three men that are relevant to the issue of "information and comprehension" of the Holocaust within the German bureaucracy? Prior to the war none of these men had a career marked by involvement in Jewish affairs. Rademacher was a judicial authority in Mecklenburg and then chargé d'affaires in Montevideo; Turner was in the Prussian Finance Ministry; and Biebow was a Bremen businessman. Nevertheless, all were Nazi party members, and all were very ambitious men

---

[20] DiM, pp. 177–9 (Marder to Uebelhoer, July 4, 1941).
[21] YVA, JM 798, Activity report of August 1941.

intent on building successful careers. By virtue of the positions they subsequently took up, each of these men became deeply involved in the Nazi treatment of the Jews and accepted unquestioningly the existence of a "Jewish problem" that Germany was obliged to solve. Each had a clear vision of his contribution to this solution. For Rademacher and Turner, the Jews quite simply had to disappear. From Turner's local vantage point in Serbia, this end meant dumping his Jews on someone else further east, in Romania, Poland, or Russia. From Rademacher's pan-European perspective in Berlin, shoving Jews from one place in Europe to another was clearly not enough. "All Jews out of Europe" was his watchword, and this goal could be accomplished only by expulsion overseas to some place like Madagascar. Hans Biebow's position was different. He came to Lodz when the attempted expulsion of the Jews failed. Something had to be done with the incarcerated Jews until Berlin decided how to dispose of them. For Biebow the ghetto was a warehouse for storing the Jews in this interim period, and his responsibility was to ensure that this "warehousing" was done at no cost to the Reich. To ensure that the Jews were no financial burden, he sought to make the ghetto economically self-sufficient.

Finally, none of these men conceived on his own of mass murder as a solution to the Jewish question. Biebow explicitly opposed Palfinger's suggestion for presiding over a "rapid dying out of the Jews" through starvation. Turner, as we shall see, renewed his request for deporting the surviving Serbian Jews even as the *Wehrmacht* firing squads were clamoring for more Jews to shoot in order to fill their obscene reprisal quotas. Certainly the expulsion of millions of Jews to Madagascar would have involved catastrophic mortality, but Rademacher was more feckless than cynical when he envisaged his Madagascar "super-ghetto" as proof of Germany's "generosity" to the Jews that could be exploited propagandistically.[22] None of these case studies provides evidence that the Final Solution was launched or triggered by middle-echelon bureaucratic initiatives from below rather than by signals from above.

How then were these three men initiated into the Final Solution, and why did they react the way they did? How, in short, did they so quickly

[22] ADAP, D, X, p. 94 (NG-2586-B: Rademacher memo of July 3, 1940).

become mass murderers? For both Rademacher and Turner, the path to the Final Solution led through Serbia. As we have seen, faced with a Serbian partisan uprising of unprecedented gravity, Turner and Foreign Office officials there urged that the Serbian Jews be deported to Romania, Poland, or Russia. As the Tighina agreement had just been reached, ending German attempts to expel Jews from the Ukraine into the Romanian sphere, any approach to that country was ruled out completely. But Rademacher did ask Eichmann about the possibility of sending Serbian Jews to Poland or Russia. Rademacher's hand-written notes record the answer of September 13, 1941: "According to *Sturmbannführer* Eichmann . . . residence in Russia and GG impossible. Not even the Jews of Germany can be lodged there. Eichmann proposes shooting." Apparently not grasping the full import of this, Rademacher drafted a message for Belgrade suggesting that "large numbers of hostages" be shot if the Jews fomented unrest. Officials in Belgrade persisted in requesting deportation of the Jews, however, even carrying their complaint of insufficient support from Berlin directly to Ribbentrop. Rademacher's boss, Luther, and Reinhard Heydrich decided to send a delegation of one Foreign Office representative, Rademacher himself, and one SS man, Eichmann's deputy, Friedrich Suhr, to Belgrade to check whether the problem of the Serbian Jews, "whose deportation had been urged by the embassy, could not be settled on the spot."[23] Heydrich had one other reason for sending his own man, namely, to check the complaints of the SS men in Belgrade that Turner was too "soft" for his job, particularly given his strong advocacy of collaboration with Serbs.[24]

Meanwhile in Serbia the army had taken a keen interest in the Serbian Jews. Ordered to carry out reprisal executions on the ratio of 100 to 1 for German soldiers killed by partisans, the army found the incarcerated male Jews to be the most convenient pool from which to draw its victims. The reprisal massacres began in early October and resulted

---

[23] For Rademacher's trip to Belgrade, see Browning, *The Final Solution and the German Foreign Office*, pp. 56–67.

[24] For Turner's collaboration policy, see: Christopher R. Browning, "Harald Turner und die Militärverwaltung in Serbien, 1941–42," *Verwaltung und "Menschenführung" im Staat Hitlers. Studien zum politisch-administrativen System*. Edited by Dieter Rebentisch and Karl Teppe, Göttingen: 1986.

in such grotesque absurdities as the predominantly Austrian troops of the 718th division shooting refugee Austrian Jews in Sabac in reprisal for Serbian partisan attacks on the German army.[25] Of all the German officials in Serbia, only Turner seemed to perceive the anomaly. "Actually, it is false, if one has to be precise about it, that for murdered Germans, on whose account the ratio 1:100 should really be borne by Serbs, 100 Jews are shot instead," he wrote. But Turner consoled himself that "the Jews we had in camps, after all, they too are Serb nationals, and besides they have to disappear."[26] If Turner, like virtually all German officials, fully shared the view that the Jews had to disappear and mass murder was one way of achieving that, it still had not dawned on him, however, that mass murder was now indeed the preferred way.

On October 18, 1941, the day after Turner wrote the letter quoted above, Rademacher and Suhr arrived in Belgrade. Turner immediately expressed to Rademacher his bitterest disappointment that his request to deport the Serbian Jews had not been honored; moreover, he continued to urge the deportation of those Jews who were still alive. The leader of the *SS-Einsatzgruppe,* Wilhelm Fuchs, urged on the other hand that the problem of the remaining male Jews could be quickly solved by continuing to supply them to meet the army's reprisal quotas. At a meeting on October 20, 1941, with Rademacher, Suhr and Fuchs, Turner hesitated and then relented. As Rademacher subsequently reported, the problem of the male Jews would be "settled" by the end of the week.[27]

The Jewish women and children remained, however, as the German army deemed itself too chivalrous to shoot them as hostages. In this regard Turner and Rademacher learned something entirely new at this October 20th conference attended by Suhr, who had the latest information from *SS* circles in Berlin. The *SS* opposition to deporting Jews to the east because there was no room, as voiced by Eichmann a month earlier, was apparently temporary rather than permanent. The Jewish women and children would first be interned in Serbia. "Then as soon

[25] Christopher R. Browning, "Wehrmacht Reprisal Policy and the Mass Murder of Jews in Serbia," *Militärgeschichtliche Mitteilungen.* 1983/1, pp. 31–47.

[26] NO-5810: Turner to Hildebrandt, October 17, 1941. Nürnberg document.

[27] ADAP, D, XIII, Part 2, 570-2 (Rademacher report of October 25, 1941).

as the technical possibility exists within the framework of the total solution of the Jewish question, the Jews will be deported . . . to a reception camp in the east,'' Rademacher reported.[28]

At this point Turner grasped the new realities of Nazi Jewish policy, and his response was instantaneous. If expulsion was out of favor, and mass murder was in, Turner wanted not only to facilitate it but above all to receive full credit for it. On October 26, only six days after the meeting with Suhr, Turner issued new guidelines for the treatment of civilians. ''As a matter of principle it must be said that the Jews and Gypsies in general represent an element of insecurity and thus a danger to public order and safety. . . . That is why it is a matter of principle in each case to put all Jewish men and male Gypsies at the disposal of the troops as hostages.''[29] Turner's help was more than just rhetorical. Army statistics of December 1941 credited police forces under Turner's jurisdiction with carrying out one third of all reprisal shootings to that date.[30]

For Turner, however, that was not enough. Turner had aroused suspicions in Berlin not only by his initial hesitancy to implement a local solution to the Jewish question but more so by his belief in the desirability of relying on Serbian collaborators, an issue that had led to steadily worsening relations between Turner and the local *SS-Einsatzgruppe*. Suhr had been sent by Heydrich not only to investigate the Jewish question but also to report on the deteriorating relations between Turner and his *SS* men. Following Suhr's visit, Turner's position in Serbia was seriously undermined by the appointment in January 1942 of August Meyszner as the Higher *SS* and Police Leader, for Meyszner took command of the *SS* units previously under Turner's control, and his rabid Serbophobia clashed totally with Turner's collaboration policy. Turner now wished to impress Berlin with his vigor and toughness on the Jewish question, especially to compensate for his alleged weakness on Serbs, and he repeatedly exaggerated his role in the murder of the Serbian Jews. In February 1942 he went so far as falsely to claim that the army had actually refused to shoot Jews, so that they had to be

[28] Ibid.
[29] NOKW-802: Turner to Feld - und Kreiskommandanturen, October 26, 1941. Nürnberg document.
[30] BA-MA: RW 40/23, Aktennotiz of December 12, 1941 (NOKW-474).

shot "exclusively" on his order by the *Einsatzgruppe* and police.[31] When a gas van was sent from Berlin in March 1942 to eliminate the Jewish women and children interned in the camp at Semlin, Turner wrote Himmler's adjutant, Karl Wolff, to claim credit once more: "Already some months ago I had all the available Jews shot and all Jewish women and children concentrated in a camp and at the same time, with the help of the *SD*, procured a 'delousing truck' that will finally clear the camp in some 14 days to 4 weeks. . . . "[32] This was not how Emanuel Schäfer, the *Sipo-SD* commander in Belgrade remembered it after the war, when he frankly testified that the gas van had been sent directly to him, and no other German agency in Serbia had been involved.[33] But in Nazi Germany exaggerated claims about the zealous killing of Jews were not always enough. Turner was still perceived in Berlin as too weak because of his consistent attempt to work with Serbian collaborators, and he was forced from his job in the fall of 1942.[34]

If, following the October 20th meeting in Belgrade, Rademacher still had any doubts about the fate of women and children unfit for labor being sent to a reception camp in the east, they were removed immediately upon his return to Berlin. There he found waiting a letter from his old friend of *Der Stürmer*, Paul Wurm, who had been visiting Berlin and had just missed Rademacher. "Dear Party Comrade Rademacher," Wurm wrote. "On my return trip from Berlin I met an old party comrade, who works in the east on the settlement of the Jewish question. In the near future many of the Jewish vermin will be exterminated through special measures."[35] By the end of October, therefore, Rademacher knew all there was to know other than the precise nature of the "special measures" to be used to murder the Jews.

---

[31] Bundesarchiv Koblenz (hereafter cited as BA), NS 19/1730, Turner Gesamtbericht to Himmler, February 15, 1942. Earlier exaggerated claims of his role in the murder of the male Jews are found in his reports of December 3, and December 15, 1941, also in NS 19/1730.

[32] BDC, Turner to Wolff, April 4, 1942.

[33] Landgericht Köln, 24 Ks 1/52 and 2/53 (Schäfer trial), II, pp. 199–204, 331–34, 342–44 (Schäfer testimony). Landgericht Hannover, 2 Ks 2/65 (Pradel trial), VII, pp. 55–7; XII pp. 238–9 (Schäfer testimony).

[34] On Turner's fall, Browning, "Harald Turner und die Militärverwaltung in Serbien 1941–2."

[35] PA, Inland II A/B 59/3, Wurm to Rademacher, October 23, 1941.

How did Rademacher react to this new understanding that Nazi Jewish policy now entailed mass murder? The answer is that he reacted with effective professional competence and ineffective personal evasion. In late November his boss, Luther, received an invitation to the Wannsee Conference along with a copy of Göring's authorization to Heydrich of July 31, 1941, to coordinate a total solution to the Jewish problem in Europe. Luther eagerly accepted Heydrich's offer for continuing SS-Foreign Office cooperation in Jewish affairs, for only in this way could the Foreign Office preserve its shrinking influence against further SS encroachment, a matter of primary concern for Luther. No stranger to Luther's determination to protect Foreign Office jurisdiction, Rademacher provided him with a list of "desires and ideas" of the Foreign Office for the conference, making clear its readiness to participate in a sweeping deportation program.[36]

By a number of accounts, not all friendly to Rademacher, the Foreign Office Jewish expert also asked to be released from his position. Luther made this release conditional upon finding and training a successor. Rademacher thus applied to the Personnel Division for a new assistant. In justification of his request for additional manpower, Rademacher wrote: "The stronger the German victory looms, the greater and more urgent become the tasks of the *Referat,* because the Jewish question must be solved in the course of the war, for only so can it be solved without a world-wide outcry."[37] Rademacher continued to work in the *Judenreferat* for another year, without the visible initiatives that had characterized his earlier work. But loss of enthusiasm meant no loss of efficiency. While still touting his beloved Madagascar Plan to any captive audience he could find, Rademacher ensured that the work of the Jewish desk was done. When he was finally replaced in the spring of 1943, Germany was well on its way to fulfilling what Rademacher considered its "obligation to solve the Jewish question."

For Hans Biebow in Lodz, initiation into the Final Solution also came in the fall of 1941. Biebow's efforts to stabilize the Lodz ghetto had come under renewed threat as early as June 1941, when the prospect was raised of interning there all the other Jews in the Warthegau as well. Biebow warned of catastrophic consequences if this were done

---

[36] Browning, *Final Solution,* pp. 76–77.   [37] Ibid., pp. 81–3.

without both enlarging the ghetto and ensuring adequate food supplies.[38] Nonetheless in mid-July the Warthegau *Gauleiter*, Greiser, ordered Lodz to accept at least 2,900 Jews from the Leslau district. The German authorities in Lodz dragged their feet and delayed this transfer until late September.[39] By then, however, they were faced with a far greater threat in the form of Himmler's intention to resettle 60,000 German and Protectorate Jews in Lodz.[40] The numbers were quickly scaled down to 20,000 Jews and 5,000 Gypsies, but the Lodz officials were still flabbergasted at the prospect. Biebow assiduously assembled counter-arguments for his immediate superiors, *Oberbürgermeister* Ventzki and *Regierungspräsident* Uebelhoer. "Were the ghetto a pure decimation ghetto, then one could contemplate a greater concentration of Jews," Biebow noted. But it was a "work ghetto" that "is today a finely tuned and thereby extremely sensitive component of the defense economy." More Jews could not be taken in for health, security, economic, and nutritional reasons, as well as for lack of space.[41] Uebelhoer forwarded these arguments to Himmler. Himmler conceded that the counter-arguments had been "excellently compiled" by Uebelhoer's experts but refused to accept them. Moreover, he noted that Ventzki, under whose name this admittedly "excellent" report had been forwarded and whom Himmler thus assumed to be its author, "did not appear to be an old national socialist." Uebelhoer was ordered as both *Regierungspräsident* and *SS* leader to devote his energies to carrying out the resettlement rather than obstructing it."[42]

Uebelhoer did not immediately give up his obstruction but instead found through contacts in the Interior Ministry that Eichmann had misrepresented the situation in Lodz to Himmler by claiming, among other things, that the economic manager of the ghetto, that is Biebow, had

---

[38] DiM, p. 184 (excerpt of monthly activity report of June 3, 1941).
[39] DiM, pp. 188–93 (Biebow to Landrat Wolun, September 2, 1941; Greiser to Uebelhoer, September 11, 1941; Ventzki to Uebelhoer, September 9, 1941; Polizeidirektor Leslau to Reichsbahndirektion Posen, September 20, 1941).
[40] National Archives Microfilm T 175/54/2568695 (Himmler to Greiser, September 18, 1941).
[41] National Archives Microfilm T 175/54/2568671-94 (Ventzki to Uebelhoer, September 24, 1941) and 2568668-70 (Uebelhoer to Himmler, October 4, 1941).
[42] National Archives Microfilm T 175/54/2568662-3 (Himmler to Uebelhoer, October 4, 1941).

explicitly agreed to the resettlement. This alleged agreement by Biebow was not possible, Uebelhoer noted, for in fact Biebow was the real author of the Ventzki report that Himmler had found so "excellent:" Infuriated by Uebelhoer's obstruction and his audacity in suggesting that the *Reichsführer-SS* had been fooled by what Uebelhoer characterized as Eichmann's "Gypsy-like horse trading manners," Himmler put the *Regierungspräsident* in his place.[43] The deportation of the 20,000 Jews and 5,000 Gypsies to Lodz began on October 15, just three days, it might be noted, before Rademacher and Suhr arrived in Belgrade.

Up to this point, the German authorities in Lodz were not aware of the impending Final Solution. It cannot be determined if Eichmann actually talked to Biebow in late September, as Himmler claimed, and if so, what Biebow learned. But in October preparations began for the death camp at Chelmno.[44] On December 8, 1941, the mass murder of the Jewish populations in the immediate area of Chelmno commenced, and on December 16, the German authorities in Lodz met with Rumkowski to inform him that deportations from the Lodz ghetto itself were imminent.[45] Then from January 16 to May 15, 1942, more than 56,000 Jews were deported from Lodz to the death camp at Chelmno. Exactly when in this sequence of events Biebow learned the real meaning behind these deportations cannot be established. But his reaction was logical and predictable. Having argued vehemently for months that the existing population in the Lodz ghetto was not adequately fed and that an influx of yet more Jews would destroy the economic viability of the ghetto and its capacity to fulfill important defense contracts, Biebow could hardly stand in the way of eliminating that portion of the ghetto population that was not productive.

Biebow in fact threw himself into the new situation with the same zeal and efficiency that had characterized his earlier activity. In the spring of 1942, the former coffee importer was in frequent contact with the commandants at Chelmno, Lange and Bothmann, to ensure the

---

[43] National Archives Microfilm T 175/54/2568543-5 (Uebelhoer to Himmler, October 9, 1941) and 256851 (Himmler to Uebelhoer, October 9, 1941).

[44] For dating, see Christopher R. Browning, *Fateful Months: Essays on the Emergence of the Final Solution.* New York: 1985, p. 30.

[45] Dobroszycki, *The Chronicle of the Lodz Ghetto,* pp. 96–7 (entry of December 20, 1941).

recovery of the valuables and clothing of the murdered Jews for his economic operations in Lodz. This salvage operation involved even visits to the death camp itself.[46] When the deportations from Lodz temporarily came to a halt in May 1942, and the Germans switched to liquidating the other ghettos of the Warthegau, some 25 men of Biebow's ghetto administration joined *SS* and police to form the notorious ghetto-clearing squads.[47] Biebow, moreover, was also interested in the "human material" that could be salvaged from the ghetto liquidations. In the ghetto-clearing operations, witnesses saw him personally involved in the selection of able-bodied workers to be sent to his workshops in Lodz.[48] In the summer of 1944, as a fitting conclusion to his career as ghetto manager of Lodz, Biebow persuaded the surviving Jews to board the trains for Auschwitz.[49]

It can be seen, therefore, that if none of these three men initiated mass murder from below, neither did they receive explicit orders from above. Unlike an Eichmann or a Höss, none was formally called before his superior and officially initiated into the new policy of mass murder. Instead new signals and directions were given at the center, and with a ripple effect, these new signals set in motion waves that radiated outward. Because of their involvement in the Jewish question, with the situations they found themselves in and the contacts they made, these three bureaucrats could not help but feel the ripples and be affected by the changing atmosphere and course of events. These were not stupid or politically inept people; they could read the signals, perceive what was expected of them, and adjust their behavior accordingly. If Turner and Biebow were more zealous in this adjustment than Rademacher, the Foreign Office Jewish expert nevertheless did all that was needed to facilitate the participation of his bureaucratic agency in the mass murder.

How typical were these three men? It should be noted that in regard to the issue of initiative from below, they were "relative" moderates.

---

[46] Zentralstelle der Landesjustizverwaltungen Ludwigsburg, 203 AR-Z 69/59 (Chelmno trial), Bd. 1, 114–121 (Meyer testimony), and Landgericht Hanover 2 Ks 1/63 (Bradfisch-Fuchs Judgment), 20.

[47] DiM, pp. 221–9.

[48] YVA, O-53/50/245-6 (testimony of Jozef Azod Kozminski) and 250-1 (testimony of Abraham Mandel).

[49] DiM, pp. 267–8.

There was no shortage of those advocating and even practicing murder before the signals came from Berlin. We have already noted the reprisal shootings of Jews carried out by the army in Serbia and the shrill advice of Palfinger in Lodz to preside over a "dying out" of the Jews through systematic starvation. One could also note other instances. The infamous Höppner memorandum of July 1941, reporting conversations among SS-men in the Warthegau, suggested to Eichmann that it would be more "humane" to kill superfluous Jews through some "quick-acting" means rather than to let them starve.[50] And when the chief health official of the General Government, Dr. Jost Walbaum, addressed 100 doctors at a meeting in Bad Krynica in mid-October 1941 on the threat of epidemics, he approved, with the following statement, the newly-decreed death sentence for Jews caught leaving the ghettos: "One must be clear about it, and I can speak openly in this circle; there are only two ways, we condemn the Jews in the ghettos to death by starvation or we shoot them." Such sentiments did not shock his audience of doctors, for the protocol notes that his frankness was greeted with "applause, clapping."[51]

For the most part, however, the Final Solution would be implemented not by such zealots, the "anticipators," but rather by the "normal" bureaucrats, the "accommodators" who waited for the signal from above. It was their receptivity to such signals, and the speed with which they aligned themselves to the new policy, that allowed the Final Solution to emerge with so little internal friction and so little formal coordination. If the irresistibility of the *Gleichschaltung* of 1933 was due not only to the efforts of political activists but above all to the pervasive self-coordination and accommodation of so many Germans to the new regime, the destructive dynamic of the Final Solution was due to a similar phenomenon regarding the bureaucratic perpetrators.

In retrospect we can see that the inauguration of the Final Solution in 1941 was a monumental event in history, when old notions of human nature and progress were shattered and mankind passed forever into the

---

[50] Raul Hilberg, *Documents of Destruction*. Chicago: 1971, pp. 87–88 (Höppner to Eichmann, July 16, 1941).
[51] YVA, O-53/145/77 (Arbeitstagung der Abteilung Gesundheitswesen, Bad Krynica, October 13–16, 1941).

post-Auschwitz era. But if this appreciation has come to us only gradually over the past four decades, we should not be surprised that such an appreciation was lost upon many of the murderers themselves. Nor should we be surprised at how quickly and smoothly the three perpetrators whom we have been studying took those last fatal steps into this new era. The personal adjustment that each had to make flowed so naturally out of the logic of his past conception of the Jewish question, and dovetailed so completely with his own career self-interest, that there was no sudden crisis of conscience, no traumatic agonizing, no consciousness of crossing an abyss, virtually no foot-dragging, and only occasional attempts to escape personal involvement, provided of course that it could be done without damage to career.

In short, for Nazi bureaucrats already deeply involved in and committed to "solving the Jewish question," the final step to mass murder was incremental, not a quantum leap. They had already committed themselves to a political movement, to a career, and to a task. They lived in an environment already permeated by mass murder. This included not only programs with which they were not directly involved, like the liquidation of the Polish intelligentsia, the gassing of the mentally ill and handicapped in Germany, and then on a more monumental scale the war of destruction in Russia. It also included wholesale killing and dying before their very eyes, the starvation in the ghetto of Lodz and the punitive expeditions and reprisal shooting in Serbia. By the very nature of their past activities, these men had articulated positions and developed career interests that inseparably and inexorably led to a similar murderous solution to the Jewish question. They did not initiate the mass murder but they were certainly too implicated and entangled to stand in the way, much less extricate themselves.

After the war, perpetrators like these three men would speak of their involvement in the mass murder as something that had happened to them; that was their fate, rather than something they had inflicted on others. It was as if they had been without volition, had never made decisions, had never been responsible for their actions. They spoke as if they too had been victims. But of course in reality they had choices and they made decisions, but these choices and decisions were spread out over time and flowed so naturally one after another that they were unconscious of any particular turning point. Elsewhere I have argued that

even for the top echelons of the Nazi leadership, the Final Solution resulted not from a single decision but rather from a series of decisions.
If this is the case for Hitler, Himmler, and Heydrich, we should not be
surprised that the middle-echelon bureaucrats' path to complicity in
mass murder was not marked by a single decisive and dramatic turning
point. Instead the path was a gradual, almost imperceptible, descent
past the point of no return.

7

Genocide and Public Health: German Doctors and Polish Jews, 1939–1941

In recent years the study of German doctors in the Third Reich has been a "growth industry" in the historical profession.[1] One aspect of the overall problem that has not yet been explored, however, is the public health policies of German doctors in the occupied territories and the relationship of these public health policies to Nazi anti-Jewish measures. Raul Hilberg has noted that the Germans cited fear of epidemics

In memory of a friend and colleague in the field of Holocaust studies, Uwe Adam-Radewald, 1940–1987.

Archival materials for this study have been collected gradually during various research trips abroad. I am thus greatly indebted to numerous sources of support: the Institute for Advanced Studies on the campus of the Hebrew University of Jerusalem; the Alexander von Humboldt Foundation; and Pacific Lutheran University. I am also grateful to Dr. Shmuel Krakowski who brought to my attention the key document that caught my interest in this topic, to Prof. Michael Kater and Dr. William Seidelmann for the initial stimulus and encouragement to undertake this study, and to Dr. William Rieke for checking the accuracy of the manuscript's medical aspects.

Reprinted in slightly revised form with permission of Pergamon Press PLC. From *Holocaust and Genocide Studies*, vol. 3, no. 1 (1988), pp. 21–36.

[1] See for example Michael Kater's *Doctors under Hitler: The German Medical Profession in Crisis during the Third Reich* (Chapel Hill, NC: University of North Carolina Press, 1988) as well as his many important recent articles; Robert Lifton, *The Nazi Doctors. Medical Killing and Genocide* (New York: Basic Books, 1986); Henry Friedlander's forthcoming book on euthanasia; Fridolf Kudlien, ed., *Ärzte im Nationalsozialismus* (Köln: Klepenhener and Witsch, 1985); Benno Müller-Hill, *Tödliche Wissenschaft, Die Aussonderung von Juden, Zigeunern und Geisteskranken 1933–1945* (Reinbek: Rowohlt, 1984); and Ernst Klee, *Euthanasie im NS-Staat. Die "Vernichtung lebensunwerten Lebens"* (Frankfurt: Fischer, 1983).

as a primary reason for ghettoizing the Polish Jews. They subsequently cited the same fear as justification for liquidating the ghettos.[2] The purpose of this study is to examine what role the German doctors in the General Government, particularly the public health officials, played in this medical rationalization of ghettoization and mass murder. I will argue that the public health policies of these doctors were an important element in the intensification of anti-Jewish measures in the General Government, and that by late 1941 most of these doctors were quite receptive to the Final Solution as a way out of a self-induced public health dilemma.

The official Party attitude toward the practice of public health in the General Government was articulated by Eberhard Wetzel and Gerhard Hecht in a 25 November 1939 memorandum of the Racial Political Office. This document was circulated among the Nazi leadership and clearly had an important influence on Heinrich Himmler.[3] Concerning the Poles, Wetzel and Hecht wrote, "Medical care from our side must be limited to the prevention of the spreading of epidemics to Reich territory. . . . All measures that serve to limit the birth rate must be tolerated or promoted. . . . Measures of racial hygiene must in no way be supported." As for the Jews, Wetzel and Hecht wrote: "We are indifferent to the hygienic fate of the Jews. Also for the Jews the basic principle is valid, that their propagation must be curtailed in every possible way." In short, the practice of public health *vis-á-vis* Poles and Jews was to be its denial or perversion for the conscious purpose of decreasing their numbers.

We know that the Third Reich was a very polycratic system, and that the civil administration of Hans Frank in the General Government quarreled fiercely with and often advocated a less ideological and more

---

[2] Raul Hilberg, *The Destruction of the European Jews* (Revised edition: New York: Holmes & Meier, 1985), I, p. 224.

[3] NO 3732 ("Die Frage der Behandlung der Bevölkerung der ehemaligen polnischen Gebiete nach rassenpolitischen Gesichtspunkten, 25 November 1939") printed in *Documenta Occupationis*, V, pp. 1 –28. For an example of the circulation of this memo, see: NG 4921 (Gross to Reich Finance Minister, 4 December 1939). For the influence of this memo on Himmler, see his subsequent memo (NO 1880) "Einige Gedanken über die Behandlung der fremdvölkischen im Osten," Helmut Krausnick, ed., *Vierteljahrshefte für Zeitgeschichte*, 5:2 (1957), 196–8.

pragmatic course of action than that of the SS. We must therefore ask whether the idea popular among the racial ideologues in Berlin of decreasing the Polish and Jewish populations through a denial of health services was shared by German doctors in the General Government.

The head of the Division of Public Health in the General Government was Dr. Jost Walbaum.[4] A member of the NSDAP since 1930 and the SA since 1932, he received a public health position in Berlin in 1933. In his earlier private practice, Walbaum had gained the friendship of Hermann Göring while treating him for his morphine addiction. In late October 1939 Walbaum was suggested to Hans Frank and *Reichsgesundheitsführer* (Reich Head of Public Health) Leonardo Conti by Artur Seyss-Inquart as a suitable appointee, and was made both *Leiter der Abteilung Gesundheitswesen* (Director of the Division of Public Health) and *Gesundheitsführer* in the General Government. He filled the key posts of his new public health domain with what he considered to be like-minded doctors.

The attitude of Walbaum and his team is best revealed in their own words in a book entitled *Kampf den Seuchen! Deutsche Ärzte-Einsatz im Osten*.[5] This book is an anthology of articles by Walbaum and his associates that appeared in June 1941, although most of the articles seem to have been written in 1940 before the closing of the Warsaw ghetto. Three themes predominate. First is their outspoken contempt for Poles. Poland was a filthy, unsanitary country of primitive, "half-civilized people" who could not maintain a health infrastructure fit even for animals.[6] Second, Walbaum and his men had in a short time overcome the prevailing "chaos" and set up an effective health administration that was intended "first of all to serve the interests of the

---

[4] The details on Walbaum's career are from his files in the Berlin Document Center (hereafter cited as BDC), and his post-war judicial interrogations in the Zentrale Stelle der Landesjustizverwaltungern in Ludwigsburg (hereafter cited as ZSt): Interrogations of 3 April and 10 December 1963, in: 206 AR 1211/60, pp. 103–6, 109–14; and of 17 October 1968, in: 201 AR-Z 49/66, pp. 132–147.

[5] *Kampf den Seuchen! Deutscher Ärzte-Einsatz im Osten. Die Aufbauarbeit im Gesundheitswesen des Generalgouvernements*, Jost Walbaum, ed. (Krakau: Buchverlag "Deutscher Osten", 1941).

[6] Ibid., pp. 11–12, 23. To quote Dr. Joseph Rupprecht: "Und was man sieht! Mit einem Wort: Dreck, Dreck und nochmals Dreck!"

German Reich and Reich Germans." Walbaum insisted that while it was not the task of the German public health administration to provide health care for Poles, nevertheless, its policies were "obviously of great benefit to the native population."[7] Dr. Joseph Rupprecht was more explicit. He noted that German doctors in the General Government implemented measures not only to protect themselves from infection but also to prevent the spread of epidemic in the Polish population as well. This effect was accomplished by forcing the Poles to carry out health measures with "German thoroughness."[8] In short, population-decimating epidemics may have looked attractive to ideologues in distant Berlin, but for Germans living in Poland they appeared in a more dangerous light.

A third major theme in this book concerned the Jews as the source of the epidemics that threatened both Germans and Poles. The German doctors argued that the Jews in particular were the source of spotted fever or exanthematic typhus (what the Germans called *Fleckfieber*) caused by a rickettsia carried by body lice. Dr. Nauck dutifully cited a paper by Walbaum on "spotted fever and ethnic identity" which emphasized that "the Jews are overwhelmingly the carriers and disseminators of the infection. Spotted fever endures most persistently in the regions heavily populated by Jews, with their low cultural level, their uncleanliness and the infestation of lice unavoidably connected with this."[9] Dr. Erich Waizenegger emphasized the same theme:

> The sickness occurs . . . especially among the Jewish population. This is caused by the fact that the Jew totally lacks any concept of hygiene. The living quarters are too small, full of filth and rubbish; ragged and unbelievably dirty clothing and linen are very seldom changed by the Jews. Thus it is easy to see that the Jewish population is infested with lice as far as its ghetto or living area extends. It is obvious that the door is thereby wide open for the spread of spotted fever.[10]

Three other doctors expressed a similar view in somewhat less dramatic language.[11]

---

[7] Ibid., p. 16.   [8] Ibid., pp. 26–7.   [9] Ibid., p. 34.   [10] Ibid., p. 145.
[11] Ibid., pp. 28, 72–4, 78, 154.

The doctors were convinced that spotted fever, if it spread among the German population, would have a far higher fatality rate than among the Jews who had developed greater resistance to it.[12] Thus effective counter-measures were a major concern. Two doctors suggested imposing forced delousing and stricter sanitation regulations on the Jews, and Dr. Nauck proposed in addition to these measures the novel idea of better food and housing.[13] However, the most frequently advocated anti-epidemic measure was the call for restricting the movement of the Jews.[14] As a result, the German doctors in the General Government became the most insistent and persistent advocates of ghettoization. In German self-interest the Poles were to be protected from epidemics, but in contrast the Jews were to be locked up with the diseases they allegedly carried.

The doctors did not systematically separate environmental, cultural, and genetic factors in their diagnosis of the Jewish propensity for spotted fever. However, ultimately the latter two factors predominated. It was because of his culture and nature, not his poverty, that the Jew lived in the filthy conditions so conducive to infestation by disease-carrying lice. The persistent medieval anti-Semitic stereotype of the Jew as the plague-carrier thus called forth as a modern medical response the revival of a medieval invention – the sealed ghetto.

How important was the role of the doctors in the ensuing policy of ghettoization in the General Government? Clearly the doctors were not the only ones advocating ghettoization. In the neighboring Warthegau, the ghettoization of the Lodz Jews was initiated prior to the intervention of medical authorities.[15] But it is my argument that in Warsaw, with the largest Jewish community in Europe, the doctors played a decisive role in ghettoization, and that this then set the pattern that was followed in the rest of the General Government.

The first initiative for ghettoization in Warsaw came from the SS-*Einsatzgruppe* commander, Dr. Rudolf Batz, who on 4 November 1939 ordered all Jews in the city to be concentrated in one area within three

---

[12] Ibid., pp. 84, 144.   [13] Ibid., pp. 146, 155, 87.   [14] Ibid., pp. 28, 72–4, 87.
[15] The ghettoization of the Lodz Jews was initiated in December 1939. For the enthusiastic support of ghettoization by the *Gesundheitsamt*, see the memo of 1 February 1940 quoted in: H. G. Adler, *Der verwaltete Mensch: Studien zur Deportation des Juden aus Deutschland* (Tübingen: J. C. B. Mohr, 1974), pp. 169–70.

days. This would have involved the immediate uprooting of 150,000 people. The military commander, General von Neumann-Neurode postponed this measure, and instead the Jewish quarter was designated a *Seuchengebiet* or "quarantine-area" and placed off-limits to German military personnel.[16] Although the Warsaw district governor, Dr. Ludwig Fischer, secured Frank's permission for a ghetto in Warsaw at this time,[17] no further initiatives were taken until the following spring. In March 1940 the idea of a Jewish ghetto on the far side of the Vistula was rejected as too disruptive to the economy, and in April a plan to deport the Jews to Lublin was vetoed by the Higher SS and Police Leader, Wilhelm Krüger.[18] At this point the Jewish Council in Warsaw was ordered to begin construction, naturally at its own expense, of a 2.2 meter high wall – a *Seuchenmauer* – around the quarantine area. The initiative in this matter is clearly recorded. "The erection of the quarantine wall was considered unconditionally necessary by the public health department" – in this case Dr. Kaminski of the Warsaw district and Dr. Walbaum himself – because the Jews had allegedly not complied with the public health regulations.[19]

Neither the wall construction initiated by the public health doctors in April nor a subsequent plan for two suburban ghettos had gotten very far, however, when ghetto building was brought to a temporary halt in the General Government in July 1940 by order of Hans Frank. Ghettobuilding was "illusory," he pronounced, in view of the imminent deportation of the Jews to Madagascar.[20]

Even before defeat in the Battle of Britain laid the Madagascar Plan to rest, however, the doctors returned to the offensive. On 20 August SS-*Obersturmführer* Dr. Arnold Lambrecht replaced Dr. Kaminski as

---

[16] Israel Gutman, *The Jews of Warsaw 1939–1943: Ghetto Underground, Revolt* (Bloomington: Indiana University Press, 1982), p. 49. Yad Vashem Archives (hereafter cited at YVA), JM 1112 (Auerswald report "Zwei Jahre Aufbauarbeit im Distrikt Warschau: Juden im Distrikt Warschau").

[17] *Das Diensttagebuch des deutschen Generalgouverneurs in Polen 1939–1945* (hereafter cited as Frank, *Diensttagebuch*), Werner Präg and Wolfgang Jacobmeyer, eds. (Stuttgart: DVA, 1975), p. 59 (entry of 7 November 1939).

[18] *Faschismus–Getto–Massenmord* (hereafter cited as FGM), (Berlin [East], 1960), pp. 108–9 (excerpt from Schön report, 20 January 1941).

[19] YVA, 0-53/102/391-99 ("Halbjahres Bericht" of Dr. Kreppel, 14 May 1940).

[20] FGM, p. 110 (excerpt of Schön report, 20 January 1941).

Walbaum's chief of public health in the district of Warsaw. The 38-year-old Lambrecht – like Walbaum – was an *alte Kämpfer* (veteran fighter) who had joined the NSDAP and SA in 1931 and the SS in February 1933.[21] Lambrecht was immediately alarmed by the spotted fever statistics in his district. In the past, he stated, outbreaks of spotted fever outside Warsaw fell way below that of the city itself. In August 1940, however, 50 cases had been reported outside Warsaw in comparison to 18 within the city. "These statistics," he concluded in a report of 3 September 1940, "make the outbreak of spotted fever in numerous places in the district in the coming winter months an absolute certainty."[22] A report to Frank in Cracow on the following day by the Division of Internal Administration, to which Lambrecht's report was attached, indicated that negotiations between Warsaw and Cracow on Jewish policy had already been underway the previous month. The results had not been satisfactory to the Warsaw authorities, who lamented that "until now clearly no unified treatment of the Jewish problem has been established in Cracow." What the Warsaw authorities wanted was simple: "The question of building ghettos for Jews in the district is particularly urgent . . . especially for health reasons."[23]

Two days later, on 6 September, Walbaum met with Frank in Cracow, presented his spotted fever statistics, and claimed that the disease was being spread from the Jewish quarter. Healthwise, he argued, it was of the "greatest importance" that all Jews be brought into ghettos as quickly as possible, especially in Warsaw.[24] On 12 September Frank

---

[21] BDC, Lambrecht files.

[22] YVA, JM 814, Report of Dr. Lambrecht of 3 September 1940.

[23] YVA, JM 814, Acitivity report for the month of August of the Division of Internal Administration in Warsaw, 4 September 1940.The Schön report of 20 January 1941 (FGM, 110) indicated that on 20 August 1940 the Division of Internal Administration had already urged the creation of Jewish residence areas but, out of economic expediency, not hermetically sealed ghettos. It is thus likely that Lambrecht's report was not only welcome ammunition in Warsaw's quest for approval from Cracow to proceed with ghetto-building but that it also persuaded other Warsaw authorities to accept tighter sealing of the ghettos despite the inevitable economic repercussions this would have. The leading role of the public health officials in pressing for ghettoization is also confirmed by: *The Stroop Report: The Jewish Quarter is No More!*, Sybil Milton, ed. (New York: Pantheon, 1979), p. 2.

[24] *Trials of the Major War Criminals Before the International Military Tribunal* (Nürnberg, 1947–9), 29, 406 (Frank *Tagebuch*, entry of 6 September 1940).

announced his approval.[25] The Warsaw ghetto was sealed on 15 November, and the other Jewish communities in the district were also ghettoized at this time. Ghettoization followed in other parts of the General Government the following spring.

The sealing of the ghettos severed the economic ties between the Jews and the surrounding community and deprived the incarcerated Jews of their already diminished opportunities to make a livelihood. Everywhere the insufficient supply of food and fuel, combined with terrible overcrowding and the influx of impoverished refugees, led to dire hardship, a dramatic rise in fatalities, and ultimately the massive outbreak of the very spotted fever epidemic that the German doctors feared. Ghettoization in short produced a self-fulfilling prophecy.

The predictability of such a phenomenon on the one hand and the subsequent, even more murderous course of Nazi Jewish policy on the other has led many historians to assume that the Nazi reference to epidemics was a mere pretext to justify ghettoization, which in turn was a conscious preparatory step for total annihilation. For example, in his classic work *Judenrat,* Isaiah Trunk has argued that "the Germans deliberately created unsanitary conditions which could not but spread contagious diseases and that "the attrition of Jewish lives through the massive fatalities inflicted by diseases and epidemics was part and parcel of the Nazis' diabolical plan to hasten the physical destruction of the Jews."[26]

In my opinion, such a conclusion is too simple. It presumes both a uniformity of view among the various German agencies in Poland and a continuity in Jewish policy from 1939 to 1941 that is impossible to reconcile with the reality of the German occupation regime in the General Government. The top Nazi officials in the General Government did not eagerly seize upon the doctors' reports or order them to produce such recommendations in order to carry out a predetermined policy. Rather the doctors initiated pressure on the top officials to persuade them to end their footdragging, reverse their policy, and

---

[25] Frank, *Diensttagebuch,* p. 281 (Abteilungsleitersitzung, 12 September 1940).
[26] Isaiah Trunk, *Judenrat: The Jewish Councils in Eastern Europe under Nazi Occupation* (New York: MacMillan, 1972), p. 143.

proceed swiftly with ghettoization. However misguided, the doctors believed them- selves to be acting in a strictly medical capacity. For example, when those Germans who did in fact want to use ghettoization to starve the Jews – Waldemar Schön, Alexander Palfinger, and Karl Naumann – urged cutting off all food supplies to the Warsaw ghetto, SS-*Obersturmführer* Dr. Lambrecht protested "energetically" against an "artificial famine" that would bring on the outbreak of epidemic. Simultaneously, however, he did urge a tighter sealing of the ghetto.[27]

Dr. Wilhelm Hagen was the Warsaw public health official who had to deal with the accelerating death rate in the Warsaw ghetto and the increasing danger that the spotted fever epidemic would jump the ghetto walls and spread to the rest of the population.[28] Unlike the Nazi cronies of Walbaum appointed earlier to the top positions of the Division of Public Health, Hagen was an old socialist. His involvement in student revolutionary politics during the Munich Republic in the spring of 1919 had cost him three months in jail, and his subsequent medical career had been devoted to public health until he was fired from his position in Frankfurt in 1933 for "political unreliability." He then pursued an unsatisfying career in private practice until 1940, when the shortage of doctors for public health positions in the occupied territories led to his appointment as *Amtsarzt* (city public health doctor) in Warsaw in January 1941.

If Hagen did not share the political convictions of most of his colleagues, he shared at least one viewpoint with them. Even 30 years later Hagen fully accepted as medical fact that for "unclarified" reasons spotted fever was endemic among the Jews. "That is a phenomenon of medical statistics that has nothing to do with politics," he

---

[27] YVA, JM 1113, conference of 2 December 1940. On the policy conflict between those wanting to starve the Jews and those wishing to utilize their labor, see Chapter 2 in this book.

[28] For Hagen's career, see: Wilhelm Hagen, *Auftrag und Wirklichkeit: Sozialartzt im 20. Jahrhundert* (Munich–Gräfeling, 1978); Wilhelm Hagen, "Krieg, Hunger und Pestilenz in Warschau 1939–1943," *Gesundheitswesen und Desinfektion*, 8 (1973), 115–128, and 9 (1973), 129–43; and ZSt, II 201 AR 1800/69 (Ermittlungsverfahren of the Staatsanwaltschaft bei der Landgericht Dortmund, 45 Js 7/69).

wrote in 1973, and provided comparative statistics for the spotted fever outbreak in eastern Europe between 1916 and 1921 to prove his point.[29] Unlike others, however, he did not see this as justification solely for isolating the Jews and containing the disease within the ghetto walls. The Jews were to be isolated, but the spotted fever epidemic was to be combated.

Hagen's medical battle against spotted fever in the Warsaw ghetto was, in his own view, thwarted from two sides. On the one hand, other German authorities constantly sabotaged his efforts. Sixty-six thousand uprooted Jewish refugees were brought into the ghetto from outside the city in the spring of 1941, which swamped Hagen's efforts to establish a 14-day quarantine period for all new arrivals. Hagen found his efforts within the ghetto constantly harassed by German ghetto administrators, who told him he "had no business" there. With totally insufficient supplies of food, fuel, and medicine, the overall death rate soared. In Hagen's estimation 8 to 10 percent of these deaths were due to spotted fever.[30]

On the other hand, Hagen was frustrated because the ghettoized Jews were extremely reluctant to comply with the public health measures he decreed, including delousing baths and quarantine. In his estimation only 20 to 25 percent of the spotted fever cases were ever reported, and bribery and passive resistance undermined all attempts at enforcement.[31] Isaiah Trunk has written, "The Nazi methods of 'fighting' infectious diseases were well known and were feared not less than

[29] Hagen, "Krieg, Hunger und Pestilenz in Warschau 1939–1943," p. 117. Elsewhere (pp. 121–2) Hagen noted that the three places where spotted fever reached epidemic proportions in the Warsaw district were the Jewish ghetto, Mokotow prison, and a camp for Russian prisoners of war, but he never drew the rather obvious conclusion that the common denominator for spotted fever epidemic was the merciless conditions in which the Germans interned their victims and was thus quite clearly a political phenomenon.

[30] Ibid., pp. 119, 121; Hagen, *Auftrag und Wirklichkeit*, pp. 169–70, 173. Hagen made no distinction between the Schön–Palfinger ghetto administration that clearly wanted to decimate the ghetto population, and the Auerswald–Bischof ghetto administration that was appointed in May 1941 to build a self-sufficient ghetto economy. Hagen seems to attribute to Auerswald the policies of his predecessors. See Chapter 2 in this book.

[31] Hagen, "Krieg, Hunger und Pestilenz in Warschau 1939–1943," p. 121; *Auftrag und Wirklichkeit*, pp. 165–6.

the epidemics themselves."[32] At the time Hagen was incapable of understanding the terror with which his health measures were perceived by the Jewish population. For them, quarantine often meant starvation. Compulsory delousing left temporarily vacated apartments vulnerable to theft. Often the delousing ruined the clothing of the Jews, and all too frequently the Jews were left standing naked in all kinds of weather for long periods of time. Unable to comprehend their reasons for noncompliance, Hagen treated Jewish evasion of his health measures as willful and blind stubbornness to be overcome only by draconic threats.[33]

On 7 July 1941, Hagen submitted a comprehensive report on the spotted fever epidemic.[34] The disease was being spread above all by Jews leaving the ghetto, and only timely measures would prevent spotted fever from assuming epidemic proportions elsewhere. Hagen bitterly criticized uncooperative German ghetto administrators and obstinate Jews, who obstructed his efforts. More German supervision and inspection, more trained personnel and more medical equipment were needed. "Considerations of cost and possible considerations of principle regarding the Jewish question must for the moment not be decisive," he argued.

Jewish police and medical personnel who evaded regulations and Jews who were caught leaving the ghetto should be flogged, he urged. "Vagabond Jews" wandering about the district should be shot.[35] But Hagen also insisted on adequate food supplies. "In order to curb misery and demoralization and reduce the pressure to break out of the ghetto, the entire provisioning of the Jewish quarter requires an increase to the

---

[32] Trunk, *Judenrat*, p. 159.

[33] Hagen denied the charge that, with pistol in hand, he had threatened a group of Jewish health workers with death for not reporting every case of spotted fever. He did admit that he had threatened the "most severe punishment." Verfügung, 24 November 1970, of Dortmund Ermittlungsverfahren, 45 Js 7/69, pp. 17, 21 (in ZSt, 11 201 AR 1800/69).

[34] YVA, O-53/105/III/760–68 ("Die Fleckfieber Epidemic im Warschauer Judenviertel. Vorschläge zu ihrer Bekämpfung"). Much of this report is reprinted in Hagen, "Krieg, Hunger und Pestilenz in Warschau 1939–1943," pp. 122–5.

[35] After the war Hagen explained this proposal for shooting "vagabundierende Juden" as a necessary compromise; others were proposing to shoot all Jews found outside the ghetto, and he thought "vagabundierende Juden" were being shot already in any case. Verfügung, 24 November 1970, of Dortmund Ermittlungsverfahren, 45 Js 7/69, pp. 19–20; Hagen, "Krieg, Hunger und Pestilenz in Warschau 1939–1943," p. 125.

bare minimum for existence," he wrote. If this was not done, "[m]ore and more Jews will attempt to escape the ghetto, because otherwise they face nothing but a certain death."

The new commissar of the Jewish ghetto, Heinz Auerswald (unlike his predecessor Waldemar Schön), did not maliciously deny that the totally inadequate food supplies to the ghetto were producing famine, and that there was a direct link between famine and epidemic.[36] At first Auerswald took a rather lenient attitude toward smuggling to alleviate the food shortage, but he became increasingly alarmed that smuggling was spreading the spotted fever epidemic.[37] He embraced Hagen's recommendations to increase the food supply and to shoot "vagabond Jews," but above all he determined to create ghetto boundaries that could be effectively guarded. To that end the ghetto had to be reduced in size, first by moving the walls inward to the middle of the streets, so openings could not be made through the back walls of border houses, and second by cutting off the smaller southern sector of the ghetto entirely.[38]

Hagen was appalled at the implications of Auerswald's plan, for the drastic resettlement and intensified overcrowding of the ghetto population were totally contrary to his quarantine and isolation measures to combat the spotted fever epidemic. Unable to dissuade Auerswald, he went over the latter's head and wrote a blistering letter to the German mayor of Warsaw, Ludwig Leist, in which he argued that "it is insanity (*Wahnsinn*) to carry out such a measure at the present time. . . . The rise in spotted fever is such, that any movement of peoples in Warsaw will lead to an unchecked spread of spotted fever."[39] The idea of eliminating the southern sector of the ghetto was given up, but even so the boundary changes uprooted 60,000 people in the ghetto.[40]

On 15 October 1941, Frank acted on the two other proposals for more food and more draconic punishment that Auerswald had put before him. The request for more food for the ghetto was rejected, because "even

[36] YVA, JM 1112, Auerswald report of 26 September 1941.
[37] *The Warsaw Diary of Adam Czerniakow*, Raul Hilberg, Stanislaw Staron and Joseph Kermisz, eds. (New York: Stein & Day, 1979), p. 248 (entry of 13 June 1941).
[38] FGM, pp. 127–8 (Auerswald circular, 18 September 1941).
[39] YVA, JM 3462, Hagen to Leist, 22 September 1941.
[40] *The Warsaw Diary of Adam Czerniakow*, pp. 285–6 (entries of 4 and 6 October 1941).

for the Polish population hardly anything more can be provided."[41] At the same time Frank intensified the second proposal by decreeing the death penalty for *all* Jews caught leaving the ghetto, not just for the so-called "vagabond Jews."[42]

The logical connection between these two decisions did not escape the attention of 100 public health, military, and SS doctors from all over the General Government, who were meeting at the Polish resort of Bad Krynica from 13 to 16 October under the chairmanship of Walbaum.[43] The featured theme of the *Tagung* (conference) was the campaign against epidemics, with the first session devoted to spotted fever. The opening statement of this session was given by Walbaum's deputy, Dr. Otto Buurman. He was a rare non-party doctor in Walbaum's entourage and was valued by Hagen as a close friend and indeed his only confidant in the Department of Public Health.[44] Buurman reiterated the premise that the diffusion of spotted fever was "incontestably explained by the undisciplined behavior of the Jews, especially those who wander about." Buurman was followed on the program by Prof. Kudicke, the special deputy for combating spotted fever. He urged a vastly intensified campaign of delousing, for even those already sick were not infectious to others if they were free of lice. Then "with great caution" Kudicke raised what he termed the "important question." Speaking "purely academically without making any value judgment," Kudicke noted that one could not successfully combat the spread of epidemic without removing its cause.

[T]he Jewish population simply broke out of the ghettos in which there was nothing to eat. . . . if one wants to prevent that in the future, then one must use the best means for this, namely provide for more sufficient provisioning of the Jewish population. This is beyond my power – I may be quite open – this is beyond the power of all of us. For me the matter is clear, and I also know that

[41] YVA, JM 21/4, Frank *Tagebuch*, entry of 15 October 1941.
[42] FGM, pp. 128–9 (Frank decree of 15 October 1941).
[43] YVA, O-53/145/57-265 ("Arbeitstagung der Abteilung Gesundheitswesen i. d. Regierung in Bad Krynica" of 13–16 October 1941).
[44] ZSt, 6 AR 1211/60, Sonderheft I, 40–45 (interrogation of Dr. Otto Buurman, 5 October 1962); Hagen, *Auftrag und Wirklichkeit*, pp. 163–4.

the difficulties are so great, that the shortage may possibly never be removed in this regard.

Thus one had to be clear, Kudicke concluded. The attempt to combat the spread of epidemic might quite simply fail.

On this discouraging note, Dr. Walbaum apparently felt the need to intervene.

> You are completely right. Naturally it would be best and simplest to give the people sufficient provisions, but that cannot be done. That is connected to the food situation and the war situation in general. Thus shooting will be employed when one comes across a Jew outside the ghetto without special permission. One must, I can say it quite openly in this circle, be clear about it. There are only two ways. We sentence the Jews in the ghetto to death by hunger or we shoot them. Even if the end result is the same, the latter is more intimidating. We cannot do otherwise, even if we want to. We have one and only one responsibility, that the German people are not infected and endangered by these parasites. For that any means must be right.

The protocol, to record the reaction of the one hundred doctors gathered at Bad Krynica, stated quite simply: "Applause, clapping" (*Beifall, Klatschen*).

Walbaum then asked if anyone else had something further to say on this subject, and Dr. Arnold Lambrecht rose to make additional spontaneous remarks. It was utopian to think one could so seal the ghetto that not a single infected Jew could leave, he said. They had tried to disinfect the ghetto but Jewish money had corrupted the disinfection teams. Thus one must naturally approve of shooting Jews found outside the ghetto without permission. He too had tried to improve the food supply to reduce pressure on the borders.

> Unfortunately the necessary food supply could not be approved, because nothing was there. But it is always better, in any case, that the Jews starve in the ghetto than that they sit scattered about the city and die there. . . . One must be logical; and it is thus appropriate to proceed against the Jews much more severely than before.

Lambrecht's remarks were greeted not just once but twice with "applause, clapping."

In this frenzied atmosphere, Dr. Hagen rose to deliver his scheduled presentation. Recent experience had shown that three factors were basic to the spread of spotted fever: hunger, overcrowding, and filth. One thousand people per week were dying in the ghetto, mostly from starvation. Thousands more Jews had been brought into the ghetto the previous spring without expanding the available space and at a pace too fast to quarantine the new arrivals. Without coal, the delousing apparatus could not be operated, hospitals could not be heated, and clothes could not be washed. Priority for the army's demands on the food supply was obvious, but the epidemic now threatened the Germans in Poland, including the army. "I must therefore take the view that three things are decisive to combat spotted fever at the moment: bread, coal, and soap." The protocol records no applause or clapping for Hagen's remarks.

Exactly two months later, on 16 December 1941, Hans Frank and his leading officials met in Cracow.[45] A large portion of the meeting was devoted to the spotted fever crisis. Walbaum reported that in November the figure for new cases was still rising.[46] The disease had now broken out in the camps for Russian prisoners of war, and German soldiers returning from the east were also spreading it. Oblivious to the evidence that he had just presented that spotted fever was not spread solely by the Jews, Walbaum urged accelerated judicial procedures for shooting Jews found outside the ghettos. District reports on the state of spotted fever followed. Governor Kundt of the Radom District seconded Walbaum's recommendation for a rapid carrying-out of the death penalty. Only then would the Jews see that the German administration was serious, he argued. Governor Lasch of Galicia expressed his "gratitude" for the "shooting order." Governor Fischer's deputy from the Warsaw District, Dr. Herbert Hummel, also complained about the slow procedures

---

[45] Frank, *Diensttagebuch*, pp. 452–8 (Regierungssitzung, 16 December 1941).
[46] Ironically, this was the last month in which this was the case, at least for the Jewish population. Beginning in December 1941 the cases of spotted fever in the Warsaw ghetto began to drop off dramatically. YVA, O-53/101 (Hummel's monthly reports from December 1941 through July 1942 record 1,971 new cases of spotted fever in December 1941, 784 in February 1942, and 67 in July 1942).

for shooting Jews caught outside the ghetto. In his district over 600 such Jews had been arrested, 45 convicted, but so far only eight executed. The judicial proceedings were too long and complicated; they needed to be simplified.

Hans Frank rose to speak in this atmosphere of concern over spotted fever, approval of the shooting order, and widespread desire for shooting Jews even more quickly. He informed his followers of the Final Solution. He noted that he had always proceeded from the position that the Jews had to disappear. He had undertaken negotiations to expel them to the east. But no one wanted the Jews there either. "In Berlin they have said to us: why all this bawling; liquidate them yourselves!" Frank did not yet know how it was going to be done, but plans were being made in Germany, and he would keep them all informed.

What can one say in conclusion? It is not, of course, my contention that the German doctors in the General Government were the primary instigators of the mass murder of the Polish Jews. But the role they played in intensifying the persecution of the Jews was considerable; their responsibility was not small. These German public health officials did not accept the more radical Nazi view of depriving the Polish population of public health services as a means of population decimation, if for some of them only out of obvious self-interest. But they viewed the Jews in a very different light. Both Nazi doctors and others like Hagen and Buurman accepted as a medical premise that the Jews – by nature and culture – were the particular carriers of spotted fever. They threw the weight of their medical prestige and authority behind ghettoization as the appropriate response. Both medical and ethical judgments were implicit in this action; the Jews were not lives to be saved but rather a danger to be avoided.

Quite predictably, ghettoization created a self-fulfilling prophecy. In the terrible conditions of hunger, overcrowding, and filth that the Germans imposed, the Jews fell victim to the very disease that had been cited to justify their incarceration. None of the public health doctors initially pursued a policy of intentionally starving the ghettoized Jews, as some other Germans did. Nonetheless they continued to urge an ever-tighter seal around the ghettos as a further medical response to the epidemic they had helped call forth, even when they clearly knew what would result if the increase in food supplies that they recommended was not forthcoming.

Food supplies were of course not appreciably increased, and the epidemic worsened. When the hope of containing spotted fever within the ghettos proved to be illusory, the doctors faced a real public health crisis of their own making. Most of them embraced Walbaum's solution: one way or another, by shooting or starvation, the Jews had to die. For Walbaum and the doctors there was no other way.

They had applauded Dr. Lambrecht's call to think logically and act severely but, left to themselves, they did not take the final step. However, the doctors served a regime of more fertile imagination and ruthless logic. Having decided to treat the Jews not as victims to be cured but as carriers to be avoided, the doctors were only a short psychological step from Hitler's belief that the Jews were no better than bacilli and vermin. Now he determined that they should be exterminated as such. What the public health officials had done in the General Government over the past two years ultimately provided justification and legitimacy for such a policy of systematic mass murder, one carried out more quickly, with greater efficiency – dare one say in an altogether more medical manner?[47] – than the gradual disappearance of the Jews through starvation and firing-squad that the doctors had embraced at Bad Krynica. We have no protocol to tell of the applause and clapping with which German public health officials greeted the news of the Final Solution, but we have no reason to believe that it would not have been enthusiastic.

Epilogue

Within 15 months of the Bad Krynica *Tagung*, both Wilhelm Hagen and Jost Walbaum had departed from their medical positions in the General Government. At issue was not their attitude toward the fate of

---

[47] One is reminded of the remark of Eichmann's defense attorney in Jerusalem, Dr. Servatius, that killing by gas was indeed a "medical matter." Hannah Arendt, *Eichmann in Jerusalem: A Report on the Banality of Evil* (Revised edition: New York: Viking Press, 1965), p. 69.

the Jews but their quarrels with the SS on other matters. In Hagen's case, the quarrel was based on his insistence that the Poles receive adequate public health services to combat tuberculosis. In Walbaum's case, several factors seem to have been decisive: his quarrelsome nature and questionable competence; his approval or at least passive toleration of Hagen's TB program, which clashed with SS racial policy as enunciated in the Wetzel-Hecht memorandum of November 1939; and most important his jealous guarding of health facilities which the SS coveted for its own use.

In the spring of 1942, Wilhelm Hagen was appointed special deputy for combating tuberculosis in the General Government. The focus of his activities was to be the protection of ethnic Germans. However, the committee which he headed prepared a plan for combating TB among both ethnic Germans and Poles that would have cost over 18 million zloty. Hagen wrote to the *Reichsgesundheitsführer* Leonardo Conti on 20 July 1942: "The honorable task of combatting tuberculosis in Poland has been assigned to me. I know that this task can be carried out only if I can also do something for the Poles, if I do some good for them." The plan was approved by Walbaum's superior, Dr. Ludwig Siebert of the Division for Internal Administration in Cracow.[48] It must therefore have been passed upward with Walbaum's approval.

Hagen's proposed TB program quickly led to open confrontation with the SS. In Warsaw he fought with the Warsaw District SS and Police Leader Ferdinand von Sammern-Frankenegg over salvaging medical equipment from the Warsaw ghetto for his program. The heated correspondence culminated in a letter from Sammern-Frankenegg to Hagen on 5 December 1942:

I vehemently refuse to accept any kind of reproach or instruction from you. It is totally intolerable that you want to issue orders to me concerning an assignment received from and carried out in accordance with the intentions of the Reichsführer-SS. It is totally out of the question that equipment from the Jewish hospitals be made available for use by the Poles, as you have in mind here.

---

[48] Hagen, "Krieg, Hunger und Pestilenz in Warschau 1939–1943," pp. 123–30, and *Auftrag und Wirklichkeit*, pp. 190, 197.

I . . . won't stand for speaking about a destruction process and about how it may no longer take place. Finally, I refuse to negotiate or correspond with you over this matter any further.[49]

Sometime in November, before Hagen received this letter from Sammern-Frankenegg, he had, in Cracow, met with officials of both the Department for Population and Welfare and the SS to present his plan for combating TB. The head of the Department for Population and Welfare, Lothar Weirauch, interrupted his presentation to inquire if these health measures were actually intended for the entire population. When Hagen confirmed this, the incredulous Weirauch told Hagen that the whole plan was in error, that Germany had no interest in maintaining the Polish population; the only good Pole was a dead Pole. As an illustrative example, Weirauch explained confidentially the fate of the displaced Poles in the coming resettlement of ethnic Germans in the Zamość region; the old people and children would be killed and the adult population placed in work camps.[50]

In despair Hagen approached an old friend, the Reich Veterinarian Leader Dr. Friedrich Weber, who advised him to write to the Führer! After consulting his wife, Hagen wrote to Hitler on 7 December 1942, advising that he had learned confidentially of plans to proceed with 70,000 children and old people from Zamość "as with the Jews, that is, to kill them." Hagen warned of the consequences: increased partisan resistance, a windfall for Allied propaganda, and a growing fear among other peoples of Europe that they might share the same fate as the Poles. Though advised by Weber to restrict himself to military and political consequences, Hagen also argued that Germany had no interest in diminishing the Polish population. "Of all the foreign workers the Pole can be considered racially as one of the closest elements to us." He thus urged the Führer not to destroy workers needed in the coming decades and not to leave Poland a "scorched earth."[51] One month later Hagen asked for an appointment with Conti to discuss his

---

[49] ZSt, II 201 AR 1800 69 (Ermittlungsverfahren of the Staatsanwaltschaft bei dem Landgericht Dortmund, 45 Js 7/69), p. 48.

[50] Hagen, *Auftrag und Wirklichkeit*, p. 198, and "Krieg, Hunger und Pestilenz in Warschau 1939–1943," p. 131.

[51] T175/38/540407-9 (Hagen to Hitler, 7 December 1942).

serious doubt whether I can still reconcile working in the General Government with my conscience. . . . Should the principle that the destruction of Poland is in Germany's advantage remain the basis of policy in Poland . . . then I request, on the basis of the crisis of conscience arising from this, to be released from my activities in the General Government.[52]

Even before his letters to Hitler and Conti could have their effect, however, the net was closing around Hagen in Warsaw. In December 1942 the Warsaw deputy for the Reich Commissariat for the Strengthening of Germandom (RKFDV), *Hauptsturmführer* Herbert Packebusch, prepared a report repeatedly denouncing Hagen and his TB program for the "basically false conception" that "Germans and Poles as sick people must be treated equally without distinction?!!" Hagen's program was an "insanity," and the point had been reached in which it "appeared advisable to proceed against Dr. Hagen and his Polish TB-program with all available means."[53]

This report was forwarded to Sammern-Frankenegg on 30 January 1943.[54] Contrary to his earlier pledge not to correspond with Hagen further, Sammern-Frankenegg wrote to Hagen again on 5 February, and reiterated the denunciations of the Packebusch report. Hagen thereupon submitted his resignation, which was accepted. He left Poland on 28 February and was assigned to medical duty with the Sixth Army in Russia on 29 March.[55]

Meanwhile, Hagen's letter to Hitler worked its way through the Nazi bureaucracy. At the end of January 1943, the party headquarters in Munich sent a copy of Hagen's letter to the Higher SS and Police Leader in the General Government, Wilhelm Krüger, with an "urgent" request for his position on the matter.[56] Krüger in turn asked Weirauch for his

---

[52] Hagen, *Auftrag und Wirklichkeit*, pp. 210–2.

[53] NO 1415 (Packebusch draft report of December 1942), cited in Hagen, "Krieg, Hunger und Pestilenz in Warschau 1939–1943," pp. 139–42.

[54] NO 1415 (Covering letter, Packebusch to Sammern, 30 January 1943), cited in Hagen, "Krieg, Hunger und Pestilenz in Warschau 1939–1943," p. 139.

[55] Hagen, *Auftrag und Wirklichkeit*, pp. 203–5.

[56] T175/38/548006 (NSDAP Hauptamt für Volkstumsfragen to HSSPF Krüger, 28 January 1943).

version of events. Weirauch denied that he had ever revealed state se-
crets or told Hagen that 70,000 young and elderly Poles from Zamość
were to be killed. Hagen, he noted, had not overcome his many years
of membership in the SPD and had no understanding for the "principles of racial politics." He, Weirauch, on the other hand, fully supported the policy of the SS that the tuberculosis campaign be aimed
solely to prevent the disease's spread to Germans.[57]

The role, if any, of Krüger's investigation in Hagen's resignation and
departure from the General Government is not revealed in the surviving
documentation. In late March, however, the letter to Hitler came to
Himmler's attention. He inquired of Leonardo Conti what had become
of Dr. Hagen, who had sent an "impossible letter" to the Führer. In
Himmler's opinion, Hagen ought to be sent to a concentration camp for
the duration of the war.[58] Conti replied that Hagen had been removed
from public health service in the General Government and severely rep-
rimanded. Hagen was an "idealist" who could still be useful and thus
Conti recommended leniency.[59] Himmler concurred with Conti's recommendation that nothing further be undertaken against Hagen.[60]
Hagen credited Conti with quickly securing his military assignment in
late March as a move to protect him from Himmler.[61]

In post-war Germany Hagen returned to public health activities and
rose to the position of President of the *Bundesgesundheitsamt* before he
retired in 1958. Honored by the Poles, Hagen was less esteemed by sur-
vivors of the Warsaw ghetto. Josef Wulf included Hagen among the bi-
ographies of 18 perpetrators in the 1961 edition of *Das Dritte Reich und
Seine Vollstrecker*. When Hagen asked the courts to block Wulf from
spreading his charge further, Wulf countered by bringing criminal
charges against Hagen. In a grotesque paradox Wulf called upon as witnesses several men whom Hagen had testified against in other post-war
proceedings, including none other than Lothar Weirauch! The criminal
charges against Hagen were dismissed, and upon the suggestion of the

[57] T175/38/548001-5 (Weirauch to Krüger, 4 February 1943).
[58] T175/38/548011 (Brandt to Conti, 29 March 1943).
[59] T175/38/548110 (Conti to Brandt, 31 March 1943).
[60] T175/38/548999 (Personal Staff of RFSS to Conti, 14 April 1943).
[61] Hagen, *Auftrag und Wirklichkeit*, p. 207.

court the civil proceedings were resolved when Wulf agreed not to discuss Hagen's activities in Warsaw in any further publications.[62]

Paradoxically, the dismissal of the convinced Nazi Jost Walbaum from his post preceded Hagen's resignation by more than two months. During his tenure as chief of public health in the General Government, the arrogant and contentious Walbaum had had running battles with many people. In April 1941 he had a stormy argument with Frank, who temporarily refused to speak with him and gave him one month to arrange for his successor.[63] Frank and Walbaum were reconciled, but one year later Walbaum was quarreling with Governer Fischer of the Warsaw district, when Walbaum tried unsuccessfully to dismiss two Warsaw doctors, including Dr. Arnold Lambrecht.[64] And in October 1942 Walbaum was quarreling with Frank's powerful State Secretary, Dr. Bühler, on the grounds that the latter was blocking his promotion to *Ministerialrat*.[65] In short, Walbaum had strained relations with the most important people in Frank's civil administration – Fischer, Bühler, and Frank himself. For the non-Nazi doctors working for Walbaum, that is, Hagen and Buurman, his general incompetence and corruption justified removal in any case.[66] It is not surprising, therefore, that when Walbaum quarreled with the SS, he had no support to fall back on.

What precisely triggered Walbaum's removal? On 27 March 1943, Herbert Packebusch wrote to SS-*Brigadeführer* Hans Hinkel, General Secretary of the *Reichskulturkammer* (Reich Culture Board) in Berlin, claiming credit for ousting both Hagen and Walbaum. "In health matters," he wrote, "my recent intervention led to the recall of not only the deputy for combating TB in the General Government but also the President of the Main Division for Health." Under Walbaum's successor, SS-*Brigadeführer* Prof. Dr. Teitge, a "clear and unequivocal policy" was now being pursued.[67] Another Packebusch letter to

[62] ZSt, II 201 AR 1800/69 (Verfügung, 24 November 1970, of the Staatsanwaltschaft bei dem Landgericht Dortmund, 45 Js 7/69).
[63] YVA, JM 21 (entry of 19 April 1941).
[64] YVA, JM 21 (entry of 26 March and Arbeitssitzung of 30 May 1942).
[65] YVA, JM 21 (entry of 2 October 1942).
[66] Hagen, "Krieg, Hunger und Pestilenz in Warschau 1939–1943," p. 139; ZStL, 6 AR 1211/60, 42 (testimony of Otto Buurman, 5 October 1962).
[67] BDC, Packebusch file.

Sammern-Frankenegg, however, made it clear that Packebusch had exploited Hagen's TB policy to tarnish Walbaum out of sheer expediency, not because of any principled stand by the latter. Packebusch noted that while "the former head of the Health Department in Cracow, Dr. Walbaum, had to be made responsible for this affair [the TB-program], that nonetheless the initiative for it came exclusively from the TB-deputy for the General Government, the public health chief in Warsaw, Dr. Hagen."[68] The real reason for the final SS attack on Walbaum is found in an informal "Dear Rudi" letter on 21 November 1942, from the managing director of the *Lebensborn* program in Munich, Max Sollman, to SS-*Obersturmbannführer* Rudolf Brandt on Himmler's staff. *Lebensborn* coveted a women's hospital in Cracow – with 90 percent Polish patients – as a site for a *Lebensborn* home. Walbaum promised the hospital, if Conti's approval were secured. As Walbaum was quarreling with Conti at the moment, he suggested that Sollmann had best approach Conti himself. Conti refused to give his approval without hearing from Walbaum, however, and the latter continued to defer to Conti while in fact not sending him any information upon which to make the decision. To Sollmann, the reason for Walbaum's evasion was clear. The infant mortality rate among ethnic Germans in the General Government was an appalling 50 percent, he claimed. Walbaum's hostility to *Lebensborn* was based on his fear that the latter would immediately do so much better that it would reflect negatively on Walbaum, who in three years had accomplished nothing. Sollmann thus asked Brandt to secure Himmler's intervention with Conti.[69] Ten days later Walbaum was out of a job.

Walbaum's dismissal would be nothing more than another example of sordid Nazi infighting unworthy of detailed attention, if it were not for his successful avoidance of both extradition to Poland in 1949 and indictment in Germany in the 1960s. Each time Walbaum cited the SS opposition that led to his dismissal as evidence for his claim that he had been a "resister" who had systematically opposed SS attempts to carry

[68] NO 1415 (Packebusch to Sammern-Frankenegg, 30 January 1943, copies to Max Sollmann, *Lebensborn*, and to Pers. Stab des RFSS), cited in Hagen, "Krieg, Hunger und Pestilenz in Warschau 1939–1943," pp. 139–40.
[69] BDC, Walbaum file (Sollmann of *Lebensborn* to Brandt, 24 November 1942).

out euthanasia in the mental institutions in the General Government.[70] In fact, of the four mental institutions under Walbaum's supervision (Kulparkow, Tworki, Kobierzyn and Zofiowka-Otwock), Kobierzyn was liquidated on 23 June 1942, when its patients were sent to Auschwitz and Zofiowka-Otwock on 19 August 1942, when its patients (all Jews) were sent to Treblinka. The other two were not liquidated after Walbaum's departure, hence making it clear that his alleged protection of them was not the reason for his dismissal. They were still in existence when liberated in 1944, although 90 percent of the patients had starved to death.[71] Moreover, Walbaum's claim that he had saved Kulparkow by making a special deal with the Wehrmacht was denied by both the chief Polish doctor there and by the army doctor with whom he allegedly dealt.[72]

The Hannover prosecuting attorney dropped charges against Walbaum in 1968 after a four-year investigation. While many points of Walbaum's testimony seemed scarcely credible to the prosecutor, he nonetheless concluded: that there was no proof of Walbaum's contribution to the murder and starvation of mental patients; that Walbaum "had had no influence on the formation of the ghettos," where in any case health matters were the responsibility of the SS "as well as Jewish doctors"; and that his comments at Bad Krynica had to be evaluated in the context of a serious health threat to all inhabitants in the General Government "but especially to the Germans living there."[73]

---

[70] Walbaum, a widower since 1922, also noted that even during his years in the General Government he continued to live with his half-Jewish mother-in-law. For Walbaum's accounts contrived for public consumption, see articles based upon materials fed to the press in the *Hannoverschen Allgemeinen* of 30 September 1964 and the *Stuttgarter Zeitung* of 15 March 1968. He also tried to sue *Der Spiegel* for libel for its statement that Germany's jurists and doctors had obeyed the Nazi regime.

[71] ZSt, 201 AR-Z 49/66, pp. 11–21 (excerpts from report of Polish war crimes commission) and pp. 153–6 (Verfügung, Staatsanwaltschaft bei dem Landgericht Hannover, 21 November 1968. The liquidation of Kobierzyn was examined in detail in 6 AR 1211/60 (Dortmund 45 Js 52/61).

[72] ZSt, 201 AR-Z 49/66, pp. 80–6 (testimony of Dr. Alexander W., 4 January 1967) and pp. 120–1 (testimony of Dr. Erich P., 29 March 1967).

[73] ZSt, 201 AR-Z 49/66, pp. 151–77 (Verfügung, 21 November 1968 of the Staatsanwaltschaft bei dem Landgericht Hannover, 2 Js 855/64).

8

One Day in Józefów:
Initiation to Mass Murder

In mid-March of 1942, some 75 to 80 percent of all victims of the Holocaust were still alive, while some 20 to 25 percent had already perished. A mere eleven months later, in mid-February 1943, the situation was exactly the reverse. Some 75 to 80 percent of all Holocaust victims were already dead, and a mere 20 to 25 percent still clung to a precarious existence. At the core of the Holocaust was an intense eleven-month wave of mass murder. The center of gravity of this mass murder was Poland, where in March 1942, despite two and a half years of terrible hardship, deprivation, and persecution, every major Jewish community was still intact; eleven months later, only remnants of Polish Jewry survived in a few rump ghettos and labor camps. In short, the German attack on the Polish ghettos was not a gradual or incremental program stretched over a long period of time, but a veritable blitzkrieg, a massive offensive requiring the mobilization of large numbers of shock troops at the very period when the German war effort in Russia hung in the balance.

This study is based entirely on the judicial records in the Staatsanwaltschaft Hamburg that resulted from two investigations of Reserve Police Battalion 101: 141 Js 1957/62 and 141 Js 128/65. German laws and regulations for the protection of privacy prohibit the revealing of names from such court records. Thus, with the exception of Major Trapp, who was tried, convicted, and executed in Poland after the war, I have chosen simply to refer to individuals generically by rank and unit rather than by pseudonyms.

Reprinted in slightly revised form with permission. From *Lessons and Legacies: The Meaning of the Holocaust in a Changing World*, Peter Hayes, ed. (Evanston, Illinois: Northwestern University Press, 1991), pp. 196–209.

The first question I would like to pose, therefore, is what were the manpower sources the Germans tapped for their assault on Polish Jewry? Since the personnel of the death camps was quite minimal, the real question quite simply is who were the ghetto-clearers? On close examination one discovers that the Nazi regime diverted almost nothing in terms of real military resources for this offensive against the ghettos. The local German authorities in Poland, above all SS and Police Leader (SSPF) Odilo Globocnik, were given the task but not the men to carry it out. They had to improvise by creating ad hoc "private armies." Coordination and guidance of the ghetto-clearing was provided by the staffs of the SSPF and commander of the security police in each district in Poland. Security Police and Gendarmerie in the branch offices in each district provided local expertise.[1] But the bulk of the manpower had to be recruited from two sources. The first source was the Ukrainians, Lithuanians, and Latvians recruited out of the prisoner of war camps and trained at the SS camp in Trawniki. A few hundred of these men, among them Ivan Demjanjuk, were then sent to the death camps of Operation Reinhard, where they outnumbered the German staff roughly 4 to 1. The majority, however, were organized into mobile units and became itinerant ghetto-clearers, traveling out from Trawniki to one ghetto after another and returning to their base camp between operations.[2]

The second major source of manpower for the ghetto-clearing operations was the numerous battalions of Order Police (*Ordnungspolizei*) stationed in the General Government. In 1936, when Himmler gained centralized control over all German police, the Secret State Police (Ge-

---

[1] For ghetto-clearing in the various districts of the General Government, the following are the most important judicial sources. For Lublin: Staatsanwaltschaft Hamburg 147 Js 24/72 (indictment of Georg Michalson) and StA Wiesbaden 8 Js 1145/60 (indictment of Lothar Hoffmann and Hermann Worthoff); for Warsaw, StA Hamburg 147 Js 16/69 (indictment of Ludwig Hahn); for Cracow, Landgericht Kiel 2 Ks 6/63 (judgment against Martin Fellenz); for Radom, StA Hamburg 147 Js 38/65 (indictment of Hermann Weinrauch and Paul Fuchs); for Bialystok, StA Dortmund 45 Js 1/61 (indictment of Herbert Zimmermann and Wilhelm Altenloh), and *Documents Concerning the Destruction of Grodno*, ed. Serge Klarsfeld (Publications of the Beate Klarsfeld Foundation); for Galicia, LG Münster 5 Ks 4/65 (judgment against Hans Krüger), and LG Stuttgart Ks 5/65 (judgment against Rudolf Röder).

[2] For the Trawniki units, see StA Hamburg 147 Js 43/69 (indictment of Karl Streibel).

stapo) and Criminal Police (Kripo) were consolidated under the Security Police Main Office of Reinhard Heydrich. The German equivalent of the city police (*Schutzpolizei*) and county sheriffs (*Gendarmerie*) were consolidated under the Order Police Main Office of Kurt Daluege. The Order Police were far more numerous than the more notorious Security Police and encompassed not only the regular policemen distributed among various urban and rural police stations in Germany, but also large battalion-size units, which were stationed in barracks and were given some military training. As with National Guard units in the United States, these battalions were organized regionally. As war approached in 1938–39, many young Germans volunteered for the Order Police in order to avoid being drafted into the regular army.

Beginning in September 1939, the Order Police battalions, each of approximately five hundred men, were rotated out from their home cities on tours of duty in the occupied territories. As the German empire expanded and the demand for occupation forces increased, the Order Police was vastly expanded by creating new reserve police battalions. The career police and prewar volunteers of the old battalions were distributed to become the noncommissioned officer cadres of these new reserve units, whose rank and file were now composed of civilian draftees considered too old by the Wehrmacht for frontline military service.

One such unit, Reserve Police Battalion 101 from Hamburg, was one of three police battalions stationed in the district of Lublin during the onslaught against the Polish ghettos. Because no fewer than 210 former members of this battalion were interrogated during more than a decade of judicial investigation and trials in the 1960s and early 1970s, we know a great deal about its composition. First let us examine the officer and noncommissioned officer (NCO) cadres.

The battalion was commanded by Major Wilhelm Trapp, a fifty-three-year-old career policeman who had risen through the ranks and was affectionately referred to by his men as "Papa Trapp." Though he had joined the Nazi Party in December 1932, he had never been taken into the SS or even given an SS-equivalent rank. He was clearly not considered SS material. His two captains, in contrast, were young men in their late twenties, both party members and SS officers. Even in their testimony twenty-five years later they made no attempt to conceal their contempt for their commander as both weak and unmilitary. Little is known about the first lieutenant who was Trapp's adjutant, for he died in the spring of 1943. In addition, however, the battalion had seven reserve lieutenants, that is men who were not career policemen but who, after they were drafted into the Order Police, had been selected to receive officer training because of their middle-class status, education, and success in civilian life. Their ages ranged from 33 to 48; five were party members, but none belonged to the SS. Of the 32 NCOs on whom we have information, 22 were party members but only seven were in the SS. They ranged in age from 27 to 40 years old; their average was 33½.

The vast majority of the rank and file had been born and reared in Hamburg and its environs. The Hamburg element was so dominant and the ethos of the battalion so provincial that contingents from nearby Wilhelmshaven and Schleswig-Holstein were considered outsiders. Over 60 percent were of working-class background, but few of them were skilled laborers. The majority of them held typical Hamburg working-class jobs: dock workers and truck drivers were most numerous, but there were also many warehouse and construction workers, machine operators, seamen and waiters. About 35 percent were lower-middle class, virtually all of whom were white-collar workers. Three-quarters of them were in sales of some sort; the other one-quarter performed various office jobs, both in the government and private sectors. The number of independent artisans, such as tailors and watch makers was small; and there were only three middle-class professionals – two druggists and one teacher. The average age of the men was 39; over half were between 37 and 42, the *Jahrgänge* most intensively drafted for police duty after September 1939.

The men of Reserve Police Battalion 101 were from the lower orders of German society. They had experienced neither social nor geographic mobility. Very few were economically independent. Except for apprenticeship or vocational training, virtually none had any education after leaving school at age 14 or 15. About 25 percent were Nazi Party members in 1942, most having joined in 1937 or later. Though not questioned about their pre-1933 political affiliation during their interrogations, presumably many had been Communists, Socialists, and labor union members before 1933. By virtue of their age, of course, all went through their formative period in the pre-Nazi era. These were men who had known political standards and moral norms other than those of the Nazis. Most came from Hamburg, one of the least Nazified cities in Germany, and the majority came from a social class that in its political culture had been anti-Nazi.

These men would not seem to have been a very promising group from which to recruit mass murderers of the Holocaust. Yet this unit was to be extraordinarily active both in clearing ghettos and in massacring Jews outright during the blitzkrieg against Polish Jewry. If these middle-aged reserve policemen became one major component of the murderers, the second question posed is how? Specifically, what happened when they were first assigned to kill Jews? What choices did they have, and how did they react?

Reserve Police Battalion 101 departed from Hamburg on June 20, 1942, and was initially stationed in the town of Bilgoraj, fifty miles south of Lublin. Around July 11 it received orders for its first major action, aimed against the approximately 1,800 Jews living in the village of Józefów, about twenty miles slightly south and to the east of Bilgoraj. In the General Government a seventeen-day stoppage of Jewish transports due to a shortage of rolling stock had just ended, but the only such trains that had been resumed were several per week from the district of Cracow to Belzec. The railway line to Sobibor was down, and that camp had become practically inaccessible. In short the Final Solution in the Lublin district had been paralyzed, and Globocnik was obviously anxious to resume the killing. But Józefów could not be a deportation action. Therefore the battalion was to select out the young male Jews in Józefów and send them to a work camp in Lublin. The remaining Jews – about 1,500 women, children, and elderly – were simply to be shot on the spot.

On July 12 Major Trapp summoned his officers and explained the next day's assignment. One officer, a reserve lieutenant in 1st company and owner of a family lumber business in Hamburg, approached the major's adjutant, indicated his inability to take part in such an action in which unarmed women and children were to be shot, and asked for a different assignment. He was given the task of accompanying the work Jews to Lublin.[3] The men were not as yet informed of their imminent assignment, though the 1st company captain at least confided to some

---

[3] StA Hamburg 141 Js 1957/62 gegen H. and W. u.a. (hereafter cited as HW), 820–21, 2437, 4414–15.

of his men that the battalion had an "extremely interesting task" (*hochinteressante Aufgabe*) the next day.[4]

Around 2 A.M. the men climbed aboard waiting trucks, and the battalion drove for about an hour and a half over an unpaved road to Józefów. Just as daylight was breaking, the men arrived at the village and assembled in a half-circle around Major Trapp, who proceeded to give a short speech. With choking voice and tears in his eyes, he visibly fought to control himself as he informed his men that they had received orders to perform a very unpleasant task. These orders were not to his liking, either, but they came from above. It might perhaps make their task easier, he told the men, if they remembered that in Germany bombs were falling on the women and children. Two witnesses claimed that Trapp also mentioned that the Jews of this village had supported the partisans. Another witness recalled Trapp's mentioning that the Jews had instigated the boycott against Germany.[5] Trapp then explained to the men that the Jews in the village of Józefów would have to be rounded up, whereupon the young males were to be selected out for labor and the others shot.

Trapp then made an extraordinary offer to his battalion: if any of the older men among them did not feel up to the task that lay before him, he could step out. Trapp paused, and after some moments, one man stepped forward. The captain of 3rd company, enraged that one of his men had broken ranks, began to berate the man. The major told the captain to hold his tongue. Then ten or twelve other men stepped forward as well. They turned in their rifles and were told to await a further assignment from the major.[6]

Trapp then summoned the company commanders and gave them their respective assignments. Two platoons of 3rd company were to surround the village; the men were explicitly ordered to shoot anyone trying to escape. The remaining men were to round up the Jews and take them to the market place. Those too sick or frail to walk to the market place, as well as infants and anyone offering resistance or attempting to hide, were to be shot on the spot. Thereafter, a few men of 1st company were to accompany the work Jews selected at the market place, while the rest

[4] HW, 2091.   [5] HW, 1952, 2039, 2655–56.
[6] HW, 1953–54, 2041–42, 3298, 4576–77, 4589.

were to proceed to the forest to form the firing squads. The Jews were to be loaded onto battalion trucks by 2nd company and shuttled from the market place to the forest.

Having given the company commanders their respective assignments, Trapp spent the rest of the day in town, mostly in a school room converted into his headquarters but also at the homes of the Polish mayor and the local priest. Witnesses who saw him at various times during the day described him as bitterly complaining about the orders he had been given and "weeping like a child." He nevertheless affirmed that "orders were orders" and had to be carried out.[7] Not a single witness recalled seeing him at the shooting site, a fact that was not lost upon the men, who felt some anger about it.[8] Trapp's driver remembers him saying later, "If this Jewish business is ever avenged on earth, then have mercy on us Germans." (Wenn sich diese Judensache einmal auf Erden rächt, dann gnade uns Deutschen.)[9]

After the company commanders had relayed orders to the men, those assigned to the village broke up into small groups and began to comb the Jewish quarter. The air was soon filled with cries, and shots rang out. The market place filled rapidly with Jews, including mothers with infants. While the men of Reserve Police Battalion 101 were apparently willing to shoot those Jews too weak or sick to move, they still shied for the most part from shooting infants, despite their orders.[10] No officer intervened, though subsequently one officer warned his men that in the future they would have to be more energetic.[11]

As the roundup neared completion, the men of 1st company were withdrawn from the search and given a quick lesson in the gruesome task that awaited them by the battalion doctor and the company's first sergeant. The doctor traced the outline of a human figure on the ground and showed the men how to use a fixed bayonet placed between and just above the shoulder blades as a guide for aiming their carbines.[12] Several men now approached the 1st company captain and asked to be given a different assignment; he curtly refused.[13] Several others who

---

[7] HW, 1852, 2182; StA Hamburg 141 Js 128/65 gegen G. u.a. (hereafter cited as G), 363, 383.

[8] G, 645–52.   [9] HW, 1741–43.   [10] HW, 2618, 2717, 2742.   [11] HW, 1947.

[12] G, 504–14, 642, 647.   [13] HW, 2092.

approached the first sergeant rather than the captain fared better. They were given guard duty along the route from the village to the forest.[14]

The first sergeant organized his men into two groups of about thirty-five men, which was roughly equivalent to the number of Jews who could be loaded into each truck. In turn each squad met an arriving truck at the unloading point on the edge of the forest. The individual squad members paired off *face-to-face* with the individual Jews they were to shoot, and marched their victims into the forest. The first sergeant remained in the forest to supervise the shooting. The Jews were forced to lie face down in a row. The policemen stepped up behind them, and on a signal from the first sergeant fired their carbines at point-blank range into the necks of their victims. The first sergeant then moved a few yards deeper into the forest to supervise the next execution. So-called "mercy shots" were given by a noncommissioned officer, as many of the men, some out of excitement and some intentionally, shot past their victims.[15] By mid-day alcohol had appeared from somewhere to "refresh" the shooters.[16] Also around mid-day the first sergeant relieved the older men, after several had come to him and asked to be let out.[17] The other men of 1st company, however, continued shooting throughout the day.

Meanwhile the Jews in the market place were being guarded by the men of 2nd company, who loaded the victims onto the trucks. When the first salvo was heard from the woods, a terrible cry swept the market place, as the collected Jews now knew their fate.[18] Thereafter, however, a quiet – indeed "unbelievable" – composure settled over the Jews, which the German policemen found equally unnerving. By mid-morning the officers in the market place became increasingly agitated. At the present rate, the executions would never be completed by nightfall. The 3rd company was called in from its outposts around the village to take over close guard of the market place. The men of 2nd company were informed that they too must now go to the woods to join the shooters.[19] At least one sergeant once again offered his men the opportunity to report if they did not feel up to it. No one took up his offer.[20]

---

[14] HW, 1648; G, 453.   [15] G, 647.   [16] G, 624, 659.   [17] HW, 2093, 2236.
[18] HW, 1686, 2659.   [19] HW, 2717–18.   [20] HW, 1640, 2505.

In another unit, one policeman confessed to his lieutenant that he was "very weak" and could not shoot. He was released.[21]

In the forest 2nd company was divided into small groups of six to eight men rather than the larger squads of thirty-five as in 1st company. In the confusion of the small groups coming and going from the unloading point, several men managed to stay around the trucks looking busy and thus avoided shooting. One was noticed by his comrades, who swore at him for shirking, but he ignored them.[22] Among those who began shooting, some could not last long. One man shot an old woman on his first round, after which his nerves were finished and he could not continue.[23] Another discovered to his dismay that his second victim was a German Jew – a mother from Kassel with her daughter. He too then asked out.[24] This encounter with a German Jew was not exceptional. Several other men also remembered Hamburg and Bremen Jews in Józefów.[25] It was a grotesque irony that some of the men of Reserve Police Battalion 101 had guarded the collection center in Hamburg, the confiscated freemason lodge house on the Moorweide next to the university library, from which the Hamburg Jews had been deported the previous fall. A few had even guarded the deportation transports to Lodz, Riga, and Minsk. These Hamburg policemen had now followed other Jews deported from northern Germany, in order to shoot them in southern Poland.

A third policeman was in such an agitated state that on his first shot he aimed too high. He shot off the top of the head of his victim, splattering brains into the face of his sergeant. His request to be relieved was granted.[26] One policeman made it to the fourth round, when his nerves gave way. He shot past his victim, then turned and ran deep into the forest and vomited. After several hours he returned to the trucks and rode back to the market place.[27]

As had happened with 1st company, bottles of vodka appeared at the unloading point and were passed around.[28] There was much demand, for among 2nd company, shooting instructions had been less

[21] HW, 1336, 3542.   [22] G, 168–69, 206–7.   [23] G, 230.   [24] HW, 2635.
[25] HW, 1540, 2534, 2951, 4579.   [26] G, 277.   [27] HW, 2483.
[28] HW, 2621, 2635, 2694.

explicit and initially bayonets had not been fixed as an aiming guide. The result was that many of the men did not give neck shots but fired directly into the heads of their victims at point-blank range. The victims' heads exploded, and in no time the policemen's uniforms were saturated with blood and splattered with brains and splinters of bone. When several officers noted that some of their men could no longer continue or had begun intentionally to fire past their victims, they excused them from the firing squads.[29]

Though a fairly significant number of men in Reserve Police Battalion 101 either did not shoot at all or started but could not continue shooting, most persevered to the end and lost all count of how many Jews they had killed that day. The forest was so filled with bodies that it became difficult to find places to make the Jews lie down. When the action was finally over at dusk, and some 1,500 Jews lay dead, the men climbed into their trucks and returned to Bilgoraj. Extra rations of alcohol were provided, and the men talked little, ate almost nothing, but drank a great deal. That night one of them awoke from a nightmare firing his gun into the ceiling of the barracks.[30]

Following the massacre at Józefów, Reserve Police Battalion 101 was transferred to the northern part of the Lublin district. The various platoons of the battalion were stationed in different towns but brought together for company-size actions. Each company was engaged in at least one more shooting action, but more often the Jews were driven from the ghettos onto trains bound for the extermination camp of Treblinka. Usually one police company worked in conjunction with a Trawniki unit for each action. The "dirty work" – driving the Jews out of their dwellings with whips, clubs, and guns; shooting on the spot the frail, sick, elderly, and infants who could not march to the train station; and packing the train cars to the bursting point so that only with the greatest of effort could the doors even be closed – was usually left to the so-called "Hiwis" (*Hilfswilligen* or "volunteers") from Trawniki.

Once a ghetto had been entirely cleared, it was the responsibility of the men of Reserve Police Battalion 101 to keep the surrounding region "*judenfrei*." Through a network of Polish informers and frequent search patrols – casually referred to as *Judenjagden* or "Jew hunts" –

[29] HW, 1640, 2149, 2505, 2540, 2692, 2720.   [30] HW, 2657.

the policemen remorselessly tracked down those Jews who had evaded the roundups and fled to the forests. Any Jew found in these circumstances was simply shot on the spot. By the end of the year there was scarcely a Jew alive in the northern Lublin district, and Reserve Police Battalion 101 increasingly turned its attention from murdering Jews to combating partisans.

In looking at the half-year after Józefów, one sees that this massacre drew an important dividing line. Those men who stayed with the assignment and shot all day found the subsequent actions much easier to perform. Most of the men were bitter about what they had been asked to do at Józefów, and it became taboo even to speak of it. Even twenty-five years later they could not hide the horror of endlessly shooting Jews at point-blank range. In contrast, however, they spoke of surrounding ghettos and watching the Hiwis brutally drive the Jews onto the death trains with considerable detachment and a near-total absence of any sense of participation or responsibility. Such actions they routinely dismissed with a standard refrain: "I was *only* in the police cordon there." The shock treatment of Józefów had created an effective and desensitized unit of ghetto-clearers and, when the occasion required, outright murderers. After Józefów nothing else seemed so terrible. Heavy drinking also contributed to numbing the men's sensibilities. One non-drinking policeman noted that "most of the other men drank so much solely because of the many shootings of Jews, for such a life was quite intolerable sober" (die meisten der anderen Kameraden lediglich auf Grund der vielen Judenerschiessungen soviel getrunken haben, da ein derartiges Leben nüchtern gar nicht zu ertragen war).[31]

Among those who either chose not to shoot at Józefów or proved "too weak" to carry on and made no subsequent attempt to rectify this image of "weakness," a different trend developed. If they wished they were for the most part left alone and excluded from further killing actions, especially the frequent "Jew hunts." The consequences of their holding aloof from the mass murder were not grave. The reserve lieutenant of 1st company who had protested against being involved in the Józefów shooting and been allowed to accompany the work Jews to Lublin subsequently went to Major Trapp and declared that in the future he

[31] HW, 2239.

would not take part in any *Aktion* unless explicitly ordered. He made no attempt to hide his aversion to what the battalion was doing, and his attitude was known to almost everyone in the company.[32] He also wrote to Hamburg and requested that he be recalled from the General Government because he did not agree with the "non-police" functions being performed by the battalion there. Major Trapp not only avoided any confrontation but protected him. Orders involving actions against the Jews were simply passed from battalion or company headquarters to his deputy. He was, in current terminology, "left out of the loop." In November 1942 he was recalled to Hamburg, made adjutant to the Police President of that city, and subsequently promoted![33]

The man who had first stepped out at Józefów was sent on almost every partisan action but not on the "Jew hunts." He suspected that this pattern resulted from his earlier behavior in Józefów.[34] Another man who had not joined the shooters at Józefów was given excessive tours of guard duty and other unpleasant assignments and was not promoted. But he was not assigned to the "Jew hunts" and firing squads, because the officers wanted only "men" with them and in their eyes he was "no man." Others who felt as he did received the same treatment, he said.[35] Such men could not, however, always protect themselves against officers out to get them. One man was assigned to a firing squad by a vengeful officer precisely because he had not yet been involved in a shooting.[36]

The experience of Reserve Police Battalion 101 poses disturbing questions to those concerned with the lessons and legacies of the Holocaust. Previous explanations for the behavior of the perpetrators, especially those at the lowest level who came face-to-face with the Jews they killed, seem inadequate. Above all the perpetrators themselves have constantly cited inescapable orders to account for their behavior. In Józefów, however, the men had the opportunity both before and during the shooting to withdraw. The battalion in general was under orders to kill the Jews of Józefów, but each individual man was not.

Special selection, indoctrination, and ideological motivation are equally unsatisfying as explanations. The men of Reserve Police Bat-

[32] HW, 2172, 2252, 3939; G, 582.   [33] HW, 822–24, 2438–41, 4415.   [34] HW, 4578.
[35] G, 169–70.   [36] G, 244.

talion 101 were certainly not a group carefully selected for their suitability as mass murderers, nor were they given special training and indoctrination for the task that awaited them. They were mainly apolitical, and even the officers were only partly hard-core Nazi. Major Trapp in particular made no secret of his disagreement with the battalion's orders, and by Nazi standards he displayed shameful weakness in the way he carried them out. Among the men who did the killing there was much bitterness about what they had been asked to do and sufficient discomfort that no one wished to talk about it thereafter. They certainly did not take pride in achieving some historic mission.

While many murderous contributions to the Final Solution – especially those of the desk murderers – can be explained as routinized, depersonalized, segmented, and incremental, thus vitiating any sense of personal responsibility, that was clearly not the case in Józefów, where the killers confronted the reality of their actions in the starkest way. Finally, the men of Reserve Police Battalion 101 were not from a generation that had been reared and educated solely under the Nazi regime and thus had no other political norms or standards by which to measure their behavior. They were older; many were married family men; and many came from a social and political background that would have exposed them to anti-Nazi sentiments before 1933.

What lessons, then, can one draw from the testimony given by the perpetrators of the massacre of the Jews in Józefów? Nothing is more elusive in this testimony than the consciousness of the men that morning of July 13, 1942, and above all their attitude toward Jews at the time. Most simply denied that they had had any choice. Faced with the testimony of others, they did not contest that Trapp had made the offer but repeatedly claimed that they had not heard that part of his speech or could not remember it. A few who admitted that they had been given the choice and yet failed to opt out were quite blunt. One said that he had not wanted to be considered a coward by his comrades.[37] Another – more aware of what truly required courage – said quite simply: "I was cowardly."[38] A few others also made the attempt to confront the question of choice but failed to find the words. It was a different time and place, as if they had been on another political planet, and the

[37] HW, 2535.   [38] HW, 4592.

political vocabulary and values of the 1960s were helpless to explain the situation in which they had found themselves in 1942. As one man admitted, it was not until years later that he began to consider that what he had done had not been right. He had not given it a thought at the time.[39]

Several men who chose not to take part were more specific about their motives. One said that he accepted the possible disadvantages of his course of action "because I was not a career policeman and also did not want to become one, but rather an independent skilled craftsman, and I had my business back home. . . . thus it was of no consequence that my police career would not prosper" (denn ich war kein aktiver Polizist und wollte auch keiner werden, sondern selbstständiger Handwerksmeister und ich hatte zu Hause meinen Bettrieb. . . . deshalb macht es mir nichts aus, dass mein Karriere keinen Aufstieg haben würde).[40] The reserve lieutenant of 1st company placed a similar emphasis on the importance of economic independence when explaining why his situation was not analogous to that of the two SS captains on trial. "I was somewhat older then and moreover a reserve officer, so it was not particularly important to me to be promoted or otherwise to advance, because I had my prosperous business back home. The company chiefs . . . on the other hand were young men and career policemen, who wanted to become something. Through my business experience, especially because it extended abroad, I had gained a better overview of things." He alone then broached the most taboo subject of all: "Moreover through my earlier business activities I already knew many Jews." (Ich war damals etwas älter und ausserdem Reserveoffizier, mir kam es insbesondere nicht darauf an, befördert zu werden oder sonstwie weiterzukommen, denn ich hatte ja zuhause mein gutgehendes Geschäft. Die Kompaniechefs . . . dagegen waren junge Leute vom aktiven Dienst, die noch etwas werden wollten. Ich hatte durch meine kaufmännische Tätigkeit, die sich insbesondere auch auf das Ausland erstreckte, einen besseren Überlick über die Dinge. Ausserdem kannte ich schon durch meine geschäftliche Tätigkeit von frühen viele Juden.)[41]

[39] HW, 1640, 2505, 4344.   [40] G, 169-70.   [41] HW, 2439-40.

Crushing conformity and blind, unthinking acceptance of the political norms of the time on the one hand, careerism on the other – these emerge as the factors that at least some of the men of Reserve Police Battalion 101 were able to discuss twenty-five years later. What remained virtually unexamined by the interrogators and unmentioned by the policemen was the role of anti-Semitism. Did they not speak of it because anti-Semitism had not been a motivating factor? Or were they unwilling and unable to confront this issue even after twenty-five years, because it had been all too important, all too pervasive? One is tempted to wonder if the silence speaks louder than words, but in the end – the silence is still silence, and the question remains unanswered.

Was the incident at Józefów typical? Certainly not. I know of no other case in which a commander so openly invited and sanctioned the nonparticipation of his men in a killing action. But in the end the most important fact is not that the experience of Reserve Police Battalion 101 was untypical, but rather that Trapp's extraordinary offer did not matter. Like any other unit, Reserve Police Battalion 101 killed the Jews they had been told to kill.

Index

Printed in the United States
By Bookmasters